W9-CKQ-664

# Christmas
## The Sacred to Santa

TARA MOORE

REAKTION BOOKS

*For my daughters, who busily ornament the Christmas tree faster than I can pick the decorations from the boxes. And for my husband, who carries the boxes for us, and who always remembers to turn on the Bing Crosby Christmas music.*

Published by
Reaktion Books Ltd
33 Great Sutton Street
London EC1V 0DX, UK

www.reaktionbooks.co.uk

First published 2014

Copyright © Tara Moore 2014

Printed and bound in China
by 1010 Printing International Ltd

A catalogue record for this book is available from the British Library

ISBN 978 1 78023 357 4

# Contents

A fur-clad Santa: *A Visit from St Nicholas* (1869), illustrated by Thomas Nast.

# Introduction

The event at the heart of Christmas was a simple, normal rite of passage: birth. It happens to everyone, but this birth set off a long-lasting ripple effect that touches the spiritual, commercial and emotional lives of people on every continent, including Antarctica. By examining the narratives that people invest in their celebration of Christmas, it is possible to lay bare the part the holiday plays in the construction of national identity. Despite its liturgical spot just below Easter, many fixate on Christmas as the high point of their annual religious cycle. These same Christians, as well as most of their secular neighbours, use Christmas to reaffirm their family and social ties through community rituals like gift-giving and parties.

The term 'Christmas' carries individual images and emotions for the millions of people who endeavour each year to celebrate it. What exactly they are celebrating varies so widely that a book about Christmas could very easily become a book about the current state of our global community. Nonetheless, at its heart Christmas is a religious festival, a fact its name clearly publicizes. The English word itself initially developed from the worship service twelfth-century Catholics called Cristes mæsse. Very quickly the festivities of the day spilled outside the church building. In *Sir Gawain and the Green Knight*, written at the turn of the fifteenth century, Arthur's court celebrates the day devoted to cristmasse, as it was then called, with feasting, stories and blood-curdling contests – such as a head-chopping challenge – that clearly had nothing to do with the sacred.

The name splashed across catalogues, banners and late December schedules ironically identifies the holy origins of a holiday that has, in the course of a few centuries, become swamped with secular meaning. Before the marked shift of Christmas towards consumerism and national identity-building in the nineteenth century, the Mass or worship service had stood at the centre of Nativity celebrations for centuries. The day was first of all remarkable for the events that went on in church, although festive feelings overflowed into the streets, and houses that could afford to make merry opened their doors for the peasantry. Today, for a large percentage of global Christmas-keepers, the communal worship of Christ at Christmas does not figure in the picture.

The history of Christmas demonstrates how the holiday has long served as a battleground of politics, both religious and civic. By the third century, church fathers had chosen to reinvent the Roman Saturnalia as a Christian winter celebration when they scheduled Christmas for 25 December. Once the church began to feel it had conquered the pagans with Christmas, the holiday became a weapon used by the church to police its own. As a visible and at times vulnerable element of Christianity, the holiday was useful to state leaders who wished to promote a specific world view. Fascists, communists, monarchs and nascent democracies have all tried to dictate the message of Christmas. Moreover, many have sought to wield Christmas as a weapon of ideology. Even now this battle continues as political correctness and humanist activists seek to mellow the message of the very visible Christian Christmas.

Within the church, Christmas is not always as peaceful as its carols suggest. The popularity of the secular Christmas serves as an obstacle to the twenty-first-century evangelical church as it battles to distance itself from worldly values and distractions. Perhaps in keeping with an event that set off the Massacre of the Innocents – the murder of all the male infants in Bethlehem – Christmas brings conflict.

The intermingling of rituals has been a part of Christmas from its very earliest official celebrations in the third century. Like the Roman church fathers, some leaders have wielded Christmas

The German tradition of hanging cookies on trees also led to the upside-down tree hung from the ceiling. With that arrangement, rodents were less likely to sample the decorations.

symbolism intentionally, but in many other instances the blend of cultures has happened organically. Today many European gift-bringing figures like Father Christmas and Joulupukki have lost some of their original identity as they have fallen into the shadow of the global figure of Santa Claus. In Finland, for example, the gift-bringer developed from a goat to a red-coated Santa who still answers to the name Yule Goat. Elsewhere Santa has been adopted and made to perform alongside other traditional rituals. Like the gift-bringers, the gift focus of Christmas has drawn enormous attention in many cultures that formerly did not celebrate a Christian Christmas.

Santa was not always a kindly, merry figure. This illustration for *Visit of St Nicholas (The Night Before Christmas)* of 1850 shows his scarier side.

The emotional punch of Christmas ensures its continuance. Modern celebrants have such high expectations of family togetherness and gift-related joy that they may not realize that the emotions associated with the holiday have differed across time and continents. For example, the benevolence factor of Christmas developed through the Stewart Christmas in England, but it only began affecting the middle classes during the early nineteenth century. Feelings of home, hearth and warmth have motivated the expatriate, as well as military personnel forced to celebrate Christmas away from their loved ones. But these feelings are not the same for every culture: in Japan, for example, the romantic demands of Christmas outweigh the family togetherness that is more common in the West.

By examining the cultural messages within Christmas, it becomes possible to expose the tension between the sacred and the secular. Neither end of the spectrum can truly own Christmas, and the different perspectives cause conflict both in the celebrants' hearts and in public arenas. In the past century Christmas has become bifurcated with, on one side, the deeply entrenched religious observances and, on the other, the vibrant secular rituals being established around the world.

People who celebrate Christmas are experts in their own tiny experience of the holiday. The realities of our modern global Christmas are difficult to fathom. The following chapters will explore how past generations have felt about Christmas, how people in the same neighbourhood might look at it in different ways, and how a simple birth in Bethlehem continues to make waves across the continents.

The brutality of the Massacre of the Innocents has inspired many artists, including Matteo di Giovanni, who painted this depiction in 1488.

# ONE

# The Original Christmas

Christmas falls on 25 December with faithful inevitability. Indeed, our entire Western system of time and dating is based on this event. It seems as though it has always been this way but, like many facets of the holiday's history, the date of Christmas contains a complex story wrapped in controversy. Pope Benedict XVI's book *Jesus of Nazareth: The Infancy Narratives* rekindled interest in the mistaken dating of Christmas. As the former pope explains, no one recorded for posterity the exact date of Christ's arrival, so by the sixth century monks and church officials were working to confirm a possible day and year for the world-changing birth.

Exactly what year that birth took place remains a bit of a mystery. Luke's gospel offers certain specific facts at the opening of the Christmas story: 'In those days Caesar Augustus issued a decree that a census would be taken of the entire Roman world. [This was the first census that took place while Quirinius was governor of Syria.] And everyone went to his own town to register' (Luke 2:1–3). Such a clear statement of facts has sent scholars scurrying to corroborate what year this was, but zeroing in on the year is not as simple as one might hope. Just about the only thing all theologians can agree on is the fact that Dionysius Exiguus calculated the wrong date for Christ's birth when he established the concept of the year AD 1. In AD 525 Exiguus created what has become known as the Anno Domini system, which translates to 'in the year of the Lord'. If given the chance, the Roman monk might have cause to defend himself, since he only set out to chart

95 years' worth of the movable feast of Easter, and would be shocked to discover that his Easter charts were used to found time for much of the modern world.[1]

Before Christ's birth, dates in the Roman Empire were reckoned from the supposed founding of Rome, which happened in 753 BC, also known to Latin scholars as 753 AUC for Anno Urbis Conditae, or in the year of the city, meaning Rome. Christianity kept a low profile for some time after Jesus' death, but eventually scholars sought to link history to the birth in the stable. When Dionysius Exiguus came along, he set Christ's birth at 753 AUC according to the Roman calendar. There was now a new starting date, one believed to be the year Christ was born. This belief continued into the sixteenth century, when historians began to suspect that Exiguus had been a bit hasty. He had not accounted for the fact that Jesus was certainly born before the death of Herod the Great, which is usually dated to 4 BC but occasionally to 1 BC. Jesus was possibly two at the time of the Murder of the Innocents, when Herod, still very much alive, ordered male infants in Bethlehem to be slaughtered, so Jesus' birth would therefore fit somewhere between 6 and 4 BC.[2]

Archaeological evidence also points to an earlier date. In Ankara, Turkey, a temple wall is inscribed with evidence of Caesar Augustus' census. The inscription, discovered in 1553, is in both Latin and Greek, and has been the destination of many scholars for centuries. In 1861 Napoleon III sent scholars to view the inscription.[3] It is part of Caesar Augustus's autobiography, which appeared on his mausoleum and which the Roman senate ordered 'cut into the walls of every temple of Augustus throughout the Empire'.[4] The inscription includes the details of Caesar Augustus's victories and programmes, including three censuses. He must have been fairly proud of these people-counting endeavours, since the censuses were number eight in his list of 35 memorable 'Acts of Augustus'.[5] During the second census mentioned on the inscription, Caesar claimed that some 4.2 million Roman citizens were listed.[6] Some scholars have dated this particular census to 8 BC. It is likely that it took several years for word to spread and for people to migrate

This Nativity scene by the Umbrian painter Pietro Perugino was once used on an altarpiece. It has been dated to *c.* 1500–1523.

home, so Joseph might well have been on his way to Bethlehem, the ancestral home of his tribe, from 8 BC to 4 BC.[7]

The two dates that rise to the top of the argument concerning the birth of Christ are 4 BC and AD 6. The latter is a favourite because it is known that Quirinius oversaw a census for the purpose of taxation shortly after being installed as provincial legate of Syria in AD 6.[8] Historians who prefer the earlier dating explain that Quirinius held other high positions and had a hand in an earlier census even if he was not yet technically governor. Others explain Luke's Quirinius passage differently, translating the word *protos* in 2:2 not as the 'first' census overseen by Quirinius, but rather as the other possible meaning – 'before', which would mean that this was the census taken before the established one Quirinius oversaw as governor.[9]

Evidence of a Roman edict in AD 104 shows that residents in Egypt were compelled to return to their original homes for a census,[10] and there are other records of conquered peoples being forced to return home to take oaths of allegiance to Rome. Evidence does exist for a regular census every fourteen years. Counting back from the known census in AD 6, the previous one would have taken place in 8 BC. But such empire-wide movements lacked efficiency, and so censuses took several years to complete. At any rate, Luke offers an account that is plausible, although it has not yet been successfully explained. As one scholar stated, 'Luke's report is astonishingly precise for an ancient historian.'[11] I recommend we leave it at that.

Though ignorant of the exact year of Christ's birth, millions celebrate it. In many churches, scripture readings during Advent begin with Matthew 1:18: 'This is how the birth of Jesus Christ came about: His mother Mary was pledged to be married to Joseph, but before they came together, she was found to be with child through the Holy Spirit.' The importance of the virgin birth is enormous and entirely without non-biblical verification. What is known is that Jewish custom of the time took an arranged betrothal very seriously, such that any breaking of the contract required a divorce. A betrothed couple were considered married but could not yet live together. If the man died during betrothal his fiancée would be considered a widow.[12] The betrothal ceremony took place in front of the parents and was sealed with a taste of wine. The culture expected a groom to be at least 25 years old, but the bride would be married just after reaching puberty.[13]

12 OR 13

A 20th-century sculpture in wood, *Mary and Child*, on display in Oslo Cathedral.

Ironically the idea of a broken home entered the birth narrative even before the main character arrived on the scene. According to Matthew 1:19, Mary's pregnancy forced Joseph to plan a quiet divorce, an action he did not contemplate lightly. The law of the Jews as well as that of the Roman Empire required that Joseph divorce an adulterous wife. Joseph also needed to take this drastic step to protect his reputation in his community, since it might otherwise appear that he had overstepped the boundaries of betrothal.[14] A vindictive man might have gone to the court of village elders and scribes about Mary's apparent infidelity. This more public option would have allowed him to keep the dowry he obtained from her family and recoup any bride price he might have paid. Instead, the righteous Joseph planned simply to hand her a certificate of divorce in front of two sympathetic witnesses, a plan that would allow her to keep her dowry.[15]

Before the quiet divorce, an angel appeared to Joseph in a dream and laid out the plan for Christ's birth. As a result, Joseph decided to continue with the marriage but to refrain from sexual relations with Mary until after the birth of her son. This decision had repercussions for both of them, and for Jesus. In Mark 6:3 Jesus is preaching in Nazareth, his home town, but the reception is grim. Three decades have not wiped way the shame of his seeming illegitimacy: "'Isn't this the carpenter? Isn't this Mary's son and the brother of James, Joseph, Judas and Simon? Aren't his sisters here with us?" And they took offence at him.' Typically a man would be known by his father's name, but his childhood associates may have been especially spiteful when they degraded him with their assumptions about his mother's adultery. Knowing something like this lay in wait for her and her son, Mary must have found the escape of a trip to Bethlehem something of a relief.

The 80-mile journey from Nazareth to Bethlehem could not have been comfortable for a heavily pregnant woman. Such a trip would have taken four or five days. Women were not expected to travel for census or oath-taking requirements but, as one historian has suggested, the young couple must have seen the benefit of having the child while they were away and delaying their return so as to keep the birth date vague.[16] Perhaps Mary did not want to be left on her own in a town hostile to her pregnancy while her husband was far away. Also, in Bethlehem they would be much closer to Jerusalem, where they would be expected to travel for religious rites following the birth of a child. And so, on to Bethlehem.

In the first century BC Bethlehem was a minor blip on the map of the Roman Empire. The Romans were drawn into the area when they involved themselves in the dynastic rivalry that weakened the ruling Hasmonean dynasty. The Romans conquered Judea in 63 BC after besieging Jerusalem, and they later supported the Herodian dynasty to replace the Hasmoneans. This area was divided into three ethnic regions: Samaria, Idumaea and Judea proper. When the Parthians invaded the region, they killed Herod's brother, with whom he had shared the role of tetrarch, and they forced out Herod, who fled to Rome. There the Roman senate installed the half-Jewish, Idumaean Herod as the region's client ruler, although he had to fight for two years and besiege Jerusalem in order to establish himself in that role.[17] By 37 BC he had settled himself back into power in the region, now designated as a 'client kingdom', meaning that Judea was a puppet state, funnelling taxes to Rome. These client rulers were 'a temporary arrangement, preparing the way to full Romanization'. That next step happened in AD 6.[18] As a Roman province, a Roman governor then controlled the region. During the time of Herod, there would have been a light Roman military presence in Judea, and Bethlehem most likely had no Roman soldiers in residence.[19]

Bethlehem figures in many books of the Old Testament. In the book of Ruth, Naomi and her daughter-in-law Ruth return to Bethlehem together hoping to find a way to survive without a male protector; of course, Ruth finds a husband and gives birth to a child who would become the grandfather of King David. As a boy, David was anointed in Bethlehem by the prophet Samuel, and the town is referred to as the City of David to this day. Centuries later, when David's descendants were dealing with the aggressive Assyrian Empire, the prophet Micah prophesied: 'But you, Bethlehem Ephrathah, though you are little among the thousands

This monument, titled *Mary and Child*, stands guard over a small chapel in St Petri's Church, Malmö, Sweden.

of Judah, yet out of you shall come forth to Me the One to be ruler in Israel, whose goings forth have been from of old, from everlasting' (Micah 5:2).

During the period of Christ's birth, Bethlehem sat just east of a main north–south thoroughfare called 'The Way of the Patriarchs' associated with Old Testament journeys. The city benefited from its location between a farming zone in the hill country and the pasture lands to the east of the city.[20] This was a tertiary town, not of vital importance and certainly overshadowed by Jerusalem five miles away.[21] Caesar Augustus's Palestine was located 'between 31° and 33° north latitude, in the same parallel as Georgia, Arizona, Nagasaki, and Shanghai', but the Mediterranean moderates the climate of this region.[22]

The Palestinian climate had long supported herds of domesticated sheep. The shepherds that attended the sheep outside Bethlehem probably made use of a herdsmen's village below the city. The herdsmen were probably ordinary nomadic Jews. Such men used metal-studded clubs and sheepdogs to protect their stock from robbers and predators.[23] Tradition sometimes suggests that these men were overseeing the sheep intended for sacrifice at the temple in Jerusalem, but nothing in the Bible supports this.

Biblical accounts seem sparse when compared to the narrative details and lore Christians have concocted in the ensuing centuries. Christmas would feel foreign without details like the royal identity of the Magi, their camels and their joint arrival with the shepherds to the infant Jesus, yet all these elements of the story are more supposition than fact. Even the popular image of Mary's birthing room, the inn stable, has been discounted by many Bible scholars. One sixteenth-century Spanish theologian faced the Inquisition when his students, showing a misguided zeal for accuracy, turned him in for claiming that Jesus was born not in an inn, but rather in a relative's guest room. Francisco Sánchez de las Brozas, like many scholars after him, argued about the Greek term *kataluma*, which has been typically translated as 'inn', and usually 'the inn', suggesting that there was a real, historical inn. However, fault can be found with this translation. Joseph would have had, at the very least, de las Brozas argued, hospitable relatives in his home town of Bethlehem. Like the family they stayed with, Joseph and Mary would have been living very close to animals and the manger used to feed them, since farmhouses of this period often had a floor for animals below and one above for people.[24] Relatives unprepared for a birth may have tidied up the manger to welcome their newest cousin. Later in Luke 22 the term *kataluma* appears again. This time it refers to the use of private house space, the upper room used for the Last Supper. Ironically, the frequent translation, 'there was no room for them in the inn', has led to countless Christmas sermons on inhospitality towards Christ, when in reality the new baby probably enjoyed warmth and welcome from his extended family.

Not only the location, but also the guest list is open to interpretation. Tradition rather than scripture has positioned gilded magi beside lowly shepherds on millions of sparkling Christmas cards. One wonders what these men discussed in the pauses between bouts of adoration. No such conversation could have existed, however. The account in Matthew 2 reports that once Herod had figured out that the Magi were not going to return with the exact location of the new king, he used the information they had related about when they had first seen the star to order male children aged two and under killed. This suggests that the star had been indicating Jesus' presence on earth for two years, so the wise men may have met a Judean toddler rather than a swaddled infant. At any rate, they did not arrive on the night of his birth.

Nicolas Poussin, *The Adoration of the Shepherds*, 1633–4. Poussin has set his painting of Christ's early days amid the ruins of a classical building. In reality Christ probably drew his first breath on the bottom floor of a relative's home.

The three Magi from Matthew's gospel did not end their travels after leaving the holy manger; rather, they developed into characters during the early modern and Middle Ages. The three Magi were being referred to as kings by the sixth century, if not before, and evidence of a cult of the Three Kings has been recorded in Western Europe since the eleventh century.[25] Like the body of that other Christmas figure, St Nicholas, their remains were to be moved around multiple times during antiquity and the Middle Ages; Empress Helena moved them to Constantinople's St Sophia, and later they moved to Milan. In 1164 the supposed relics relocated from Milan to Cologne, a symbol of that city's twelfth-century identity as the capital of western Christendom.[26] Starting around 1440, when African slaves were being sold in Germany, German artists began to represent one of the three Magi as black.[27] These three Magi had gained classical names during the fifth century – Balthazar, Caspar and Melchior – but the names did not gain much ground until the magi took to the stage in religious plays in the fifteenth and sixteenth centuries.[28] While emperors once preferred to be aligned with these blessed, kingly figures, the Magi eventually became the special friends of children, and many Spanish-speaking cultures see them as the gift-bringers.

The newborn Jesus would have been busy even without the visit from the Magi. At eight days old, in keeping with Mosaic Law, he needed to be circumcised and named. At 40 days old he accompanied his mother to the temple in Jerusalem. All devout mothers sought purification after childbirth, and Mary's previous trip to Bethlehem meant that she was just five miles away from the holy city when her time came.[29] At the temple, a prophet and prophetess recognized the baby as the Jewish Messiah and blessed the young couple. At some point after this the magi arrived to offer their gifts, because Matthew has the holy family fleeing Palestine and Herod's wrath immediately after the wise men's departure: 'When they had gone, an angel of the Lord appeared to Joseph in a dream. "Get up," he said, "take the child and his mother and escape to Egypt"' (2:13).

Perhaps the devout can be forgiven for reading so much into the brief details the gospel offers about the Magi and the holy birth.

Jesus's Moses → Egypt

Through the centuries, the relics of the Three Kings have moved from Constantinople to Milan and finally on to Cologne, where they have rested since 1164. Their reliquary is made up of three separate sarcophagi.

The Nativity story as we know it today is contained within fewer than 100 verses. Of the four Gospels, only two mention Christ's birth in a narrative form. Matthew includes Joseph's angelic message and the only notice of the Magi. Luke details Jesus' prenatal experiences (his cousin John the Baptist responded to him while they were both in their respective wombs), Mary and Joseph's journey to Bethlehem and the angels' notification of the shepherds. Nonetheless, throughout the Old Testament, prophets and poets prophecy details by which the Messiah's birth would be known.

Herod's scribes probably referred to these prophecies when the Magi trudged in seeking the whereabouts of the new king of the Jews. Herod did not know the answer, but his own wise men checked their records, probably referencing Micah 5:2, which promises a ruler from Bethlehem. Isaiah 7:14 presages the virgin birth and Psalm 72:10 hints at the gift-bearing magi about a thousand years before they started on their starlit trip. Another associated prophecy comes from Hosea 11:1, telling that the Messiah would be called 'out of Egypt', and indeed, the Holy Family fled to Egypt for a brief time before returning to Judea with their unique toddler.

The reason the Holy Family sped away to Egypt has to do with the man in charge of Judea during that time. Herod the Great is an iconic figure from this period, and his bloody exploits were recorded by the historian Josephus two generations after the Judean leader's death.[30] About Herod Josephus wrote, 'He was of great barbarity towards all men equally, and a slave to his passion.'[31] Herod's father had come to the aid of Julius Caesar, and as a result the Romans installed Herod as the governor of Galilee; later the visiting Mark Antony responded well to Herod's gifts of coin and reciprocated by making the young man a tetrarch.[32] An uprising forced Herod to flee to Rome where, in 40 BC, the Roman senate appointed him king of Judea. The rule was not easy; he came into conflict with Cleopatra while she held sway over Mark Antony, and some fertile land was removed from Herod's control.[33] Following the Egyptian queen's suicide, Herod was well placed to court Octavian's favour. Rather than a small-time local chief, Herod was a well-travelled politician, acquainted with the emperors of his day.

Herod was also known as a great builder. During a quieter period of his reign he built several palaces, including the astounding palace at Herodium.[34] He built an artificial harbour at Caesarea and, perhaps most famously, renovated the Temple in Jerusalem. Two previous temples had stood on that same sacred ground: Solomon's Temple and the Second Temple, built following the Babylonian Captivity of the Jews. In 20 BC Herod oversaw the renovation of the Second Temple, and his work stood for 90 years until the Roman Siege of Jerusalem under Titus. At that point, the Jews' holy temple was destroyed.

Perhaps his close association with the greatest authority in the empire caused him to guard his own powers so cruelly. Herod had Mariamne, a wife he dearly loved, killed because, as a princess from the previous dynasty, which he had helped to subdue, she posed a threat to him. Mariamne had borne him two sons, and even after her death Herod groomed them for power, but these sons rose up as foreboding rivals for the people's affection. Herod provided the intelligence needed for a court to condemn them to death.[35] He ordered a third son executed five days before his own impending death from syphilis.[36] One further sign of his sadism was his plan to have a large number of local elders taken hostage and executed upon his death. Herod had hoped to prevent any celebrations in Judea that news of his death would bring; if the people would not grieve for him, they would grieve for their elders. However, when Herod died, his sister freed the hostages before they could be killed.[37]

One part of his will that was obeyed was the division of his kingdom between three of his remaining sons. The dynasty was weakened as a result. One of the three sons, Herod Antipas, would also become a key figure in the Gospels; he famously had John the Baptist beheaded. Leading up to Jesus' crucifixion, Pilate wished to pass on the responsibility of deciding what to do with Jesus, so he sent the Galilean to Herod Antipas, who was conveniently in Jerusalem for Passover. Herod's son had been eager to meet Jesus to see him do miracles, but when the famous teacher refused to perform, Herod Antipas mocked him and sent him back to Pilate for execution (Luke 23).

Herod the Great might have taken some twisted comfort in the fact that his own son had a hand in killing a person who had evaded Herod's own murderous plot some three decades earlier. At that time, as king of Judea, Herod had feared the Magi's claims of a new king of the Jews. During the Magi's visit, Herod had become suspicious that a newborn rival for his throne might one day become a nuisance. He gleaned information about the age of the supposed king and asked the Magi to return with the child's whereabouts. The Magi, warned in a dream to avoid Herod, did not return with the information he was waiting for, so the king of Judea took steps to ensure that the child would not slip through his brutal net. All male children aged two and under would be slaughtered.

This episode has been called the Massacre of the Innocents. Artists have long envisioned a widespread pogrom, but evidence about Bethlehem's population seems to contradict this traditional image. There were no more than 1,000 people in Bethlehem during

Herod's reign, and one scholar's population estimates suggest that there would have been a maximum of twenty male babies born in a two-year period. Furthermore, natural infant mortality would have claimed some of these vulnerable children.[38] So, in all likelihood, the Massacre of the Innocents ended the lives of a dozen children.

The biblical scholar Richard T. France finds no supporting proof for the massacre outside Christian circles, but the absence of other records does not negate the truth of Matthew's history. This relatively small-scale massacre was in keeping with Herod's defence of his throne in his later reign and, in fact, would have been a minor blip on his slaughter record. Herod is known to have executed other groups when he felt they threatened his throne, and in one case the murder resulted from a prediction that Herod would be replaced by a new authority.[39] Another scholar notes that the main historian of the era, Josephus, who was writing two generations later, crafted his history for a Greco-Roman readership who would find little to remark about in the death of infants. After all, at this period infanticide was common among Greeks, and Romans had a law that allowed a father to condemn a newborn to death by refusing to pick it up after birth.[40]

Jesus escaped falling victim to Herod's inelegant trap because his parents fled with their toddler son to Egypt. That part of the story does have a sense of immediacy; Joseph awakened Mary and her child in the night and began their unplanned trip to Egypt. There they remained for an unknown amount of time until Joseph learned of Herod's death. Historians largely agree that Herod died in March of 4 BC after a desperate attempt to find relief from his syphilitic symptoms including 'fever, itching, pains in the colon, swollen feet, inflammation of the abdomen, gangrene of the penis, lung disease, convulsions, and eye problems'.[41] His death brought safety for Jesus and his family, but not peace. His heir's inept choices and an ensuing revolt during the following Passover led to the crucifixion of 3,000 Passover pilgrims.[42]

Rather than wait for any normal communication of the king of Judea's demise to trickle into Egypt, an angel appeared in a dream to Joseph to tell him it was safe to return to Israel. Joseph's three reported angelic conversations all came in the form of dreams. In all there are five angelic visitations during the infancy narrative of Christ – one to Mary, three in dreams to Joseph and one to the shepherds outside Bethlehem – in addition to the dream that warned the Magi to avoid Herod. Like the angel that brought Mary news of her pregnancy, the one who spoke to Joseph was male. The women who today play the role of angels in the many live Nativities are an extension of the modern perception of angels rather than what texts tell us. Despite the common secular perception of angels, Christian and Jewish scriptures attest that angels were created by God before he made man. The angels of the Bible are spiritual beings who can, during times of need, take physical form, but there is nothing to connect them to the spirits of dead humans.

While little is known about the life of angels in heaven, when they are sent to do service on earth they have a fairly narrow range of duties. Revelation shows the role as bringers of plague; elsewhere in the Bible they are warriors involved in an unseen spiritual battle. However, they are used by God throughout the scriptures most often as messengers to men. In fact, Old Testament Hebrew authors used the word *mal'akh* and New Testament authors the Greek word *angelos*, both of which mean messenger.[43] Galatians 3:19 shows Paul passing on the Jewish belief that angels conveyed the law to Moses, who became its mediator.

The account of the Annunciation names the angel Gabriel who visited Mary. Gabriel is also mentioned in the book of Daniel, when the angel speaks to Daniel in a dream to explain what he is seeing during the dream-vision. He also carried a message to the priest Zechariah before the birth of the prophet John the Baptist. One of only three named angels, Gabriel means 'the strength of God'.[44]

No name is given to the first angel to appear to the shepherds. After what must have been an already startling proclamation, the supernatural announcement becomes even more dazzling: 'Suddenly a great company of the heavenly host appeared with the angel, praising God and saying, "Glory to God in the highest, and on earth peace to men on whom his favour rests."' Some translations present

The angels named in the Bible are all male. Typically, when churches organize live nativities, women and girls take the roles of angels, as in the Live Nativity Angel Choir in Wintertown, Pennsylvania, 2012.

this heavenly host as the armies of God, and indeed they are more often at work on military matters when mentioned in the scriptures.

Following that awesome communication, the shepherds continue on the path we know so well. They troop into the small town of Bethlehem and find the house with visitors who have placed their newborn child in a manger normally used for feeding animals. They see a woman resting after her labour, a couple overwhelmed with the joy of a safe delivery and a new baby. What they find does not dull the power of the angels' appearance, because the shepherds return to their nomadic lifestyle as evangelists, spreading the news of the miracle, amazing their audiences with their story. Meanwhile the family becomes accustomed to their new charge, but relishes the excitement of the night of his birth. Luke, arguably the most pro-women author of the New Testament, records a delicate, insightful image from this event: 'Mary treasured up all these things and pondered them in her heart' (Luke 2:19).

The events of the first Christmas may appear simple, certainly far simpler than its commemorative celebration today. In the midst of shopping lists, baking and finding a moment of peace and quiet in between Christmas services, parties and choral concerts, we might covet the Holy Family's minimalistic existence. Nonetheless, the planning that went into pulling off that first, tentative Christmas Day was as fragile as a newborn's first breath.

# TWO

# Early Celebrations and Customs

It took some time for the Christian church to institutionalize the birthday heralded by the Old Testament. In AD 325 Constantine the Great declared that the Roman Empire had a new state religion: Christianity. The Roman church had scheduled Christmas, known then as the Feast of the Nativity, by 336.[1] Early records of this feast's acceptance are sparse, but we know that a preacher in Antioch made Christmas part of a homily in 386, calling the festival 'new-fangled', since it had been in Antioch for only ten years.[2]

Once Christianity had become the power religion among the Romans, finding a yearly date to celebrate its Messiah's birth became a luxury in which the Church could indulge. In the Bible, only Pharaoh and Herod Antipas celebrate birthdays, and Herod probably did it as a mark of his acceptance of Roman culture. Unlike the Greeks, Romans celebrated the birthdays of adults, although the evidence is not as clear on children's birthdays. The birthday person took the lead in orchestrating their own birthday, firing up their home altar and interacting with the gods who allowed their life to continue; friends could join in and often gave gifts, but the birthday ritual focused on the self.[3]

Astronomers and historians have worked together to try to identify the star that called the wise men from the East to Bethlehem. The Bible records offer some tantalizing details. The Magi saw the star and followed it to King Herod in search of the new Jewish king: 'We saw his star in the east and have come to worship him' (Matthew 2:2). Herod's scribes suggest Bethlehem as the proper destination,

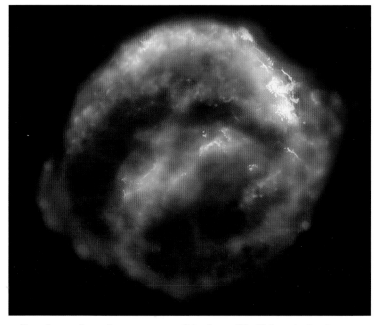

One theory about the appearance of the Star of Bethlehem is that it was a supernova that attracted the attention of the Magi. NASA has used infrared and optical light to study the remnants of Kepler's supernova, which was easily observed by the naked eye when it was first seen in 1604.

but the star seems to continue to lead the Magi there: 'the star they had seen in the east went ahead of them until it stopped over the place where the child was' (Matthew 2:9). Before he let the Magi out of his clutches, Herod asked them about the star's appearance, and, later, he used this knowledge to order the deaths of all male children two years of age and younger.

Since it is believed by some that Jesus was actually born in 6 BC, certain astronomers hypothesize that the heavenly event was Pisces, or the formation of Mars, Saturn and Jupiter very close together. If not Pisces, another possibility for the event is a supernova, like the one that occurred in 1054, which lasted for two years and could be seen at its peak during the daytime. However, such an occurrence received plenty of attention, so it seems unlikely that a supernova between 6 and 4 BC would be recorded by only one Judean writer, Matthew.[4]

If not a supernova, the event may have been a conjunction of the planets. In May of 7 BC, Jupiter, then thought to be the royal star, passed near Saturn in a conjunction in the region of Pisces. Astrologers associated events in Pisces with the land of the Hebrews, so the stargazing Magi would have known where to go. Another possibility is the conjunction of Jupiter and Venus in June of 2 BC, when the two planets seemed to merge in a brilliant light. The only difficulty with using modern computers to chart ancient planetary movements is the fact that the single gospel account says the star moved and then stood still over Bethlehem. This does not fit planetary movements, which are constant.[5]

Of course, the early church fathers did not have computers charting ancient planetary movements, so they suggested dates based on other criteria. Logic was not always part of the process. Climate dictates that Bethlehem is too rainy to keep sheep in fields during December and January, and lambing has long brought shepherds into the fields at night in March, April and May. Consequently, these springtime months seemed the most likely for the event.[6] Nonetheless, the local church in Rome took the initiative to claim, in 336, that 25 December was Jesus' birthday.[7] Meanwhile, the churches of Cyprus, Mesopotamia, Asia Minor and Armenia retained 6 January as the date for Christ's birth.

There are two compelling reasons for the December date. First of all, the Annunciation had been factored to fall on 25 March. Some thinkers had argued that this date, the spring equinox, was the appropriate birthday of Christ since it brimmed with symbolism of spring's rebirth and new creation.[8] God's son and His resulting new creation must have sprung from this date too, they argued. However, later voices like the historian Sextus Julius Africanus pointed out that this must instead be the date of Christ's physical conception on earth. So, with Jesus' conception date tracked down, it is possible that church historians timed his orderly birth to follow exactly nine months later.[9] In the twentieth century scholars did not argue about the actual date of Jesus' birth; instead, they filled journals with articles about the means by which early church leaders concocted possible dating systems.

If holy maths, or something like it, could be categorically proven to be truly responsible for the 25 December date of Christmas, than scholars following the Calculation hypothesis would be cheering in a bar somewhere. Their competitors, proponents of the History of Religions hypothesis, have their own strong points to bring to the debate. In the old Julian calendar, 25 December was already heralded as the winter equinox, the shortest day of the year. As such, it was held to be the birthday of the sun god of Persia as well as that of the popular divinity with which that sun god had been conflated, Mithra.[10] Mithra was a favoured god of Roman soldiers, and they planted temples to him at many of their outposts, including one in the City of London, where the stone foundation of the temple was uncovered in 1954. As a male cult, Mithraism had plenty of appeal. A text referred to as the *Chronography* from 354 reveals the planning that went into fixing church dates as church authorities considered Roman and pagan mythology and solar events. They picked the winter solstice for Jesus' birthday and the summer solstice, 25 June, for that of his cousin John the Baptist.[11]

Saturnalia, originally a feast in honour of Saturn, was already a popular celebration among the Romans running from 17 until 23 December, and the holiday season lasted until Kalends, on 1 January, the day Roman officials took office. This extended holiday was cause for feasting, parades and ritual worship. Records show that Saturnalia gifts included wax dolls, thought to be perhaps the happier interpretation of earlier child sacrifices to the sun god.[12] In 274 the Emperor Aurelian declared that the winter solstice, then 25 December, would be a public festival honouring the sun. When the Roman Christians chose the same date for their Christmas celebration, they were staking a claim on the day's festive possibilities. This blending of traditions between Mithra, Saturnalia, Kalends and Jesus marks a meaningful start to Christmas's continuing evolution based on intermingled rituals and narratives, a characteristic of the holiday that is in full force in the twenty-first century.

The Eastern Church was also honouring Christ's birth on 25 December by 380, but this meant a revision of the Epiphany holiday as they had been celebrating it. Earlier the church in Constantinople had celebrated Jesus' birth and baptism on Epiphany, but they separated the two and adopted the Catholic Church's December date. Catholics would later revise Epiphany to be a feast for the Magi, but parishioners in the East did not follow suit.[13] Even today the Eastern Church celebrates Epiphany as Christ's baptism, while churches in the West, if they celebrate it at all, keep it as the revelation of Christ to the Magi.

In the West, many celebrants showed great loyalty to the date, even when it shifted. An added level of scheduling confusion came with the controversial shift to the Gregorian calendar, which Pope Gregory XIII instituted by papal bull in 1582. Pope Gregory's scientists had found that the Julian calendar had calculated the year to be eleven minutes shorter than it really is, and the error was amounting to eighteen hours per century. The spring equinox, and therefore Easter, was moving ever backwards towards early winter; hence the papal bull. Catholic countries like Spain, France and Italy obeyed immediately, but Protestant countries felt no reason to comply. This meant that you could celebrate Christmas on 25 December in France,

The rites of the Roman Saturnalia included sacrifices to the god Saturn, parties and gift-giving, as depicted in this engraving of 1866.

sail across the Channel, and celebrate with the British on their Christmas, which, to the enlightened Gregorian calendarist, would seem like 6 January. Eventually Britain instituted the calendar change for itself and its colonies in 1752. The switch meant that Britons had to give up eleven days in September of that year, causing Christmas to fall (for those who embraced the new calendar) on 25 December. Those who chose to celebrate Old Christmas Day feasted on 5 January, waiting to see if the Glastonbury thorn – a traditional indicator of Christmas – would bud on Old Christmas. They hoped such indefatigable proof would force the rest of the world to revert to the sanity of the Julian calendar.[14] The famous thorn complied, according to legend, but the world did not. Thomas Hardy still used the confusion over the real Christmas Day's date in his late Victorian novels. By then the practice seemed very rustic.

Plenty of controversy can be found around Christmas, even today. An urban myth that haunts Christmas is the concern over the use of 'Xmas' as a post-modern abbreviated form of the word that takes 'Christ' out of it. What had long been referred to as 'the Nativity' became, in Old English, 'Christes Maesse' around 1050, and the abbreviation of Xmas was in use by the 1100s. The Greek word for Christ begins with a character that looks like an X, known as 'chi', prompting the frequent abbreviation of both 'Xian' and 'Xmas'.

The practice of Christmas spread alongside Christianity. After all, who doesn't like a party? Pope Julius I declared it a holiday in 350.[15] The Egyptian church was celebrating it by 432, and it had reached England by the sixth century. Scandinavians adopted it over the next two centuries, but only after mixing the holiday with their own pagan Yule. The popularity of Yule traditions may be one reason that Christmas has outshone Easter, the liturgical heavyweight, in the colder climates.[16] In the late sixth century Pope Gregory had instructed Mellitus, an abbot in Britain, to encourage the new converts to celebrate the holy days of the church however they liked, even if that meant following pagan customs; the Christian God would now be the focus of formerly pagan devotions.[17] By the thirteenth century Christmas had spread throughout Europe.

HELLEBORUS *niger, flore albo, etiam interdum valde rubente* 12
*True Black Hellebore, or Christmas rose.*

Georg Dionysus Ehret, *Helleborus niger*, 1745. A legend surrounds
this flowering evergreen, also known as the Christmas rose. Apparently, in
past centuries, the little flower bloomed only on Christmas Day according
to the Julian calendar, causing attentive gardeners to reject the
Gregorian dating system.

In Norway, the pagan population had to transition from the beer-drinking traditions of the Viking Yule, or *jøl*, into the Christian Christmas. In the tenth century King Haakon the Good, who had been raised and converted in the English court, ordered that *jøl* celebrations coincide with the Christian Christmas, and that everyone drink beer and make merry or pay a fine.[18] It took the work of several more kings to Christianize Norway, and regional law-making bodies typically established laws that required beer-drinking, most likely to encourage the adaptation of old ways of toasting the Norse gods.[19] The Norwegians adopted the gift-giving rituals from the Roman Kalends, and the church regulated other rituals associated with the religious Christmas. In all of Europe, however, the Norwegians are the only people still to refer to the midwinter holiday as their pre-Christian ancestors did – it is not Christmas to them, but *jøl*. When the Reformation hit Norway, a dearth of clerics led to two equally sacred days of rest and worship, a scheduling boon still enjoyed today.[20]

Boniface's mission work in Germany in the mid-eighth century was the first successful effort to Christianize the Saxon tribes there. He worked in conjunction with another missionary, Leoba, who established monasteries that served to showcase the fruits of Christian living to the surrounding tribes.[21] Christmas developed there much as it did in other European nations adopting Christianity. There is a sense that the Germans have a special historical tie to Christmas, but this perception did not develop until a millennium after the holiday was first brought to Germany. During the nineteenth century Germans succeeded in convincing themselves and their neighbours that the German Christmas had a particularly unique character.[22]

As missionaries carried the vestiges of Roman culture and the blossoming Christian faith north into Europe, they also brought new ways of thinking about the year. The Roman months replaced pre-Christian month names, and Christians also introduced the schedule of religious festivals, including Lady Day, Martinmas and Christmas. St Willibrord, Benedictine missionary to England and to the German Saxons, created a calendar matching up the feast days with the Roman calendar in the early eighth century. These feast days served both as a way to celebrate and as a means of educating the people in the new faith.[23]

Like missionaries, politicians have long known how to calculate the effectiveness of Christmas. Charlemagne scheduled his coronation in Rome for Christmas Day in 800, which might also be seen as the birth date of the Holy Roman Empire. Similarly, after arriving in England in September and a decisive victory in October, William the Conqueror became king in Westminster Abbey on Christmas Day 1066. We must recall that 25 December was seen not only as the birthday of the king of kings, but as the date for celebrating the kingly Magi.

The development of Advent as a season of preparation came along in the sixth century, spreading slowly across Christendom. Monks in sixth-century Gaul fasted from St Martin's Day, 11 November, until Christmas, and laypeople eventually followed suit. Later that Lent-length fast lost its catchy name, Quadragesima of St Martin, and it shrank to just the four weeks leading up to Christmas; then it was demoted to a less austere form of preparation, and one the laity was not always expected to perform.[24] In seventh-century Rome the liturgical year started with the vigil of Christmas, but a change in the religious celebration of Christmas caused the church year to open instead with Advent and its four weeks of preparation.[25]

In England, Christians probably did not face the month-long weight battle that now characterizes the Christmas season. In the fifteenth and sixteenth centuries the wealthy skipped roasts and pies, but ate instead soups and fish. Christmas Eve's restrictions kept cheese, meat and eggs off the table, so the meal that welcomed Christmas Day truly gave cause for celebration. A nobleman's kitchens might provide several swans and barrels of Malmsey wine.[26] Elsewhere nobles feasted their neighbours, both rich and poor, with open-house hospitality.

The Twelve Days of Christmas, which now seems to be mostly represented by the repetitive song and television programming, simply comes from the convenient scheduling of the festival period.

The Victorians idealized country-house Christmas traditions
from the 1500s, especially the presentation of the boar's head.
Engraving by Edmund H. Garrett, 1886.

Instead of the run-up to Christmas, the twelve days marked the
period following the Advent fast, from Christmas Day until Epiphany, the real party of the season. The Council of Tours of 567 first
bundled the twelve days into one celebration, but this probably
only ratified what had been going on in practice.[27] In England, the
Christmas season had lasted for just nine days until a decree by
ninth-century King Alfred extended the event to Epiphany, bringing the total festive days to twelve.[28] During these twelve days some
localities required people to take a rest from their work, especially
spinning and carding of wool, the typical winter activity on a farm.

The final night of Christmas, which fell on 5 or 6 January, depending on one's location, was called Twelfth Night and involved feasting and costumed celebrations. Shakespeare probably wrote *Twelfth Night* for a Christmas-time entertainment, and he certainly included a plot that emphasized disguise and merriment. History records various dramatic celebrations on Twelfth Night, including masques put on for Elizabeth I, James I and Charles I. The cost of one Christmas masque in 1633 ran to £20,000.[29]

During the 1990s an urban legend developed, suggesting that the song 'Twelve Days of Christmas' contained elements of a secret Catholic catechism, but there is no supporting evidence for this. The song is probably French in origin, and it served as the basis of a Twelfth Night memory game with forfeits. In addition to games, Twelfth Night had its own special menu. A traditional French Twelfth Night included a cake, a forerunner of the King Cake of New Orleans, in which celebrants sought a hidden bean or pea. Whoever found it wore the crown for the night as a celebratory monarch. Mary Queen of Scots celebrated with such a cake in 1563, and her own attendant Mary Fleming found the bean and reigned for the night, complete with a gown and jewels borrowed from the real monarch.[30]

The extended season of Christmas became a time of reversals. Feasting, cross-dressing and Lords of Misrule entertained the population of Europe. The Christmas season upended the strict hierarchical structure of church and social life, often relieving the strain of the oppressed masses. In Scandinavia Christmas celebrants continued a similar practice into the 1700s. During a Christmas game, single people conducted a ceremony that 'consecrated' a Christmas bishop wearing blackface. This faux bishop had the power temporarily to marry people. The marriages lasted for one night, suggesting that the custom's detractors had some reason to quibble with the morality of the practice.[31]

In medieval cathedrals, monasteries, religious schools and parish churches throughout Western Europe, choirboys would select one of their own number to take on an incredibly public role. The boy bishop would temporarily assume many of the duties of the real bishop, even presiding over services in bishop's clothing. While this must have been great fun for the boy bishop, it is easy to see how it must have been a grating experience for the adults in charge. Some cathedral authorities added rules about who could be elected, and others simply took the democratic power away from the trouble-making choristers. Nonetheless, the populace loved the tradition, and the naysayers had a hard time restricting it over the several centuries it held sway as an expected part of the Christmas season. Selecting boy bishops took place in England from the early thirteenth century until 1559, and it lasted until 1721 in at least one French diocese.[32] At Salisbury Cathedral the practice dates back to before 1222.[33] There a boy bishop might expect to spend several weeks travelling through the district, feasting and visiting the homes of rich patrons who found great amusement in being instructed in ecclesiastical behaviour by a choirboy.[34] In Padua the boy bishop would demand wine from the real bishop, and the feasting that characterized medieval Christmases reigned during this topsy-turvy time as well.

Boy bishops, sometimes called Nicholases, may have grown out of two specific December holy days. St Nicholas became popular in Europe after his bones became European citizens, having been transferred from modern-day Turkey to Italy at the end of the eleventh century. Boys may have taken to dressing up as this historical bishop in early December. On 28 December, Holy Innocents Day, attention turned to the young choristers, and it is believed that the two holy days were combined; certainly, the election of boy bishops was traditionally held on 28 December. The boys' choir would take the seats of the church authorities, and the canons would have to sit in the choir and perform the choirboys' duties during the services overseen by the boy bishop. The boy bishop could give an often ironic homily that had been written for him and lead much of the Mass but not, however, the Canon – the game did not extend that far.[35]

Similarly, eighteenth-century Jutland schoolchildren enjoyed the topsy-turvy nature of St Thomas's Day, 21 December, when they could ignore all their masters' rules. Their antics included card-playing, dancing, yelling and burning the switch that the masters used to punish them.[36]

In 1541 Henry VIII forbade the practice wherein 'children be stranglie decked and apparayled to counterfeit priestes, bishoppes, and women ... rather to the deryson than the true glory of God'.[37] Queen Mary allowed the practice, but her sister put an end to it, perhaps just as it was dying a natural death and the public found entertainment in a growing number of other venues.[38] The rest of Europe also saw the end of the practice in subsequent years. Nonetheless, for centuries the boy bishop had served as a safety valve for populations burdened by the authority of the Church, and it also gave the boys a chance to drive their superiors to distraction. Other than a very few parish churches that have bravely revived the boy bishop, most twenty-first-century churches would probably rather forget all about it.

London seemed the place to be for Christmas revelries in the sixteenth and seventeenth centuries, so much so that royal decrees went out telling gentleman landowners to leave the capital before Christmas so that they could oversee festivities on their own rural estates. In 1589, James I famously tried to revolutionize Christmas into a country holiday with repeated requests and decrees to his noblemen to go home. Ben Jonson's Christmas masque, written and performed for James I in 1616, idealized the elements of the rural, traditional Christmas, partly as a rhetorical device to convince the nobility to head home and lead celebrations for their labourers. The stunning, expensive feasts and theatricals James I and his son held probably did not help their cause, since they made London the Christmas hotspot for less motivated nobles.

One of the traditions King James's nobles could look forward to was the crowning of a peasant as the Lord of Misrule. The Roman Saturnalia lent Christmas this tradition of hierarchical buffoonery. Christmas-keeping and feasting required considerable organization, and some royal English courts and noble estates appointed a Lord of Misrule or King of Christmas to oversee the dramatic delights and other festivities. The tradition became popular among royalty at the end of the fifteenth century.[39] Henry VII paid money to a

Lord of Misrule. Edward VI and Henry VIII had their own Lords of Misrule, usually choosing a new one each year.[40] The custom's popularity peaked under Henry VIII.[41] Certainly, wherever the king was for Christmas, a Lord of Misrule could be found as well.[42] Edward VI's Lord of Misrule kept a busy schedule during the season, which included in 1552–3 a mock naval battle on the Thames and a joust on hobby horses. In other years he paraded into the City and gave mock speeches surrounded by a retinue of morris dancers and bagpipers, with someone tossing money to bystanders. Edward's successor, Mary, had her brother's Lord of Misrule executed for political reasons, and that put an end to the practice at the English court.[43]

Royalty were not the only ones to establish a Christmas administrator. The Inns of Court in London not only prepared rich young men for the legal profession in an Oxbridge-like setting,

The Lords of Misrule were put in charge of Christmas event planning from the medieval period until the practice was banned in the 16th century. Engraving by Edmund H. Garrett, 1886.

but provided an education in Christmas-keeping. Sometimes lasting from 21 December until 10 January, the Christmas season at the Inns of Court included singing, dancing, dicing and dramatic entertainment, usually presided over by a Christmas King. On Christmas Day the young men did not neglect church, and they followed the service with a traditional meal of boar's head. Additional entertainment, which sounds cruel to modern ears, included a mock hunt complete with a cat bound to a fox; hounds set upon these sorry creatures inside the hall among the celebrants. As one historian has noted, 'Student parties have never been renowned for sensible activities.'[44] During plague years – and there were several in the early sixteenth century – Christmas at the Inns of Court was cancelled.[45] During the years when Christmas cheer prevailed, the Inns of Court continued the tradition of a drama, sometimes with a cast of 60 or more, and served as a practice ground for budding writers such as George Gascoigne and William Baldwin.

During the fourteenth century, urban Britons might have taken in a play as part of their Advent season. Staging plays outdoors in cold climates limited the development of drama during Christmas, and the Nativity story was often portrayed during summer performances. However, some dramatists gave the Christmas season a chance. Lincoln Cathedral staged an Epiphany drama for most of the fourteenth century, and Tintinhall and Tewkesbury also put on biblical plays, although they were not always about the Nativity.[46]

A form of Christmas theatre may have been the transition point from pagan tree-decorating ceremonies to the Christian Christmas tree. The paradise play, about Adam and Eve, was especially popular at this time of year, since their feast day was 24 December. The sole prop for the play, a fir tree hung with apples, caught the imagination of audiences and lingered there long after church authorities had banned the plays because of their growing vulgarity. Influenced by the play's decorated fir, Germans brought the paradise tree into their homes. A candlelit, multi-tiered shelf called a pyramid held symbols of Christmas and was already in use as a holiday decoration, both in Germany and in Moravian homes in eighteenth-century Pennsylvania. Eventually someone probably combined the tree of the play with the pyramid, thus creating a Christmas tree like one we would recognize today.[47]

Ancient festivities had already accustomed Europeans to celebrating with trees. Pagans had celebrated midwinter with trees in ancient times, when druids decorated oaks for Odin and Balder. One Roman tradition during Saturnalia was to place trinkets, candles and representations of the sun god on trees. Two legends have arisen about Christian authorities promoting the cause of the festive tree. One tells how Boniface, the missionary to Germany, struck down an oak tree, a symbol of paganism, to stop a child sacrifice. He redirected the stunned pagans' attention to an evergreen tree and told them to revere it as the infant Christ's tree. The other myth suggests that Martin Luther brought an evergreen into his home and decorated it for Christmas. Regardless of who decorated the first official Christmas tree, the tradition was lively enough in the Salzburg area in 1755 for authorities to ban the removal of evergreens from the surrounding forests.[48]

And Christmas-keepers have continued to demonstrate the Salzburgers' zeal for the holiday in subsequent centuries, often without any limit to the consumption of materials to that end. The monumental meaning of Christmas drives us on. Much of the modern significance of Christmas is a patina of legends overlaying the biblical accounts and the work of scholars who have only sometimes got it right. This holiday has grown into a machine, but at the heart of it is a tiny child whose real birthday, it is safe to say, has been lost to history.

# THREE

# Christmas in Art and Culture

It is a cold, miserable, muddy late December outside Stalingrad in 1942. In the German Sixth Army morale is slipping, and creature comforts are nowhere available. In the poor light of his cramped bunker, ordained pastor and staff physician Kurt Reuber meticulously sketches an image of Mary and the infant Christ on the back of a Russian map. Conditions are poor for making the sketch – his pencils, he complains, are lost in the mud – but the act of devotion sustains him. Certainly, when he unveils the three- by four-foot image to the men in other bunkers, their reaction uplifts him: 'How they sat there! Like being in their dear homes with mother for the celebration.'[1] At his unit's Christmas gathering, Reuber's sketch captivates them all: 'They stood as if entranced, devout and too moved to speak in front of the picture on the clay wall . . . This earthly object became for me a symbol of the eternal all – and then in the end it was Christmas and the Madonna appeared before us.'[2]

The sketch found a spot on the last flight out and escaped the Red Army, which surrounded the German Sixth. Reuber was not so lucky. Within a month of his Christmas celebration, he was a prisoner of war, destined to die in a prison camp two years later.[3] I still remember first seeing a reproduction of Reuber's work more than a dozen years ago in an alcove at Coventry Cathedral. The simplicity of the drawing attracted me, as did its comforting curves and the austere medium. The story of suffering and courage that produced this Christmas artefact makes it a valuable object of meditation. Furthermore, the *Madonna of Stalingrad* represents what

The simple, curving charcoal lines of Kurt Reuber's *Madonna of Stalingrad* eloquently express the comfort available at Christmas 1942.

Christmas art is capable of. The gospel accounts offer limited descriptions of the night of Christ's birth, but artists have not allowed such lacunae to limit the presentation of that scene. Early Christian art and music reinterpreted the scant data offered by the gospel writers.

Unlike Reuber's fellow soldiers, denizens of the twenty-first century, inundated as we are with Christmas images, jingles and decor, have become largely desensitized to the role of effective Christmas art. This was certainly not the case in the past. Since the fourth century, Christmas art has been used to instruct the masses in religious devotion and, more recently, the community expectations of Christmas.

Iconography, the study of symbolism in art, offers a way for historians to follow ideas embedded in depictions of the Nativity.

Scholars of iconography see each artist's image of a biblical text as not just illustration but actual interpretation.[4] The earliest surviving example of the Nativity in art is in the form of sarcophagi dating from the fourth century, found in Rome and Gaul. Early representations might show only a swaddled infant or the infant and the animals. Placing such signs on stone coffins was meant to represent Christ's divinity and his promised salvation.[5] The more elaborate Nativity scenes on sarcophagi were already introducing the misinterpretation that the shepherds and the Magi visited Christ together on the night of his birth.[6]

In the sixth century Eastern Orthodox works began to show Mary reclining, recovering from the exhaustion of labour. At the same time, two apocryphal scenes of the Nativity lent themselves to Eastern Christian art: the midwives who delivered Jesus and the child's first bath, as described in the apocryphal Arabic Gospel of the Childhood of Christ.[7]

Late twelfth-century Christian art shows a new state in the relationship between Mary and her newborn. While previously Mary had seemed indifferent, artists now attempted to show tenderness between the Holy Mother and the infant Christ. It seems the realities of human life had entered the depictions of the Nativity, with some pieces even showing Mary breastfeeding her child.[8]

The 1300s brought to art the Adoration of the Child motif, which was a more devotional arrangement. Through body language and facial expressions, it became clear that instead of just recovering from birth, Mary and Joseph were worshipping the infant. The mysticism of this era dictated this new motif.[9] From the mid-sixteenth century onwards, the Adoration of the Child transformed into the Adoration of the Shepherds, where the shepherds join the holy parents in staring worshipfully at the child. Sixteenth-century Nativity art focused on the poverty of the Holy Family, a switch from earlier centuries when Mary might have been shown with serving women. Rembrandt's Nativity scene of 1646 emphasizes the poverty of the manger's inhabitants.[10]

An anonymous Flemish painting of the Nativity scene dated to 1515 may be the first depiction of Down's syndrome in art. The

This is the oldest known artistic representation of the first Christmas. Unlike later sarcophagus Christmas scenes, this one correctly shows a toddler Christ welcoming the Magi. Panel from a Roman sarcophagus, 4th century CE, from the cemetery of St Agnes in Rome.

painting, *The Adoration of the Christ Child*, shows several figures arranged around the naked infant Christ. An angel kneels next to Mary, and this angel shows several physical traits that an author for the *British Medical Journal* has identified as characteristic of Down's syndrome: the angel has a 'flattened mid-face, epicanthal folds, upslanted palpebral fissures, a small and upturned tip of the nose; and downward curving of the corners of the mouth'; in addition, the left hand has short fingers.[11] John Haydon Langdon-Down would eventually identify the syndrome in 1866, so all prior historical representations of it are intriguing. The psychiatrist who co-wrote the essay identifying the angel with the syndrome reflected: 'It is impossible to know whether any disability had been recognised or whether it simply was not relevant in that time and place.'[12]

As printing technology improved, engravings became a relatively inexpensive way for a wide audience to access art. Many eighteenth- and early nineteenth-century engravings emphasized the joviality of the Stewart Christmases past. Soon engravings were also used to teach a new type of Christmas, the one focused on domesticity and children. It was, after all, the engraving of Queen Victoria and her family around their table-top Christmas tree in the *Illustrated London News in* 1848 that validated the Christmas tree's place in the national celebration of Christmas. Similarly, Thomas Nast's Santa engravings for *Harper's Weekly* established the particular rotundity of a jolly Santa we expect to see today.

As with the visual arts, the appearance of Christmas in poetry evolved over time. The fourteenth-century poem *Sir Gawain and the Green Knight* takes Christmas court scenes as its setting:

> Christmas time. The king is home at Camelot
> Among his many lords, all splendid men –
> All the trusted brothers of the Round Table
> Ready for court revels and carefree pleasures.[13]

The alliterative verse in Middle English explains that King Arthur's fifteen days of revelry are interrupted by the appearance of a tall, entirely green knight on a green horse who challenges the court to a beheading game. One might like the odds of 'you chop my head off and then I'll chop off yours', but when Sir Gawain gallantly accepts the dare, he finds not only that the green man survives his beheading, but that his detached head can dole out specific instructions about how Gawain must find him and offer his own neck before a year is out.

The Gawain poet, as the unknown writer has been named, fits in the revels of one more Christmas season before the quest concludes. Gawain completes his seemingly hopeless quest, and discovers his own faults in the process. As one *Gawain* scholar has written, 'Gawain and his fellow-members of the Round Table require an education into the meaning of the feast they are celebrating, and the Green Knight is to be the instrument of that education.'[14] Thus the purpose of the Christmas setting is not just one of gratuitous festive description; it touches on the deep religious culture of the poet's time.

When English poets of the fifteenth century pounced on the idea of Christmas in verse, it was a largely new development. Their carols, less sacred then a typical hymn, were religious in nature but more informal, perfect for a party of wassailers enjoying Christmas out of doors.[15] The carols formed the main body of Christmas poetry during the fifteenth and sixteenth centuries in England, as they did in Italy, France, Spain and Germany.[16]

The seventeenth-century English metaphysical poets George Herbert and Henry Vaughan drafted severely religious Christmas verse with a mystical overtone, as in Vaughan's plea,

> I would I had in my best part
> Fit rooms for Thee! Or that my heart
> Were so clean as
> Thy manger was![17]

In contrast, the country clergyman Robert Herrick's heartier poetry sounds brazen and exhilarating:

Illustration from *King Arthur and the Knights of the Round Table* by Michel Gantelet (1472). Sir Gawain is the nephew of King Arthur and a Knight of the Round Table. The poem about his quest begins at Christmastide.

> Come, bring with a noise,
> My merrie merrie boyes,
> The Christmas log to the firing;
> While my good dame, she
> Bids ye all be free,
> And drink to your hearts desiring.[18]

Hymns dominated the Christmas poetry of the eighteenth century, and the religious tone continued through a vein of Victorian seasonal verse. The flowering of the periodical market, made possible by cheaper printing methods and an increasingly literate society, cried out for Christmas poetry to fill December volumes.[19] Socially minded Christmas poems might rhapsodize about overworked seamstresses or the dreariness of Christmas in the workhouse. The popular comic periodical *Punch* included no end of droll poems about the ironies of Christmas. On a more serious note, Thomas Hardy was not alone in writing poems about ghosts and the horrors of war, an especially effective approach during the season of peace.

Many people can quote at least a few lines from one American Christmas poem, 'A Visit from St Nicholas', which is more often referred to as ''Twas the Night before Christmas'. Title pages in countless versions of this poem attest that it was written by a New Yorker and professor of classics, Clement Moore; however, this attribution may be the result of literary theft. Tradition holds that Moore wrote the poem for his six children, who had apparently requested it, just in time for Christmas 1822.[20] A snooping relative is supposed to have found the poem and had it printed in a local New York paper a year later. Oral testimony, however, suggests another author, one Henry Livingston Jr, a Revolutionary War major, farmer and general Renaissance man living in Poughkeepsie, New York. Livingston's daughter passed on a tale about how her father shared his poem with guests one Christmas morning, and that one of those guests, the governess to Clement Moore's children, requested a copy, which took on a life of its own. Certainly the rhyme scheme and absurd topic of the poem suggest a match with Livingston's other poetry. Furthermore, a volume of verse Moore produced made claims that all the poems were his, when in fact several came from the pen of his wife and other, uncredited poets.[21]

Whoever the author, the poem itself has had a traceable impact on the development of the modern Christmas. Our idea of Santa Claus as portly and merry stems directly from the description given in 'A Visit from St Nicholas'.[22] Prior to that, gift-bringers might be threatening or menacing, like the Pennsylvania German Belsnickel. Also, some of those gift-bringers were associated with drunken carousing, so their merriment was not of the child-friendly variety. Perhaps more importantly, in the same way that early dictionaries served to standardize spelling, this early printed description of the Americanized St Nicholas largely froze him in that attitude.[23] And the poem that first entertained an audience in 1822 today continues its lively career. Furthermore, the poem's distinctive limerick-like metre, rhymed anapaestic tetrameter, makes it a tempting subject for parody.[24] Thus advertisements annually co-opt the poem, and there are even a host of alternative versions of 'A Visit from St Nicholas', including those voiced by a pirate and a marine, and one written to honour The Beatles.

While Christmas poems can be trivial in nature, they have also been used to make very sombre statements. Thomas Hardy, the late Victorian novelist and poet, took Christmas for his subject in several poems. In his later years, the Christmas poems are typically gloomy, mostly because Hardy uses the ideal of Christmas as a contrast to the depravity he saw in early twentieth-century culture. Published in the London *Times* in 1915, 'The Oxen' recounts the rustic belief that cattle would kneel down as the bells tolled in Christmas out of reverence for the animals who witnessed Christ's birth. The poem's narrator expresses jealousy for earlier generations who, like his childhood self, could believe in such a folk tradition. It seemed the horrors of the First World War had eradicated the ability to embrace fully something so antiquated. Yet the speaker ends the poem by asserting that even now he would consider going to the barn to see if the oxen really did kneel, 'Hoping it might be so'.[25] Later Hardy's poetic use of Christmas became even darker. For example, his epigrammatic poem of four lines, 'Christmas: 1924',

THE

# Night Before Christmas;

## OR

### KRISS KRINGLE'S VISIT.

BY

## CLEMENT C. MOORE.

### WITH OTHER CHRISTMAS POEMS.

ILLUSTRATED BY NIOE.

PUBLISHED BY WILLIS P. HAZARD,

## AT KRISS KRINGLE'S HEAD QUARTERS,

### 724 Chestnut St., Philadelphia.

This 1858 edition of Clement Moore's poem not only shows the development of the gift-bringer's appearance, but demonstrates that the title was still in flux. This Philadelphia publisher has rechristened the poem to highlight Kris Kringle instead.

cynically notes that mankind has failed to internalize the message of peace so often heralded during Advent, and points to the use of poison gas as a more realistic, if disturbing, marker of humanity's evolution.

Perhaps one of the best-loved works by the Welsh poet Dylan Thomas is his strikingly expressive prose reminiscence about how we perceive Christmases past. Thomas drafted the first version of 'A Child's Christmas in Wales' for a BBC Wales Children's Hour radio broadcast in 1945.[26] Rather than tell a story, the piece captured different scenes that emphasized the nostalgia of childhood Christmases: 'All the Christmases roll down the hill towards the Welsh-speaking sea, like a snowball growing whiter and bigger and rounder, like a cold and headlong moon bundling down the sky that was our street.'[27] Snow features heavily in the reminiscence, not only as a symbol of the memory itself, but as the marker of how special a child's experience is even long after childhood has ended: 'I can never remember whether it snowed for six days and six nights when I was twelve or whether it snowed for twelve days and twelve nights when I was six.'[28]

Like 'A Visit from St Nicholas' and 'A Child's Christmas in Wales', Dr Seuss's *How the Grinch Stole Christmas* features every year as a narrative tradition that helps Christmas-keepers recognize what they wish to embrace about the holiday. The Grinch first appeared in a poem of 1955 published by Theodor Seuss Geisel in *Redbook*. Two

John Morgan, *Snowballing*, 1865. Poetry, novels, paintings and, more recently, films have emphasized a nostalgia for snowy Christmases.

years later the Grinch made his Christmas debut simultaneously in *Redbook* and in book form. Seuss claims to have found his inspiration for the destructive Grinch in his own reflection in the mirror. He certainly embraced his grinchiness, since he selected a personalized registration plate for his car reading 'GRINCH'.[29] 'Grinch' became a short animated film narrated by Boris Karloff in 1966, with Seuss contributing the screenplay. Like Scrooge, the Grinch transforms on Christmas morning. Where the converted Scrooge rushes out to buy things, the altered Grinch stands in the snow on the top of Mount Crumpit and comes to appreciate the beauty of a non-commercial Christmas: 'Then the Grinch thought of something he hadn't before. What if Christmas, he thought, doesn't come from a store. What if Christmas, perhaps, means a little bit more.'[30] As one Seuss expert has remarked, the author himself benefited, as his estate continues to benefit, from the popularity of the Grinch: '[Seuss] might have enjoyed the irony of having written a successful commercial against commercialism.'[31] Further irony exists in the fact that American television viewers now have cause to complain about how the network showing the 26-minute film of 1966 now has to cut out beloved parts to fill the half-hour time slot with more commercials.[32]

Dr Seuss is one in a long line of authors who found the production of Christmas books to be a rewarding endeavour. The first really lucrative burst of Christmas books came in the form of literary annuals, anthologies of sentimental poetry and engravings. Before these ornately designed volumes arrived on the scene in the 1820s, booksellers' December advertisements offered popular eighteenth-century novels as gifts – *Gulliver's Travels*, *The Vicar of Wakefield* and so on. The stories on the gilt-edged pages were not in themselves particularly Christmassy, but these volumes' role as gifts opened the door to a new way of seeing books at Christmas-time.[33]

In America, one author stands out as a beacon of Christmas genius. Washington Irving crafted a picturesque version of Christmas at a rural English estate and packaged it for his American audience. The appealing tale featured in a serialized set of essays and short stories that Irving, then living in England, had published in America. His most famous works, 'The Legend of Sleepy Hollow'

Books about Christmas enjoyed rising popularity starting in
the 1840s, and publishers strove to produce colourful, illustrated
volumes such as *A Booke of Christmas Carols: Illustrated from
Ancient Manuscripts in the British Museum* (1846).

and 'Rip Van Winkle', also appeared in this series, entitled *The
Sketch Book of Geoffrey Crayon, Gent.*

Irving's delightful account of a fictitious Yorkshire Christmas at
Bracebridge Hall drips with nostalgia designed to delight American
readers, many of whom had recently emigrated from England.[34]
The picture of the English Christmas is also nostalgic in that the
sketches lovingly describe fading elements of older Christmas ways,
including morris dancers, the yule log and wassailing. The squire
overseeing the Christmas festivities has a deep devotion to continuing the Christmas customs he sees disappearing elsewhere. These
scenes, published for Christmas 1819, include a loving description
of an immense, communal Wassail Bowl, 'being composed of the
richest and raciest wines, highly spiced and sweetened, with roasted
apples bobbing about the surface'.[35]

As Washington Irving recorded in his sketches, ghost tales suited
the long evenings beside a midwinter fire, and eventually this oral
tradition took its place as a feature of Christmas literature. A few
ghostly Christmas tales appeared in the eighteenth century, but

the genre really took off during the Victorian Christmas craze.[36] Christmas ghosts were especially good at locating a lost inheritance for the worthy but down-on-his-luck protagonist.

Dickens's *A Christmas Carol* is, after all, a ghost story, and Dickens continued the theme in other Christmas publications. That first, inspired Christmas story had been crafted with the idea that a luxurious volume would make a superb Christmas gift book. Dickens demanded that it include four etchings coloured by hand as well as having gilt page edges and a cloth cover. These choices, and the way his contract was set up, meant that even though the first print run of 6,000 books sold out in three days, the volume brought little actual profit to the desperate Dickens. The author had calculated a personal profit of £1,000, but in the end he earned only £137 from that first print run. Furthermore, because of lax piracy laws, he very quickly saw his work earning profit for others.[37]

Many prominent writers quickly followed Dickens's lead in designing books for Christmas purchase. The early wave of Christmas books typically followed Dickens's careful design for *A Christmas Carol* and the four Christmas books he subsequently wrote: a small, single volume that stood out in an era of three-volume novels; a red cloth cover decorated with gold lettering; and, inside, a sentimental tale that almost always ended with a merry reconciliation.[38]

Victorian superstars like George Eliot, William Makepeace Thackeray and Lewis Carroll all embraced the financial boon of Christmas by writing specifically for that market. The upswing in December sales possibilities during the 1840s and '50s actually altered the working habits of authors, illustrators, typesetters and publishers as they rushed to have books to market in time for Christmas.[39] Not all their books actually dealt with Christmas themes, since by the 1870s Christmas books were needed more to supply presents or fill the additional leisure time of the Christmas holiday than to instruct readers on how to celebrate the reinvented festival. Readers first met Sherlock Holmes, for example, in the pages of a periodical's Christmas number in 1887.

Today the British Christmas book market still hums along without overtly Christmassy content. Britons are especially attentive

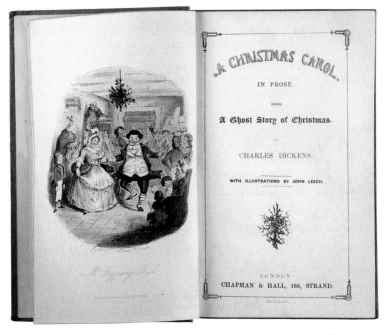

The first edition of *A Christmas Carol*, with its hand-coloured etchings. Design decisions like this, combined with the relatively low price of five shillings, undermined the book's ability to bring in a profit.

to what books sell as Christmas gifts, and each year newspapers run specialized reviews deconstructing the books as gifts in much the same way that crowded Victorian Christmas book reviews did more than a century ago. Cookbooks, coffee-table books and even cleverly written grammar books are popular in the struggle to fill the space under the tree. The book lists offered to consumers are not entirely genuine evaluations of quality, however. In 2006 W. H. Smith charged publishers £200,000 per book for a slot on their recommended reading list, and Waterstones charged £45,000 for a promotion package for half a dozen books with highly ambitious marketing campaigns.[40] Both plans were intended to boost those books' Christmas sales. Books may need special mention to stand out among the volumes for sale in December; since 2002 there has been a noticeable increase in publishers' Christmas offerings. More and more best-selling fiction writers such as John Grisham, Anne

Perry and James Patterson are producing Christmas volumes in the hope that their books will turn into traditional Christmas reading and, for the author, a reliable, long-lasting source of income.[41]

Today's musicians have a similar goal when they write Christmas ditties, and they throw their efforts into the perky, inescapable soundscape of Christmas. While radio stations may broadcast Christmas music ranging from the classic to the obnoxious, the Church has a special hold on the music of Christmas. This musical ascendency started with pieces inserted into the Catholic Mass. The Mass has staple pieces, such as the Kyrie and the Gloria, but it also has movable responses that vary depending on the liturgical season. By the late medieval period these rotating parts allowed for the early inclusion of seasonal music at Christmas time, although it was very different from the carols we sing today. A Christmas Mass of the twelfth century would have a Gregorian chant for the Gradual, a responsive chant that commented on the scripture that had just been read.[42]

Famous composers have contributed greatly to the sacred music ringing out in churches during the holiday season. Johann Sebastian Bach, for example, composed his Cantata No. 147 for the fourth Sunday of Advent. Today the piece's tenth movement is better known as 'Jesu, bleibet meine freude', its first line, which in English is translated as 'Jesu, Joy of Man's Desiring'. This Baroque cantata fulfilled part of Bach's contract with the St Thomas School in Leipzig, where he was serving as music director and cantor.[43] Bach contributed another quintessential piece of Christmas music with his Christmas Oratorio, BWV 248, which delighted its first audience on Christmas Day in Leipzig in 1734. Now the piece is a mainstay of Christmas in St Marienkirche in Berlin. As one long-time choir member there remarked, 'It makes Christmas Christmas.'[44] Bach certainly had Christmas in mind when he composed the piece, which takes three hours to perform in its entirety. Each of the six parts highlights a feast day in the Christmas season.

*A Christmas Carol* was adapted for the stage almost immediately, usually without Dickens's permission. This broadside advertises one such theatrical, scheduled for March 1844.

# Theatre Royal, Adelphi,

(Lessee, THOMAS GLADSTANE, 411, Strand)

## First Night of a NEW ROMANTIC DRAMA!

☞ FIFTH WEEK OF THE

### Original CHRISTMAS CAROL!

The Only Dramatic Version sanctioned by C. DICKENS, Esq.

SECOND WEEK OF

### Antony & Cleopatra Married & Settled

### Last Six Nights of RICHARD THE THIRD.

MONDAY, March 4th, 1844, and During the Week,

A Drama of Peculiar and Novel Construction, in *THREE STAVES*, founded on and called a

# CHRISTMAS CAROL;

OR,

## PAST, PRESENT & FUTURE.

Which will be presented with New Scenery, Novel Mechanical Effects, Dresses, Dances, and appropriate Old English Ballad Music.

Scenery by Messrs PITT and FINLAY. Dresses by Mr GODBEE and Miss GRUNDY. Machinery by Mr COOPER.

Music by Mr FRAMPTON, Sen. Music by Mr E. ROWELL, Sen.

*And the Piece Produced and Directed by Mr EDWARD STIRLING.*

☞ AUTHOR'S NOTE—I have endeavoured in this Ghostly little Book to raise the Ghost of an idea which shall not put my readers out of humour with themselves, with each other, with the Season, or with me—may it haunt their houses, and no one wish to lay it.

## Stave the First—The First of the Three Spirits.

Ebenezer Scrooge, (the Money Lender—a Christmas lister—'a name only good upon 'Change') Mr O. SMITH,

Mister Bob Cratchit, .... ( a Poor Clerk with Fifteen Shillings a Week and Six Children ) .... Mr WRIGHT,

The Ghost of Old Jacob Marley, ( Dead as a Door Nail ) Mr R. HUGHES,

Mr Fezziwig, .... ( a London Trader—'one great substantial smile'—only, rich and jovial ) .... Mr S SMITH,

Dr. Dilworth, .. (a Pedagogue) .. Mr JOHNSON, Master Scrooge, .. (a School Boy) .. Master LIGHTFOOT,

Young Scrooge and Dick Wilkins, ( Fellow Apprentices ) Mr BRAID and Mr LESLIE, Post Boy, ....Mr HONEY,

The Dirty Little Boy from over the way, Master MOUNCER, Fiddler, Mr SHAW,

Mrs Fezziwig, ( Beaming and Loveable ) Mrs WOOLLIDGE,

Bella Morton, .... ( Scrooge's first, his only love, save gold ) .... Miss WOOLGAR,

The Ghost of Christmas Past, ( "it was a strange Figure—like a Child" ) Miss E. CHAPLIN,

Little Fan, ( Scrooge's Sister ) Miss MOTT, Mary, the Tenant—Sally, the Cook—their Friends, Neighbours, &c.

## CHAMBER OF SCROOGE, THE MISER.

Air....THE BAFFLED KNIGHT.

" A gloomy suite of rooms, all enough and cheap, nobody lived in it but Scrooge"....Christmas Eve....Invitation....Christmas Lover.

Christmas Hater....The Clock....The Master....CAROL....Air....DISTANT BELLS.

"Bless, bless you, merry gentlemen, may nothing now dismay"....MARLEY's GHOST....Three Warnings.

Air GRIM KING OF GHOSTS. The First of the Spirits....Christmas Past....A Spell. Air....LITTLE MUSGRAVE.

Vision of the Past....School Days....Solitary Scholar.

### A CHILD'S STORY BOOK.

Chapter First. Tableau First....FORTY THIEVES, Ali Baba, Master Guthry

Chapter 2. Tableau 2....VALENTINE & ORSON, Valentine, Master Guianius, Orson, Master Walter

Chapter Third. Tableau Third....ROBINSON CRUSOE

Robinson Crusoe, Master Barbare, Friday, Master Hill, The Parrot, Master Jones

### HOME FOR THE HOLIDAYS.

Air....HURRY ALONG.

Mr Fezziwig....." I was apprenticed here,".....A Good Master,.....Happy Servants....London Apprentices 90 Years ago.........The Betrothed.

Air....LOVE LIES BLEEDING.

An Early Contract destroyed....." I pity and release you for the love of him you once were."

# FEZZIWIG'S BALL.

" One Christmas Ball in the old warehouse, Fezziwig always gave it, bless him ! "

## Stave Second—The Second of the Three Spirits.

Scrooge, .... ( the Miser ) .... Mr O SMITH,

Nephew Fred, .... Mr MAYNARD, Bob Cratchit, .... Mr WRIGHT,

Master Peter Cratchit, Master BRUNTON, Master Tom Cratchit, Master SCOTT, Sea Captain, Mr JONES,

Tiny Two, (" alas! poor Tiny Tim—he bore a little crutch, & had his limbs supported by an iron frame") Miss MAYNARD,

VISION OF DOOM—Ignorance, Mr CRANE, Want, Mr HOLMES, Mariners, Messrs ROUGH & RAINS,

Butchers, Grocers, Ballad Singers, Passengers, Watchmen, Small Purchasers, Visitors, &c.

Mrs Bob Cratchit, ( Wife to Mr Bob—dressed out but poorly in a twice turned gown, but brave in ribbons') Mrs F. MATTHEWS

Martha Cratchit, Miss LEE, Belinda Cratchit, Miss O. HICKS, Sally Cratchit, Miss JOHNSON,

The Ghost of Christmas Present, .. ( with a Song, "A Jolly Giant, glorious to see") .. Mr FORMAN.

## SCROOGE'S CHAMBER. — THE DREAM.

" Ghosts, spirits! all bumbug!"....Air, LADY FRANCES NEVILLE'S DELIGHT, ONE O'CLOCK.

The Jovial Appearance of Christmas Present on his Throne of Plenty, Health & Comfort.

Song by G. H. RODWELL, Esq.— Air, "EXACTLY WHAT IT OUGHT TO BE," The Journey of Life.

" He was a Jolly Giant, glorious to see."

## CLARE MARKET, by Gaslight.—CHRISTMAS EVE.

Air....CHRISTMAS COMES BUT ONCE A YEAR.

Grocers, Poulterers, Fruiterers, decked out with their goodly cheer...... Purchase of Bob's Goose....." What a lovely image."

The Poor Man's blessing, Content. The Poor Clerk's Heart....Merry Christmas, Home, home! Air, TRIP AND GO, Street Carol

## Bob Cratchits, Camden Town.—Christmas Dinner.

Air, OLD KING COLE....Careful Mother...Nice Children....Family Party...The Father and his Little Child...Tiny Tim.

The Dinner....The Goose...The Pudding ....Air, LOTS OF PLUM PUDDING! ....A Feast...Its Wonder...Blind Man's Buff.

The Mine—Working of the Spell—" Let the lessons live with you."—Destiny, Ignorance & Want.

## Stave the Third.—The LAST of the SPIRITS.

Scrooge, .... ( the Miser ) .... Mr O. SMITH,

Nephew Fred, .... Mr MAYNARD, Bob Cratchit, .... Mr WRIGHT,

Master Peter Cratchit, Master BRUNTON, Tiny Tim, Miss MAYNARD,

Old Joe, .... ( a Receiver of Stolen Goods—'a grey-haired rascal nearly 70 years of age") .... Mr SANDERS,

Mr Topper and Mr Floss, ( Worldly Friends of Old Scrooge ) Mr ALDRIDGE and Mr FREEBORN,

Mr Bilok, ( an Undertaker's Man ) Mr HONEY, Visitors, Guests, &c.

Mrs Dibler, ( a Laundress) Mrs WOOLLIDGE, Mrs Fred, Miss BUTLER, Sally, ( a Nurse ) Miss WILSHIRE,

Mrs Bob Cratchit, Mrs F. MATTHEWS, Martha Cratchit, Miss LEE,

Spirit of the Future, .. ( a solemn Phantom, dressed & hooded, coming like a Mist along the ground ) .. Mrs D. LEE

BOB CRATCHIT, CAMDEN TOWN.—CHRISTMAS DINNER.

# THE ROYAL EXCHANGE.

Air, Money Bags.——GHOST OF THE FUTURE.

" Willjes can't he hurt to me!"....The Money Lenders...Mourners...Worldly Fellowship...Sympathy of the Rich...Mourners of the Heart...Sympathy of the Poor..." My little little child, Spirit of Tiny Tim. thy childish essence was from Heaven"....Spectral Warning

Handel's *Messiah* may be associated with Christmas, but initially this oratorio was offered at Easter-time in 1742. The very first performance, in Dublin, raised money for charity, and the funds freed 142 men from debtors' prison.[45] The biblical texts were selected by Charles Jennens, and focus on Christ's Passion and Resurrection. Nonetheless, the chorus 'For Unto Us a Child Is Born' fits the Christmas season perfectly, and it resounds throughout sacred and secular performances during Advent. Similarly, the 'Hallelujah Chorus' receives more attention during Christmas. According to legend, audience members rise during this performance because the timpani startled George III out of a nap. When the king bounced up, the audience stood in deference to him and his seeming passion for the music.[46]

The carols that ring out each Christmas season hail from the tradition of non-liturgical songs. Carols might be religious, or they might be secular or pagan. Christmas music expert Ronald M. Clancy has estimated that four or five thousand carols exist, although many of these have been relegated to obscurity. Carols tended to be in Latin before the fourteenth century, but today they are known for their folk-like, Christmassy character, and their 'religious impulse that is simple, hilarious, popular, and modern'.[47]

Church choirs would surely be shocked if they were handed notations of the original carols. The word 'carol' comes from the French for a ring dance. Originally intended as a blend of dance and song, probably with a leader singing the verse and the dancers the chorus, the early carols covered fairly bawdy topics. Creative clerics would start their own traditions of Christian carols that continue to ring out today.[48] The popular, lilting 'Coventry Carol' comes from medieval mystery plays of the sixteenth century: 'Lully lulla, thow little tyne child.'[49]

The beloved carol 'Silent Night' defines Christmas Eve church services. The tale about Franz Gruber's ingenuity in the face of a broken organ in 1818 has charmed fans of the song, but it is more likely that the young organist/guitarist had composed the music some years before. Joseph Mohr, the priest who wrote the lyrics, almost certainly wrote them two years before the organ breakdown in Oberndorf, Austria. Nonetheless, the two did scramble to produce what would become a beloved piece of music. One version of events has it that the carol might have dropped into obscurity had a workman not found the sheet music while repairing the organ in Oberndorf. Consequently, the song spread to travelling singing groups. Prussia's Frederick Wilhelm IV liked to hear the song every Christmas Eve. As a result, Austrians adhere to a Christmas-time rule: 'Silent Night' is not played until after 5 p.m. on Christmas Eve, either in churches or in commercial spaces.[50] The rest of the world is ignorant of this regulation, and the English version soothes celebrants throughout the season. The most well-known English translation was by a New York City clergyman in 1859. It is believed that American First World War veterans involved in the Christmas truce brought a fondness for the carol home from Europe with them, further establishing it as a favourite in America.

The 'Silent Night' lyricist, Mohr, endured an ironic ordeal as a result of the song's success. In 1912, decades after his death, the

The fact that the legends surrounding the composition of 'Silent Night, Holy Night' may not be entirely true does not diminish the sacred beauty of the first full score, from 1818.

authorities in the town where he was buried decided to dig up his skull to craft an accurate bronze bust of him. Somewhere along the way enthusiasm for the bust waned, but the skull remained separated from its body, gathering dust. A quarter of a century later it found a resting place in the wall of Oberndorf's Silent Night Memorial Chapel.[51]

It seems that each of the Christmas carols that fill the airwaves in December has its own story. 'Joy to the World' came from the pen of Englishman Isaac Watts, a Nonconformist clergyman and educator. Psalm 98 inspired the lyrics, first published in Watts's collection of 1719, *The Psalms of David*. Watts penned the words as a meditation on Christ's Second Coming, but Christmas celebrants have found reason to pipe up with the joyful anthem. Eighteenth- and nineteenth-century Methodists like Watts had a habit of publishing poetic pieces as hymns. Such lyrics at that time would be published without musical notation; the tune to 'Joy to the World' was added by Lowell Mason in the early nineteenth century. It is believed that Mason used strains of Handel's *Messiah* to compose the well-known melody, but the tune was different enough for it to garner its own name in early hymnals: it was known as 'Antioch'.[52]

The Moravians have long elevated music within their corporate worship, and their zeal for Christmas melodies comes as no surprise. A song leader would instruct his congregation to repeat the lines of his extemporized lyrics after first selecting one of the well-known tunes that could be applied to nearly any poem written as a hymn. Such was the case with the initial singing of the 'Bethlehem Christmas Hymn', which went on for an astounding 37 stanzas when in 1755 Count Zinzendorf belted it out for his congregation in Bethlehem, Pennsylvania, to repeat line by line.[53]

With the exception of the High Church denominations – Roman Catholics, Anglicans, Episcopalians and some Lutherans – Christians enliven the weeks of Advent with the beloved Christmas carols. Church groups drive around to sing carols for elderly church members, or they might stroll down the halls of nursing facilities, carol books in hand. While Britain has a tradition of collecting money for charity during carolling, American carollers sing for free, often trolling the halls of retirement facilities or bringing the gift of song to neighbours.

There is great comfort to be found in musical rituals. Many of the oldest church members have been singing Christmas carols for their entire lives, or at least since their Christmas-wary denominations finally welcomed the carols in the early decades of the twentieth century. Today's Sunday School children will doubtless sing the same eighteenth-century biblically themed carols when they themselves are grandparents.

Any discussion of the sacred sounds of Christmas would be incomplete without mentioning the tolling bells of the Christmas Feast. Bells began to become a part of English churches during the seventh century. In the seventeenth century English bell mechanics allowed the bells to ring in a full circle, causing each bell to intone two peals per revolution. This advance brought about the mathematically complicated change-ringing phenomenon that characterized Christmas bell-ringing in many towns. The long association between bell-ringing and Christmas has secured the place of bells in holiday decorations. One author of a 1908 book on church bells bemoaned the inaccurate representation of bells that abounded in Christmas cards even in his day.[54]

Change-ringing created sounds that left a deep impression on eighteenth- and nineteenth-century writers. The bells spoke to Henry Wadsworth Longfellow, who wrote his poem 'Christmas Bells', now better known as 'I Heard the Bells on Christmas Day', in the midst of the American Civil War. He wrote the poem, which later became a beloved Christian hymn, one Christmas morning during a tumultuous period in his life: his wife had died from burns and his son had left home without his permission to fight in the war that was tearing his country apart. With such gloom in his life it is no wonder that he should have created a persona who bows his head to the burdens of life, but the poem continues with a glad epiphany of hope: 'Then pealed the bells more loud and deep: / "God is not dead, nor doth He sleep; / The wrong shall fail, the right prevail / With peace on earth, good will to men."'

A study of nineteenth-century British poetry of Christmas reveals an astounding number of lines discussing this Christmas certainty: the bells would toll as Christmas rolled in. The bells become noisome characters in *The Chimes*, the Christmas book Charles Dickens prepared the year after *A Christmas Carol*'s success. Bells also feature in the Christmas stanzas of Alfred, Lord Tennyson's *In Memoriam*, a lengthy poem assessing the evolution of grief over the course of three Christmases. The tradition continued unbroken for many years. However, British bells were forced to take a break during the Christmases of the Second World War because unrestrained ringing would have signalled invasion, not celebration.[55] Today Christmas bells do not feature heavily in British or American society. Many churches leave the bells silent entirely during Christmas Eve and Christmas Day celebrations. However, churches in New York City ring out simultaneously at midnight on Christmas Eve, and the city echoes with the joyous reverberations.

Christmas celebrants no longer count on church bells to notify them of when Christmas is scheduled because the holiday begins much earlier and popular media has taken on the task of announcing it. Christmas carols, piped into shopping spaces, create a nearly inescapable soundscape. The ubiquitous soundtrack of the holiday may be the only place where some people in America, Britain, Australia and other countries encounter the Nativity origins of Christmas.[56] In 2011, over 160 American radio stations had switched to playing only Christmas songs by the time Thanksgiving took place on 24 November. This move drastically increases ratings and adds younger listeners, since families listen together to traditional Christmas songs, even those sung by long-dead Christmas icons.[57] Musicians have plenty of encouragement to keep Christmas songs coming. If a new song becomes a hit, or even if it simply replays often enough to fill time on those all-Christmas radio stations, the musicians concerned can count on money coming in for years.

While the most enduring Christmas carols have their beginnings in the Church, the secular songs of Christmas also demand some attention here. Films such as *Love Actually* and *About a Boy* belittle the art of all-pervasive Christmas tunes, but listeners greatly desire the familiar favourites. Polling companies take stock of listeners' opinions of Christmas songs, and the radio stations that gear up to play some 744 hours of Christmas music are pretty interested in what is going to attract an audience. A poll of American Christmas listeners in 2007 found that Madonna's cover of 'Santa Baby' and any version of 'Grandma Got Run over by a Reindeer' cause listeners to change the station. One station in Washington, DC, scrapped the cheery song about Grandma's holiday demise, claiming it 'was

Rembrandt van Rijn's *The Adoration of the Shepherds*, 1646, is less elaborate in its depiction of the scene than many earlier Nativity works. Instead, this painting catches the informal intimacy of the moment in the biblical account.

too polarizing'. The morbid song started out as a local hit in San Francisco in the early 1980s after its debut in 1979. Despite listeners' negative feelings, the man who first recorded the song, bluegrass artist and veterinarian Elmo Shropshire, has claimed that his royalties have only increased, quadrupling since the 1980s.[58]

The most-loved songs – polls identify Americans' favourites as Bing Crosby's 'White Christmas' (1942) and Nat King Cole's 'The Christmas Song (Chestnuts Roasting on an Open Fire)' (1946) – are repeated frequently on Christmas music stations. Music analysts surmise that nostalgia drives the popularity of Christmas songs, especially these top two. Being featured in a Christmas film that turns into classic seasonal viewing is another strong indicator that a song will have longevity.[59] Christmas songwriters hope their contributions to the season's soundtrack will eventually become part of the nostalgia, as well as supplying them with a reliable royalty cheque. 'Have Yourself a Merry Little Christmas', for example, earned $2 million in just one year in the late 1990s. The song, originally written in 1944, is cannily marketed by its current owner, music publisher EMI. Radio stations pay a few cents and television companies pay a few dollars each time they play the song. Recording artists pay thousands of dollars to remake the song, and if their version sells more than a million copies, their contract could easily require them to pay EMI $75,000. Film studios might pay $25,000 to use the song, and its use in advertisements is also lucrative.[60]

The seasonal ballad 'Fairytale of New York' by The Pogues and Kirsty MacColl was first recorded in 1987 and has since become a classic of Christmas listening in the British Isles. The song has been in the Christmas Top 20 list repeatedly since 2005. Despite this popularity and the setting of the song's narrative in New York City, it has not caught the attention of mainstream American Christmas-keepers. Framed as a song sung in a drunk tank on Christmas Eve, it tells the tale of unhappy and somewhat vulgar lovers disillusioned with each other. Shane MacGowan tells how he and Jem Finer wrote the song following a bet they had in 1985 with Elvis Costello to write a Christmas hit. It took two years to write the song, and its success has certainly fulfilled The Pogues' side of the bet.[61]

Many musicians have taken an even more cynical approach to writing Christmas songs. In 1966 Simon and Garfunkel created a sombre version of a carol in the vein of Thomas Hardy's Christmas poetry, in 'Seven O'Clock News / Silent Night'. Songs such as Harvey Danger's 'Sometimes You Have to Work on Christmas (Sometimes)' and 1940s classics like 'Have Yourself a Merry Little Christmas' and 'Blue Christmas' explore how disappointing Christmas can be. Others, including 'Dead, Dead, Dead' from a South Park holiday album and 'Year End Letter' by Garfunkel & Oates, simply mock the December business that captivates much of the Western world.[62]

Like music, television has worked its way into the holiday rituals of Christmas-keepers. Ironically, economic considerations have been one of the formative reasons for installing some of the most classic Christmas films in their time-honoured positions. In the 1950s Hollywood was loath to sell film rights to broadcasting stations, but British filmmakers felt American television offered a bountiful opportunity.[63] They exported Christmas films like *Scrooge* (1951) with Alastair Sim, which represented a particular post-Second World War, Christmas-on-the-ration version of Dickens's novel. Slowly, American studios began releasing their older Christmas films to television too. These films – *Christmas in Connecticut* (1945), *Holiday Inn* (1942) and *Miracle on 34th Street* (1947) – became beloved through repetition on television.[64]

Movies that fell into the public domain became especially popular because they aired so often. The 1935 *Scrooge* fell into this category, as did the Jimmy Stewart Christmas classic, *It's A Wonderful Life*. Directed by Frank Capra, *It's A Wonderful Life* had flopped in 1946, but when the corporation holding the rights neglected to renew them in 1974, television stations spread the film lavishly over the airwaves. These two films would be 'the holiday mainstays of the 1970s and 1980s'.[65] Similarly, Bob Clark's Depression-era tale of childhood, *A Christmas Story*, flopped in 1983 but revived under cable broadcasts in the 1990s.[66]

Variety shows have a place in Christmas viewing as well. In the United States, variety shows by Bing Crosby, Andy Williams and Bob Hope featured every year from the 1950s onwards, and Hope's

planning each Christmas line-up two or three years in advance. The head of BBC1 scheduling recognizes some stress in the job of creating 'event TV' for the millions of Christmas viewers.[70] In addition to season premieres or much-anticipated series denouements, British viewers can rely on being able to watch certain well-loved films, such as a selection from the *Harry Potter* or *Pirates of the Caribbean* franchises or an animated family favourite such as *Shrek* or *Toy Story*.

Changing media habits can upend Christmas viewing traditions. Not only has *How the Grinch Stole Christmas* been abridged by the American network, but, in Britain, Sky bought the rights to air *Elf* in 2013, ending the traditional start of the Christmas-season viewing with that light-hearted film on Channel 4. As one blogger for *The Guardian* explained, 'The Channel 4 Christmas broadcast of *Elf* brought people together year after year. It was like a Royal Wedding for republicans, or the Olympics for people who don't understand sport.'[71] Sky subscribers can now view the film whenever they like, but this type of viewing-on-demand approach disrupts the tradition of watching Christmas films simultaneously as a nation.

American Christmas Day television viewing does not contribute to a sense of national identity the way it does in the UK, but some regions have special traditions. Residents of New York City have watched a yule log burning on their televisions for over 45 years. The seven-minute loop of crackling fire and Christmas music first came out in 1966 on a local channel, and now the same log burns each Christmas on televisions across the country. Today apartment dwellers in need of a fireplace to complete their Christmas decor have over twenty cable options for tuning in to various burning logs during Christmas. Those who love this television tradition claims it offers a beautiful, contemplative image in the bustle of the holiday. Fans have even created a web-based action group to keep the original programme on the air.[72]

Christmas art might flood into our homes in the form of Christmas cards, or keep us in a chipper mood, ensuring a longer stay at a shopping centre. So much of what we have come to expect about Christmas has reached us through the arts and, through them, Christmas-keepers are linked to the global culture of Christmas.

What a difference our experience is today from that bleak Stalingrad Christmas of 1942, when Reuber was drawn to create the *Madonna of Stalingrad*, a symbol of what, even in hopeless desolation, Christmas imagery can offer.

# FOUR

# Christmas Outlawed

Despite the highly secular form of the modern Christmas, the holiday has often been taken as a gleaming symbol of Christianity or some contested branch of that faith. As such, Christmas has faced persecution throughout the ages. Christmas has been banned in the West for appearing too Catholic to Cromwell's Parliament, the puritanical Massachusetts Bay Colony and the Presbyterian Church of Scotland. Even without legal prohibition, the religious beliefs of dissenting families have forced them to find creative, tragic and, at times, comical ways to avoid a holiday the rest of their culture treats as popular and even nationalistic. Politics rather than religion has ousted Christmas in other eras; communism, especially, has attempted to sound the death knell for Christmas under various regimes. Even when atheist governments permit Christmas to remain, as was the case in Nazi Germany, the authorities co-opt the holiday to pursue political ends. A loud debate about Christmas's current identity seems to have similar overtones, especially in the United States, Great Britain and Australia. The so-called war on Christmas has picked up every December since the turn of the twenty-first century. This clash is a far cry from the controversy that surrounded Christmas six centuries ago.

While the Church grew, missionaries often used Christmas to unite Christians across Europe. However, once Christianity became violently divided between Catholicism and Protestantism in the West during the sixteenth century, Christmas suffered. In England, Henry VIII established the Anglican Church, and Elizabeth I secured it, but many Protestant Christians felt that the Anglican Church still retained too many elements of Catholicism, and wished for deeper reform. During this period, jolly Christmases characterized the Catholic approach to the holiday, and some Protestants protested. Christmas actually posed a challenge for recusant Catholics, citizens who refused to participate in Anglican services. Some may have tried to hide their Catholicism. During this period Catholics could be executed or have their property confiscated. Their characteristically jovial midwinter celebrations – especially feasting and card playing – could give them away. Ironically, sixteenth-century Catholics who had already been imprisoned, including a group of priests at Wisbech, were free to celebrate Christmas within their prison cells.[1]

The rowdiness of the English Christmas had long caused conflict with the more sombre church leaders and observers. In the sixteenth and seventeenth centuries these Puritans felt they possessed a purer form of Christianity, which did not include Christmas. A book from the 1580s complains that 'more mischief is that time committed than in all the year besides, what masking and mumming, whereby robbery whoredome, murder and what not is committed?'[2] Decorating with greenery just seemed so pagan to Puritans, and that was enough to discourage the practice. Others deemed Christmas feasting traditions, including special ales and expensive meats, wasteful. Some Protestants also complained about the attention Jesus's mother received during Christmas; Catholics revered Mary, and celebrants had a hard time avoiding her in representations of the biblical birth narrative.[3] The reformed Kirk took power in Scotland in 1560, and by the next year it had done away with Christmas, as well as Epiphany and various saints' days.

The Scots Presbyterian censure of Christmas leaked southward into England in 1643 when the English Long Parliament signed a treaty with Scotland and submitted to their reform of the Church of England and its saint-related holidays.[4] With Charles I ousted, the Puritans who took over Parliament worked to rout Christmas as well. A committee endeavoured to clear the church calendar of all saints' days and festivals, retaining the Sabbath only as special cause for holy celebration. In 1644 Christmas Day coincided with the monthly fast day, the last Wednesday of the month, and Parliament sent out a decree that 25 December should be kept as an especially solemn fast to make up for blasphemous Christmas excesses of the past.[5] Puritans tried to rebrand Christmas as 'Christ-tide', ridding the celebration's name of the reference to the Catholic Mass. They did not entirely trust their wordsmiths, so parliamentary Puritans took legal action as well. During the summer of 1647 Parliament banned the Christmas, Easter and Whitsun holidays, and they decided that Christmas Day of that year should be a day of penance rather than of feasting. The ban needed some reinforcing, and on Christmas Eve 1652 Parliament stated that 'no observance shall be had of the five and twentieth of December, commonly called Christmas day; nor any solemnity used or exercised in churches upon that day in respect thereof.'[6] Shops remained open, churches

*Bringing in the Greens*, 1886, engraving. The pagan associations of Christmas greenery further outraged Puritans.

avoided decorations and ministers chose a non-Christmas text and topic or faced imprisonment.[7] The mandate resulted in soldiers policing shops to ensure that commerce did not pause for Christmas. Parliament did its part by scheduling itself to meet on Christmas Day every year from 1644 until 1652.[8] By 1657, simply attending church in London on Christmas Day could lead to imprisonment.[9]

It should come as no surprise that a large percentage of English citizens were loath to surrender Christmas as quickly as their Parliament wished. Following laws banning Christmas greenery in church and public places, guerrilla decorating teams fought back with cuttings of holly, rosemary and ivy. Less subtle revolts came in the form of riots in Ealing, Middlesex and Canterbury which targeted markets and shops that remained open on Christmas Day.[10] Shopkeepers anticipated disturbances, and in 1646 they requested that Parliament offer protection for shops open on 25 December.[11] The following December saw Christmas riots in towns and cities all over England, with people dying in an uprising in Norwich.[12] Thirteen years later the nation welcomed back their monarchy and their Christmas, as well as other church holidays. Twenty years of oppression had changed the holiday considerably; Charles II did not fully enter into royal Christmas excesses, but then Christmas in England has always been evolving.

In Scotland Christmas did not return with the restored monarchy. The Presbyterian leadership of Scotland had criminalized Christmas cooking in 1583, and bakeries selling Yule bread could hope to reduce their fines only if they revealed who exactly was buying the clandestine products.[13] Even in the nineteenth century Christmas food was still forbidden by the church leadership: elders would check the kitchens of their congregants to verify that they were free of the taint of Christmas preparations. In at least one case, a secreted Christmas dinner caused a fire during the elders' visit and gave away the housewife's holiday zeal.[14]

Scottish law had done away with Christmas in 1638, but the populace redirected their energy to the secular celebration of New Year, called Hogmanay in Scotland. Some of the popular aspects of the London Christmas crept into Scotland in the 1870s and

Edmund H. Garrett, *Christmas Plenty*, 1886. Christmas rowdiness
seemed like foolishness to the pious Puritans, who attempted
to censor Christmas for a little more than a decade.

following years, but visitors to Scotland in the 1940s might have
noticed that Christmas still did not cause much of a stir north of
Hadrian's Wall. A ubiquitous Christmas hit the mainstream in
Scotland only in the middle of the twentieth century.

The early, antagonistic views of Christmas spread beyond the
British Isles, with early settlers in America taking their opinions
about Christmas with them. French settlers kept Christmas with
religious observances and games.[15] Captain John Smith, who settled
the Virginia Colony, welcomed the day as one of rest and feasting.
Further north the reception of Christmas was much more controversial. The pilgrims of Plymouth worked through their first
Christmas, but the following year their community faced a serious
Christmas conflict. Not all the settlers were Dissenters, and some
of the young men, known as Strangers, wished to keep Christmas

in 1621 rather than work. Religious contemplation was allowed, but when the young men began playing games in the streets while their neighbours put in a full day's work, Governor William Bradford took offence and ordered them back inside. For years the Puritans of the Massachusetts Bay Colony tried a strategy of enticing non-Puritan neighbours away from Christmas traditions by offering pious examples of ignoring the holiday, but somehow this approach failed to dampen the appeal of Christmas. In 1659 the leadership took legal action to prohibit Christmas. When the English monarchy was restored, Charles II ordered Massachusetts to reinstate Christmas, but the Puritans dragged their feet from 1665 until 1681, when they relented to his demand. Nonetheless, four years later the English governor's Christmas service was forcibly relocated from the meeting house to the Boston Town Hall by armed Puritans.[16]

Early American Quakers, Baptists, Presbyterians and Puritans had no Christmas spirit, but throughout the colonies Anglicans, Moravians, Dutch Reformed, Huguenots and the transported criminals of Georgia had no qualms about observing the holiday's varied rituals. In the southern colonies the weather and the more lenient Anglican Church permitted cockfighting, card playing and horse racing for Christmas treats.[17] Unlike those in New England, southerners drew on the English country Christmas for their inspiration.

Christmas can become an unstoppable force, especially if the celebrants are devoted to defending their traditions to the death. The apartheid conditions of the slave economy in the British West Indies faced heightened tension during Christmas-time. Between 1649 and 1833, insurrectionists planned approximately 70 slave uprisings. Just over half of these recorded conflicts took place over Christmas or during the month of December. The white slave owners were aware that this was no random distribution; relaxed social rules gave slaves greater entitlement to congregate, travel and celebrate at Christmas as a type of merry Saturnalia. Slaves looked forward to the traditional three days of leisure and relative freedom, and planters could not suppress the expected holiday for fear of their lives. One planter, a Colonel Martin, tried to cancel his slaves' Christmas holiday, and his disgruntled workforce killed him. On

Nevis, when an overseer failed to hand out extra food for Christmas, the slaves protested by killing cattle.[18] Plantation owners warned newcomers not to meddle with the Christmas the enslaved people had come to expect and to defend, and as a result the slaves maintained their holiday freedoms until Parliament put an end to slavery.

Long after the governments of the British Isles and America had repealed laws forbidding Christmas, some Christian sects continued to expunge Christmas from their private calendars. In a memoir of his childhood, Edmund Gosse, raised in Devon in the west of England by a Dissenting father, recalls how his father's rebellious maids offered him a secret slice of plum-cake in 1857; his tortured soul could not bear it, and he revealed to his father that he had 'eaten of flesh offered to idols!' Upon hearing this, his father violently attacked the offending cake and buried what remained of it in the dust heap outside.[19] Today members of Philip Gosse's denomination do celebrate Christmas, and Presbyterians the world over heartily participate in the holiday their ancestors banned. Other groups avoid Christmas, however. Some evangelicals eschew what they see as pagan or secular aspects of the holiday, such as the Christmas tree and Santa. Others offer that the Bible does not command the celebration of Christ's birth, and they would rather err on the side of caution. Jehovah's Witnesses, for example, avoid Christmas, along with Easter and birthdays, because they wish to avoid the pagan origins associated with such rituals.

Today denominational squabbles over Christmas have moved out of Western parliaments and into local churches, where Christians wrestle with their own consciences without fear of fines or imprisonment. Twentieth- and twenty-first-century laws against Christmas have been more prevalent not in largely Christian societies, but in regions where politically atheist agendas have targeted Christmas as a holdout of Christianity. The modern Christmas has a vibrant secular life, but some communist and fascist regimes would rather stamp out Christmas or recreate it as a new, political propaganda machine.

Christmas had been a popular and widespread cultural symbol in Russia before the twentieth century, but following the Russian Revolution, the Bolsheviks did not welcome reminders of Christmas.

While Christianity was not outlawed, the state heartily wished its citizens to become atheists, and it used ridicule as well as force to convince them. Most churches were closed, and many clergymen and laypeople were imprisoned or executed. Religious holidays were replaced with Communist Party festivals. During Christmas Eve and Christmas Day, celebrated on 5 and 6 January 1923, cells of Komsomol, or the Union of Communist Youth, staged mock celebrations, intending to ridicule Christianity and other faiths. The resulting procession through the streets of Moscow lampooned priests, rabbis, the Buddha, the Virgin Mary and the Roman Catholic Pope. A similar event in Gomel put God on trial and condemned him to be burned in the square on Christmas Day. One witness recalls that the masses avoided these shocking displays, and those who happened upon the processions stood mute, afraid of challenging the Party but also unable to adopt the mock festival as their own or find pleasure in the insulting displays. The Party sensed the restrained discontent of the public and curtailed the overt ridiculing of faiths shortly afterwards.[20]

Some saints needed to be routed from the popular imagination as well, especially St Nicholas. Instead of continuing the St Nicholas Day traditions that stretched back centuries, the Communist Party scheduled alternative entertainment for children on Christmas Eve – theatricals, mostly satires about the Kerensky regime and the dangers of bourgeois life outside Russia.[21]

To popular dismay, the Bolsheviks banned Christmas trees in 1929, until Stalin ushered evergreens back into Russian society in 1935 by christening them New Year's trees. Like the Scots before him, Stalin rebranded the secular aspects of Christmas as New Year traditions. Families met, feasted and exchanged gifts in a largely propaganda-free environment. Although the Russian Revolution brought in the Gregorian calendar, the church in Russia has adhered to the old Julian calendar, with Christmas falling on 6 January; so following state-approved celebrations on 1 January, Russian celebrants often gave up Christmas.[22] Nonetheless, some Russian Christians celebrated the religious nature of Christmas in secret or, more safely, in exile.

In 1991, after 70 years of clandestine Christmases under the Soviet Union, Russia followed the Russian Orthodox schedule by planning the old Christmas Day of 7 January once again, now as a state holiday. Celebrants were free to be open in their celebrations.[23] Christmas certainly returned with a bang, and Moscow strung banners and set up Nativity scenes in Red Square. On Christmas Eve, Red Square hosted tens of thousands of celebrants who had come for fireworks, bell-ringing and musical performances. Television and radio programmes set up a continuous re-education about the Christmas story and the deep roots of Christmas tradition in Russia. The Kremlin opened its doors for a Christmas charity ball to raise money for orphans.[24] Nearly a year later, on 25 December, Mikhail Gorbachev resigned from office and handed missile launch codes to President Boris Yeltsin, an event that marked the peaceful end of the Soviet Union.

As in Russia, Christmas had enjoyed popularity in Cuba before the revolution in 1959, but the atheist regime cancelled Christmas in 1969, claiming that it interfered with the sugar harvest. Christmas symbols were banned, but families could celebrate in discreet private gatherings. Fidel Castro reinstituted Christmas as a public holiday

In China Santa stands for commerce. This rooftop Santa mans his post above a Beijing toyshop throughout the year.

82

in 1997 in anticipation of Pope John Paul II's impending visit. Cuban society began to see a small trickle of Christmas cheer in the form of decorations for sale and Christmas lights, even in government-run shops. In the early twenty-first century, Cubans enjoy greater religious freedom than at any time since the revolution. They may not find Christmas sales at government-run stores, but they do celebrate a subdued Christmas as a religious and family holiday.

Laotian celebrants may have to wait much longer for the type of flexible Christmas-keeping now seen in Cuba. Christmas celebrations can endanger people in communist Laos, where Theravada Buddhism dominates the culture. The only government-sanctioned church of Laos schedules Christmas celebrations to run for twelve days starting on 4 January. In January 2011 a group of eleven Christians obtained permission to hold a Christmas vigil, but the group was arrested during their feast and charged with holding a secret meeting. In Laos, being identified as a Christian can mean forced 're-education', as well as imprisonment and death threats. Underground Laotian Christians often celebrate Christmas weeks before 25 December to avoid the attention of government authorities. In December 2011 Christmas-keepers were arrested and led away wearing handcuffs and wooden stocks following a Christmas meal preceding a worship service.[25]

Christmas is perhaps bleakest in North Korea. Few first-hand reports leak out of the country, but those that do point to a decided lack of religious freedom. A BBC reporter visited one of the few sanctioned churches in Pyongyang, noting that the church was decorated for Christmas Day. These churches are believed to have been built solely for purposes of government propaganda, to 'prove' North Korea's claims of religious freedom. Nonetheless, foreigners always have minders when they attend services there. Outside the capital, Christians, the only ones who might care to celebrate Christmas, do their best to keep their priorities secret. Accounts suggest that Christians in North Korea face arrest, imprisonment and torture.

Meanwhile, in China, celebrating Christmas has become a recent popular trend, although Christians still face heavy persecution. The commercial profit of Christmas does seem to jar with the strict religious regulations. In 2011 Xintan, an eastern village, held a legal Christmas arts and culture fair to celebrate the region's production of $78 billion worth of Christmas exports. A few days later, when a house church held an outdoor Christmas party in the same town, police burst onto the scene and put an end to it.[26]

While some regimes continue to contend with Christmas, one twentieth-century regime sought to stage-manage it. Like the Bolsheviks, the Nazi Party wished to curtail the religious aspects of Christmas, but in Germany Christmas could not easily be stamped out. Leaders of the Party sought to wrest control of Christmas from the church and use it as a political tool. While they did not outlaw the holiday, their attempts certainly put pressure on censoring certain aspects of it. The National Socialists had plenty of symbolism to work with, especially since the nineteenth century had bequeathed a legacy of thought that left Germans feeling they had a unique and particularly authentic ownership of Christmas.[27] Hitler's approach to Christmas messages in the 1920s and '30s was not exactly inclusive; he tended to blame Christmas consumerism on various ethnic or political groups and to charge them with leading the German people away from their natural heritage as domestic Christmas-keepers.[28] Since much of the Nazi leadership was anti-Christian, they planned to do away with the Nativity aspect of the midwinter festival in favour of the pre-Christian Jul. The changes were gradual, however, to appease the largely Christian population. The Party incorporated ideas of a 'Nordic' Christmas into public celebrations, and the Hitler Youth re-enacted elements of the winter solstice rituals.[29]

During the Nazification of Christmas, the National Socialist party encouraged Germans to celebrate German nationalism through the *Volksweihnachten*, or people's Christmas.[30] In the 1930s the Nazis distributed guidelines for the new, neo-pagan Christmas; they institutionalized it as propaganda.[31] The Ministry of Propaganda even put out books about Christmas, and the government used radio broadcasts to unify the people around a special German Christmas.[32] While some Germans resisted the demands of the new German Christmas, others enthusiastically embraced the chance

Propaganda minister Joseph Goebbels participated in Christmas events, but he was also part of the team working to systematically reimagine the holiday to suit the Nazi agenda. This photograph dates from 1936.

to involve themselves with symbols of privilege in an exclusionary racial state.[33] In the late 1930s the Nazi regime took more open steps towards reimagining Christmas, banning carols and Christian-themed plays from schools. The *Weihnachtsman*, or St Nicholas, traded places once again with Knecht Ruprecht, an old European Wild Man figure, and the Nazis drew associations between their Christmas icon and the ancient Norse hero Wotan. St Nicholas's Day became Wotan's Day, or *Ruprechtstag*.

Goebbels censored the type of Christmas music allowed on the radio, removing holiday hymns, except for 'O Tannenbaum'.[34] Nazi propagandists offered new lyrics to replace the Christian themes in Christmas carols that were still sung in churches. Christ was replaced with Hitler in a reworking of 'Silent Night'; children in state-run orphanages learned this version.[35] But the clergy fought to retain the traditional Christian lyrics.[36] One Protestant group even wrote to the Nazi Party to request that Christmas and winter solstice be cleanly separated into two holidays, so that the Christians could retain their focus on Christmas.[37] This compromise failed, and by Christmas 1941 Christmas cards had been forbidden; the

Third Reich even banned New Year cards, their covert replacement, ostensibly to conserve paper.

The National Socialists de-Christianized Christmas, but they also emphasized the powerful role of women in the holiday. Women's domestic duties were invigorated with a national importance and women were told to bake holiday biscuits shaped like fertility symbols and Wotan's wheel. Women's Christmas-time roles not only brought homemakers into the public sphere; they also valorized women. New duties allowed women to fan the flame of Nordic traditions, but only the ones Nazis wished to see supersede nineteenth-century Christmas customs.[38]

While German citizens deliberated over how to treat the new Nazi Christmas, occupied nations responded with outrage. In Nazi-held Norway, Christmas decorations became a way to express discontent with the invaders. At first the occupying Germans outlawed civilian displays of the Norwegian flag, but defiant card-makers turned the flag into a principal element of Christmas cards. The cards were getting out of hand, as far as the Nazis were concerned. The Nazi government retaliated by outlawing the comic Christmas elf, or *nisse*, who had been appearing on Christmas postcards decorated with Norwegian flags and ribbons. Simply wearing the traditional *nisse* hat could result in punishment, since it represented resistance to the occupying regime.[39] At the same time, cards wished recipients a 'God *norsk* jul', or a 'Merry *Norwegian* Christmas', referring to the celebration as it had been before the Nazis arrived. Previously the phrase had been simply 'God jul'. The occupiers did not appreciate the revised sentiment. Nazi authorities rounded up all the offending cards they could find and ordered post offices to confiscate those they saw in the mail.[40] The Norwegians eventually celebrated their first free Christmas in 1945, and the *nisse* and national flag returned to the spotlight.

While the rest of the world has imported Christianity, the Middle East is the exporter of the religion, as well as of the symbols that grace billions of Christmas cards. Many Islamic countries tolerate Christmas, but in Saudi Arabia the holiday can happen only furtively at best. Saudi law bans all non-Muslim public religious

*They Sacrificed Themselves so that We Can Stand in the Light*, 1941–4. Nazi propaganda was eager to revise the meaning of Christmas symbols to promote its own objective.

activities, and even Western embassy workers have to carry out fairly covert Christmas celebrations. Christmas cards can be bought, but shops keep them hidden, treating them like the contraband they are. Religious police have detained shopkeepers for selling the trappings of Western holidays, such as Halloween. Expatriates have a tradition of making their own Christmas decorations since they cannot be purchased, and Christmas-related items are often confiscated from travellers. One florist reported that live trees from Holland were seized at the airport and destroyed.[41]

Christmas's cultural cachet has improved in Kuwait. Back in the early 1980s, Sunni fundamentalists there sponsored a bill that would ban all public Christmas celebrations, even for foreigners. Today Christmas creates traffic jams around Christian churches as Kuwaiti Christians and foreigners flock to worship.

In Malaysia, where the state religion is Islam, police attempted to assert laws about assembly to limit Christmas carolling during the Christmas season in 2011. A church was asked to hand over a list of carollers after the group failed to obtain the proper paperwork for their activities, but Christians protested at this, and the police backed down.[42] Malaysians enjoy freedom of religion, and it was supposed that the assembly law, rather than Christianity, was the cause of the kerfuffle.

In Iraq, where Christianity certainly predates Islam, Christmas is not outlawed; however, Christians attempting to celebrate their high holy day face threats. In October 2010 gunmen broke into a Christian service in Baghdad, killing two priests and 50 worshippers. The following Christmas was extremely difficult for Iraqi Christians who did not flee the violence. In 2013 a car bomb exploded by the exit of a church as Baghdad Christians were hugging each other as they left Christmas Mass, killing 24 people and wounding many more.[43] Although Iraq is considered a birthplace of Christianity, the number of Christians has dropped to half the level it was at the beginning of the u.s.-led invasion in 2003. Christmas events at the site of the massacre were cancelled, and many other churches in Baghdad, fearful of aggression, followed suit. Some Iraqi Christians began a new tradition of leaving the south to celebrate Christmas in the relatively safe northern cities.

Violence against Christians in Egypt has marred Christmas celebrations there as well, although, legally, Coptic Christians have the right to worship freely. Christians were understandably wary of going to church at Christmas in January 2011, following an attack on a Coptic church just a week earlier during a New Year service. However, on Christmas Eve (according to the Copts' Julian calendar), thousands of Muslims stood outside churches all over the country to serve as human shields and give their Christian neighbours an opportunity to worship surrounded by brotherly love. Following the Arab Spring of 2011, the celebration in January 2012 enjoyed the participation of the Muslim Brotherhood, a large parliamentary party, and other Muslim government officials.[44] Although Salafist sheikhs require adherents to refrain from joining in any Christmas celebration or verbal greeting, other Egyptian scholars issued a fatwa to counter the Salafists' ban on Christmas.

Indonesian Christians have the right to celebrate Christmas under their federal government, but their Muslim neighbours are otherwise limited by the fatwa issued by the Council of Indonesian 'Ulama' (CIU). In 1981 that organization issued a fatwa forbidding Muslims to take part in Christmas celebrations. Before the fatwa, Christians had been inviting Muslim friends and neighbours to Christmas events, and Muslims felt welcome to participate. Muslim leaders in the CIU worried that Muslim citizens would fail to interpret all Christmas events as religious ritual, and that exposure to other rites would endanger their faith. The government was especially perturbed by this hard stance as it spurred on Indonesia's religious rivalry just as religious tolerance was finally being achieved. Under pressure from the government, the chairman of the CIU was forced to resign over the fatwa, although it continued to be supported and has never been rescinded.[45] Today Indonesian Muslims walk a very fine line at Christmas-time; they are permitted to wish their Christian friends 'Merry Christmas' as long as the sentiment contains the unspoken subtext that Christ is only one non-divine prophet among many.

Christmas-keepers in the West certainly enjoy more freedom than their counterparts in these Islamic countries; however, some fear that secular laws are beginning to encroach on their expression of Christmas. The Puritan-inspired laws against Christmas have been off the books in America and the United Kingdom for several hundred years; nonetheless, the twenty-first century has brought a new fear of Christmas bans. Recently a host of American figures have touted the 'Christmas is under attack' slogan; these personalities include Rush Limbaugh, Bill O'Reilly and the Alliance Defense Fund. The typical culprit is the American Civil Liberties Union (ACLU), which annually attracts comparisons to the Grinch for its role in policing Christmas in the public arena. Actually the ACLU has defended citizens' rights to celebrate Christmas in several cases. In 2003 it stepped in to help carollers who were forbidden to sing Christmas carols in a women's prison in Rhode Island. In

Massachusetts in 1996 two women who had lost their racetrack jobs for refusing to work on Christmas Day on religious grounds found some backing from the ACLU, which filed a friend-of-the-court brief. The organization took the same action in cases in which Massachusetts students were suspended for handing out candy canes and Christian messages to schoolmates.

Despite these past cases, the ACLU's activities sometimes warrant the Grinch comparisons. Most complaints about Christmas's intrusion into the public sector target the holiday's presence in government-run public schools and municipal decorations. In 2003 the ACLU became involved when the mayor of Cranston, Rhode Island, invited residents to decorate City Hall's lawn. The mayor's office received a complaint from the ACLU, not about the inflatable Santas, the menorah or the flamingos, but about the Nativity scene one resident brought to the lawn. Other holiday icons can be reduced to the trappings of folk rituals, but the crèche remains ever sacred; after all, it represents the birth of a deity.[46]

Local governments may not please everyone when they attempt to decorate their towns for Christmas. This toy soldier guards a small-town borough office in Pennsylvania Town, 2012.

This borough-owned Nativity scene stands opposite the giant toy soldier.

Debates about Christmas have been heard at the Supreme Court of the United States several times. Every year since 1923, the president had flipped the switch to illuminate the Christmas Pageant of Peace. In 1969 Richard Nixon took his turn, and the American Jewish Congress and the ACLU took issue with the National Park Service's co-sponsorship of the Washington, DC, event.[47] In the ensuing case, *Allen v. Hickel* (1970), plaintiffs complained about the life-size Nativity scene included in the display of otherwise secular Christmas icons. The Supreme Court ruled that the Nativity's inclusion was in line with the Constitution.

The Supreme Court case *Lynch v. Donnelly* (1984) set the precedent for legal Christmas decorations on public land and came to be known as the 'plastic reindeer rule'.[48] The 5–4 ruling overturned two lower court rulings by deciding that including a Nativity scene with secular Christmas decorations on public land did not suggest a government-endorsed religion. In an oft-quoted ruling, the Court explained that the Constitution 'affirmatively mandates accommodation, not merely tolerance, of all religions, and forbids hostility toward any'. Justice O'Connor's opinion stated that 'Celebration of public holidays, which have cultural significance even if they also have religious aspects, is a legitimate secular purpose.'[49] In the United States, Australia and the United Kingdom, the fear of lawsuits rather than actual legal action may be the most active force in policing Christmas speech acts.

In the UK Christmas has faced similar problems in recent years. However, many stories of Christmas-curbing have been blown out of proportion or poorly reported. For example, every year it is claimed that the city of Birmingham has banned Christmas in favour of a renamed festival, 'Winterval', but this is untrue. The Winterval event happened in the mid-1990s during November, and did not replace Christmas, which still rolls merrily along in the West Midlands.[50] In the mid-1990s Glasgow City Council began 'Shine On', a programme of city decorations and street performances aimed at securing Glasgow's title as the UK's Christmas-shopping hotspot. The media sometimes cites this as an example of Christmas censorship, but the Glasgow city website clearly identifies the event as the 'Christmas Shopping Festival Shine On Glasgow'. With so much money changing hands at Christmas, it is in the best interests of cities to brand their particular Christmas shopping experience uniquely. Sensational media coverage of holiday plots seems often to be a way to sell newspapers rather than to spread real information.

Some Christmas traditions really have been banned – perhaps for logical reasons. In Wimborne, Dorset, re-enactors dressed as seventeenth-century militiamen typically fired blanks from their muskets at the moment the town Christmas lights went on, but in 2008 the 400-year-old practice was banned. The deputy mayor argued that the sudden noise frightened children who had gathered for the festive spectacle, although re-enactors always warned the crowd of the imminent noise.[51] In the Philippines the police themselves have been in trouble for firing loaded weapons at Christmas. In 2010 the Philippine National Police Chief Director General once again reminded officers not to shoot their weapons into the air to celebrate Christmas and New Year. Since the warning typically has no effect, departments are instructed to place plaster or tape over the barrels of guns so that, after the holidays, trigger-happy officers can be easily spotted. In 2008 nine people were wounded in the

Philippines by stray bullets, and the number climbed to fourteen in 2009.[52] The habit of firing guns at Christmas has been around for centuries, and has been linked to scaring away evil spirits. Berchtesgaden, Germany, for example, is known for 'shooting in Christmas', as the tradition is called; the noisy ritual was first recorded in the seventeenth century but probably began much earlier. In many rural parts of the United States, Christmas Eve and, more especially, New Year's Eve are marked with the legal, if noisy, firing of guns.

A discussion of banned Christmases would be bleaker without the inclusion of the long, cheerless winter in C. S. Lewis's *The Lion, the Witch and the Wardrobe*. In this tale, the White Witch maintains a frost for 100 years, and her power is such that it is always winter but never Christmas. In this tale of discovery and redemption, the appearance of Father Christmas heralds the victory of good over the witch and her evil forces. Her bleak, century-long winter expresses an evil regime, one that controls the very calendar of its citizens. When the witch's power begins to fade, a spiritually astute Father Christmas finally invades the land, spreading Christmas cheer and the message that Aslan, the Prince from Beyond the Sea, will soon rule again.

In our own world regimes have similarly tried to hold back the holiday or manipulate its message as propaganda. They recognize that Christmas is a malleable symbol, but citizens tend to reject revisions to the holiday if such changes are made too suddenly. Threats of torture and imprisonment can send Christmas celebrations underground, where they simply wait until they can emerge and evolve once more.

# FIVE

# Christmas Away from Home

Homesickness strikes adults more than children during the holiday season. Adults have decades invested in traditions, and their sense of identity – be it cultural or religious – is inseparable from how they perform Christmas rituals. Anyone with this investment will feel low if they find themselves separated from their normal Christmas routine. When isolation cannot be avoided, new rituals develop, allowing celebrants to try to drown out feelings of dislocation and the disappointment of missing Christmas.

Europeans carried special versions of the feast of the Nativity with them when they left to settle other lands. Often these early immigrants slavishly recreated their homeland's experience of Christmas as a way of underlining their continuing part in that now distant community. Newspapers from the mid-nineteenth century to the early decades of the twentieth regularly asserted the Britishness of Christmases celebrated in Victoria, British Columbia, or Sydney, Australia. British settlers in Burma (Myanmar) in the 1920s would gather together to reminisce about Christmases at home, meaning past Christmases spent in Britain, and records show their desire to do justice to the British Christmas in the Burmese jungles.[1]

With such high expectations, one can imagine the despair Christmas brought to some expatriates. Nineteenth-century poetry explores the emotions of melancholy and loss experienced by soldiers and émigrés far from their families at Christmas-time. Few Christmas poems capture holiday homesickness as clearly as

Rudyard Kipling's 'Christmas in India', first published in 1886 for an Anglo-Indian audience:

> Oh the white dust on the highway! Oh the stenches in the
> byway!
> Oh the clammy fog that hovers o'er the earth;
> And at Home they're making merry 'neath the white and
> scarlet berry –
> What part have India's exiles in their mirth?'

The narrator meditates on the short-lived toasts he knows family in England will direct his way, and ends with a depressing realization of his own plodding existence, made more unbearable, it seems, by its dislocation from the snowy Christmas of home.[2] Letitia Elizabeth Landon and others also wrote on this theme, exploring the melancholy of Christmas homesickness. In England, the Victorians were the first to establish Christmas as a celebration of home and hearth, so any separation from that scene necessarily affected their perception of the holiday and one's place in its performance.

Certainly the contrasts between Christmas in Europe and Christmas in the colonies were sharp and, at times, overpowering. One newly arrived New Zealand magistrate noted that there was so much green during his first Christmas in the bush in the 1860s that the sight mocked his memory of the beloved evergreens of his homeland. Despite the differences, he found new acquaintances with whom to celebrate Christmas.[3]

A Norwegian American immigrant wrote in 1912 of how, in the early days of his new life, Christmas seemed shabby compared to the holiday as he and his countrymen had known it in Norway. Norwegian immigrants grieved the loss of their native Christmas, feeling that Americans failed to keep the holiday. In Norway, the thirteen days of Christmas had given peasants a break from their labours, but in America people often worked through Christmas, and the Norwegian transplants felt the need to keep up with the busy pace of their new progressive society. Others lamented the lack of religious respect for the day of Christ's birth; Norwegians celebrated with piety and multiple family devotions. One man who emigrated at the age of seventeen still bemoaned his lost Norwegian Christmas half a century later.[4] He may have missed the sweet flour-based flatbread called *hardanger lefse*, traditionally made at Christmas in some regions of Norway since the time of the Vikings. Homesickness was an unpleasant guest at many immigrants' Christmas tables, especially since it highlighted the social and spiritual differences between their new culture and the one they had left behind.

Eventually, however, Norwegian immigrants banded together in settlements, and their Christmas celebrations sought to recapture their mother country's festivities exactly.[5] For example, obtaining the cask necessary for making the Christmas beer may have been difficult on the prairie, but in time the immigrants would have access to established supply chains. A. A. Veblen, brother of the famous economist Thorstein, remembers his family's Christmas practices following their migration in 1854. Norwegian immigrants would slaughter a pig, brew beer, make candles, take a bath – everyone using the same water, of course – and spin and sew new articles of clothing in preparation for Christmas Eve.[6] In time Norwegian Americans adopted the American habit of giving shop-bought presents, which had not been a part of the Norwegian celebration.

Norwegian-American settlers missed their community Christmas traditions, including this sweet flatbread, *hardanger lefse*.

This adaptation proved acceptable because it emphasized the plenty that had drawn immigrants to America in the first place.[7] Moreover, many immigrants had left Norway as peasants and settled in America as members of the middle class. This shift affected the evolution of the immigrant Christmas by bringing children and the evergreen tree to the centre of the holiday.[8]

Immigrants continue to experience the same holiday homesickness that has depressed their kind for centuries. Recent interviews of German emigrants to New Zealand have found that women especially miss the overall patchwork of elements that makes up the Christmas of their past experience: foods, cold temperatures, family events, early sunsets and long winter nights. Women carry on baking traditions brought with them from Germany, although the climate does require some food substitutions. Recent immigrants attest that their holiday experience is just like the one they had in Germany, despite the great differences. Those New Zealanders who continue their German Christmas have found it difficult to open the heart of their holiday, Christmas Eve, to non-German New Zealanders who lack the same cultural priorities. Mainstream New Zealanders like parties and balloons, but those of German heritage still cherish the Christmas tree and the quiet family gathering with singing and presents. Some even draw the curtains to block out the summer sun and replicate the early evening of the German midwinter.[9] For others, especially those who do not have children to instruct in their German heritage, the difference from their childhood Christmas is too great, and they bypass Christmas altogether.

Eventually transplanted people find ways to make Christmas their own, although it might take a few generations. The Dominions of the British Empire eventually developed a sense of self-confidence, and this was expressed in their evolving experiences of Christmas. Comparisons in southern hemisphere newspapers moved from beleaguered self-pity to proud assertions of difference. The native-born generations that followed the first convicts and immigrants to Australia were crafting their own Christmas by the 1860s. Australian newspapers recorded the growing use of native plants to decorate for Christmas, an ideological shift from earlier times when immigrants had wished to use only holly and other evergreens to capture the Christmas of their childhoods.[10] Colonists also needed to work weather into their new Christmas tableau. The warmer climate allowed for a host of outdoor activities, and by the 1890s, Boxing Day had become one of Australia's favourite holidays because of its focus on community activities and pleasure.[11]

The warm Australian Christmas allows for the huge gatherings known as Carols by Candlelight which take place on Christmas Eve. The tradition began in 1937 in Melbourne where the population is glad to share a summer evening set to music. Similar events happen in every capital city and in many smaller cities and towns. The larger events attract 100,000 people or more.[12] The lyrics of some traditional carols have been revised to befit an Australian Christmas; the Australians have excised the sleigh and snow from 'Jingle Bells', replacing them with a Holden ute (an Australian-made utility vehicle) and the pleasures of a hot day spent out of doors: 'Oh! Jingle bells, jingle bells, jingle all the way, / Christmas in Australia on a scorching summer's day.' The massive national carol-singing habit has also promoted many original carols, such as 'Six White Boomers', about the kangaroos that pull Santa's sleigh, and 'Wiggly Wiggly Christmas', first promoted by the popular Australian children's performers The Wiggles.

Despite the heat, the Australian Christmas table still includes hot turkey and flaming Christmas pudding; however, iced oysters and prawns are expected as well. Families might picnic on the beach. Across the Tasman Sea, New Zealanders decorate with the native, red-blossomed pohutukawa tree, which is traditionally dear to the traditions of the Maori. New Zealanders like to head to the beaches and celebrate Christmas in their holiday homes, called baches or bachelor pads, although whole families retreat to these small, rather basic beach cabins. New Zealanders might have an English Christmas menu or they might grill venison or other exotic meats on their barbecues. The summer fun and family gatherings make Christmas sound like an American Fourth of July picnic, only with more immediate family and different food on the table. Like Australians, New Zealanders like to find plenty of active summer sports to tempt Santa to the southern hemisphere, and he can be seen on the beaches, surfing, or paddling a traditional Maori canoe.

If you travel about 2,000 miles south of New Zealand you will reach Antarctica. Those who find themselves in Antarctica at Christmas-time are either taking a cruise or working feverishly on scientific projects. While the cruise ships tend to carry Christmas decorations and entertainment with them, the scientists exist in a far more Spartan environment. Far from family, surrounded by colleagues, they are denied the television programming, street decorations and shopping habits that might characterize their Christmas season back home because Antarctica, of course, lacks television, streets and shops. Outdoor Christmas lights are unnecessary because, so close to the solstice, 25 December receives nearly 24 hours of daylight in Antarctica. Those who enjoy the comforts of base life pause from their research on Christmas Day to communicate with family via the Internet and prepare costumes for the party held in the evening. The American Amundsen/Scott base at the South Pole holds a Christmas tradition of racing in a 3-kilometre circle around the pole so that competitors run through all 24 time zones during the sprint.

The scientists in Antarctica pause in their labours
to commemorate Christmas in 2008.

Expatriates in many of those time zones have to find new means of celebrating Christmas. Christian missionaries in the field usually celebrate Christmas with mixed emotions. One young father in Kenya empathized with the lyrics of 'I'll be Home for Christmas, If Only in My Dreams'. Lacking the Christmas-themed commercials and television programming as well as the plentiful decorations one would see in American or European shopping centres, a family newly settled in the missionary life might easily miss the cultural prompts that signify Christmas. Family and friends at home must outsmart developing-world postal systems and ship presents early. Today missionaries, like soldiers stationed abroad, might spend part of the day on Skype, participating two-dimensionally in family celebrations at home.

Embassy workers also have schedules that require them to miss out on Christmas at home. In 1985 one *Times* reporter used a Christmas pudding to buy his entry into the British Embassy in Ulan Bator, Mongolia, then the most remote British embassy in the world, accessible only by train or camel at that time. He recorded the Christmas plans of the nine British and one Frenchman in that capital city, who would together be eating what may have been the only Christmas dinner in Mongolia that year. Their holiday meal, two turkeys, had been delivered via the Queen's Messengers in white bags deceptively similar to the untouchable diplomatic bags, allowing the Christmas fare to bypass customs.[13]

Perhaps the people who spend Christmas furthest from home, astronauts, have had some of the greatest challenges performing traditional Christmas rituals. In 1968 three Americans celebrated Christmas while orbiting the moon, and a billion people tuned in as the *Apollo 8* astronauts broadcasted a Christmas programme. The men shared Christmas greetings and read the account of the Creation from Genesis. Other astronauts have spent the holiday in space, including the *Skylab 4* crew of 1973, who built a metallic Christmas tree out of food cans. While shuttles cannot expend space and lift to bring presents to the inhabitants of the International Space Station, the crew does possess one tiny Christmas tree and makes plans to talk with family and enjoy a feast with an amazing view.[14]

Despite a tight schedule, scientists aboard the International Space Station
do not neglect Christmas, as this photograph from 2005 shows.

For centuries soldiers could count on peace at Christmas-time.
Medieval European armies traditionally called for truces during the
twelve days of Christmas, although even then the institution of the
truce might be used to plot surprise attacks. This practice lasted in
a limited fashion until the turn of the twentieth century. During the
South African Boer War, for example, the armies enjoyed a Christmas truce in 1899. These combatants were not strangers to truces;
Sunday truces were the norm during this war as the Boers' religion
forbade them to fight on the Sabbath.[15]

In one famous tactical engagement of the preceding century,
George Washington took strategic advantage of Christmas Day
festivities, utterly ignoring any unspoken rules about Christmas-
time truces. In 1776 the British had far superior numbers, and they
had been chasing Washington's poorly provisioned army southwards.
In the deep cold of this late December, Washington anticipated that
most of his forces would be leaving when their enlistment concluded
at the end of December. Before the bulk of his forces either died
or abandoned the war, Washington decided to bypass the tradition
of pausing warfare during winter. Instead, he used the cold and
the element of surprise to outwit the Hessian troops who were

comfortably quartered in Trenton, New Jersey. Washington's spies assured him that Colonel Rall, the Hessians' commander, enjoyed parties and late hours, so when Washington began to move his own troops across the Delaware River late on Christmas Day in the middle of a snowstorm, he was fairly certain that the Hessians would be sleeping late on 26 December. This proved to be the case, and Washington's troops picked off the Hessians as they clambered out of their houses in response to the early morning shots and shouts. A citizen had sent a note warning Rall of the invasion, but the Hessian colonel was in no mood to read it during his evening of celebration; his death the next day was probably a direct result of the Christmas party – at least legend would have it no other way. In the end, Washington's gamble worked. Possibly slowed by their hearty celebrations the previous evening, 920 Hessian soldiers became prisoners of the bedraggled Continental Army.[16]

The Hessian defeat spawned a narrative life of its own. The British blamed it on the Hessians' drunkenness, although continental witnesses claimed that the Hessians had not appeared drunk after capture. Spurred by the anger of Prince Friedrich Wilhelm II over the defeat, the Hessian command held courts martial and interrogated returning Hessian prisoners of war in the years following the Boxing Day battle. The episode had tarnished the reputation of this highly marketable mercenary force. Blame was eventually placed on Rall and his dead officers, and the hearings downplayed any holiday lack of discipline.[17]

When servicemen and women miss out on Christmas at home, it becomes the job of the government to supply the ingredients for Christmas cheer. When the supply chain fails, politicians face censure backed by cultural outrage. The Crimean War was the first international conflict that drew large numbers of British troops away from home following the upswing in Christmas's popularity among the middle classes of Britain in the 1840s. The war started in March 1854, and, by the following Christmas, the miserable conditions of the troops and general mismanagement of supplies caused protests and, eventually, the resignation of the prime minister. In a letter dated Christmas 1854, Florence Nightingale remarked that the wounded she was seeing were starved, frostbitten, ragged and in desperate need of cold-weather clothes.[18] The general public heard shocking details via the London *Times*. Now that Christmas had become part of their cultural identity, the British at home could not bear to imagine the ill-used soldiers pining for their much-delayed Christmas food baskets. By the following Christmas the supply chain had improved. Christmas hampers containing tinned meats were available and Christmas cakes arrived from England. Mary Seacole, who had set up an improvised hospital for the troops, also cooked up plum pudding and mince pies for a clientele of officers.

The governments involved in the First World War worked hard to provision their troops with holiday paraphernalia right from the start. Nearly all the combatants taking part in the war were from nations that relished their Christmas celebrations; indeed, in Flanders, the troops who fought each other were ruled by the grandchildren of Britain's Queen Victoria. In the run-up to Christmas 1914, the German and British governments prepared supplies to send to the wet, muddy, miserable front to carry Christmas cheer into the trenches. The Germans sent 75-cm (30-in.) decorated Christmas trees and food, and the British army distributed over two million boxes of smoking gear in Princess Mary's name. Private companies also supplied British troops with sweets, plum puddings and cigarettes.[19] Neither side planned an official Christmas truce, mostly because they did not want to encourage a lull that might further sap any sense of mission the beleaguered troops still maintained. Despite orders against fraternization from both commands, in the weeks before Christmas 1914 soldiers began reaching across battlefields in unplanned, temporary and localized truces.

In one spot between Ypres and Lille, Bavarian soldiers placed their lit Christmas trees above the trenches, which caught the attention of the British troops and symbolized the soldiers' shared interest in celebrating Christmas. Propaganda from both sides had characterized the enemy as savage and uncivilized, but the lighted Christmas trees twinkling above No-Man's-Land attested to their emotional brotherhood. Both regiments agreed on an impromptu truce. Similar events must have been taking place simultaneously all over the front

Seventeen-year-old Princess Mary initiated a collection to send military personnel brass boxes containing smoking supplies or sweets. The effort to deliver the boxes in time for Christmas 1914 greatly taxed the postal system.

on Christmas Eve, and the epidemic of peace became widespread. On some battlefields British soldiers crept closer to hear the Germans' singing, and elsewhere Germans and British celebrants posted banners reading 'Merry Christmas' and waited to see if the other side would respond. French officers, who seemed to have more invested in a war on their own soil, were also willing to agree to temporary truces. In Flanders, some British regiments made makeshift soccer balls out of sandbags or ration tins and organized a Christmas Day scrimmage with the Germans, sometimes in No-Man's-Land itself. Elsewhere the Germans merely watched as welcome observers as the British played, or the two sides competed in bicycle races.[20]

The localized truces lasted until Boxing Day in many spots. The transition from unofficial, local truces back to trench warfare was not smooth along the front, and a few celebrating soldiers died when snipers on the other side decided that Christmas had ended. Some officers had prevented the truce altogether. In other locations the sides bid each other a respectful farewell, followed by a few over-head shots to signal that the war had recommenced. Generals began inspecting the trenches, forcing soldiers to resume half-hearted firing on their new acquaintances. Routine troop rotations also moved friendly regiments away from each other and brought in fresh soldiers. By the time families at home read the letters describing the amazing connections made in No-Man's-Land, bullets were flying once more in Flanders.[21]

Truces did not halt the carnage of the Second World War. While Christmas came to Britons at home, rationing, blackouts, deployment and air-raid threats gave the beloved holiday an alien quality. Children had been evacuated from cities in the four months before Christmas 1939, but many wished to return home permanently when no bombs fell and Christmas crept closer. Some 50,000 evacuees did rejoin their families that season, and some never went back to their billets. In the end, just over half of the original 700,000 children remained evacuees following those first relatively quiet months on the home front.[22]

Rationing started in January 1940, just after the first war Christmas, but it was to be a constant companion for Father Christmas until 1953.[23] In 1940, Christmas-keepers had a chance to practise serving a festive menu 'on the ration', but food allowances became progressively skimpier. The Ministry of Food relented a little for the holiday,

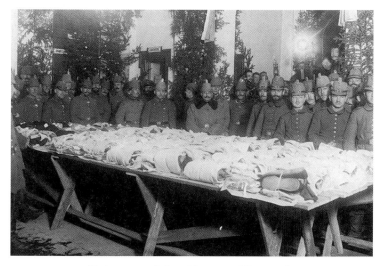

Christmas made it to German soldiers on the
Eastern Front during the First World War.

allowing additional suet for puddings in 1941 and extra meat, sugar and margarine for 1944. Nevertheless, meat was in such short supply that often only families with connections or a farm celebrated with much meat; for the rest, magazines contained recipes for meatless mock-turkey composed entirely of vegetables.[24]

Other elements of Christmas during the war years included a dearth of decorations because of restrictions on paper that also temporarily curtailed wrapped presents. Families found creative ways to retain the surprise of the Christmas gift, but finding gifts became an increasing challenge. By 1944 magazines were recommending matches as a delightful Christmas present.[25] Homemade and refurbished gifts became the norm, and volunteers worked tirelessly to ensure that children, and especially evacuees, enjoyed some special treat at Christmas.

The gifts that did exist might be exchanged in the safety of air-raid shelters. In England in 1940, fears of invasion cast an especially depressing light on Christmas festivities. Churches, whose bells would toll in the event of an invasion, were prohibited from ringing their bells on Christmas Day. Air raids tended to cease before Christmas Day, but several northern industrial cities experienced raids ending on Christmas Eve 1940, and the civilian casualties were high. That same year a massive firebombing in London on 29 December destroyed much of the City of London, including seven churches that had celebrated Christmas for the last time.[26] St Paul's Cathedral was saved by its doughty fire-watchers, who protected the largely wooden roof from the 28 incendiary bombs that fell on it.[27]

For Prime Minister Winston Churchill, as for many other citizens, Christmas of 1941 was spent at work. In Churchill's case, however, war efforts took him far from English rationing. He rushed to join President Franklin Roosevelt shortly after the Japanese bombing of Pearl Harbor in early December, and when his arrival in the States filtered through the news outlets, Christmas presents started flooding the British Embassy and the White House, where Churchill had set up his own map room. The prime minister was far too involved in following the unfolding events in the Pacific to note that American and Canadian fans had sent him 8,000 cigars as well as brandy, clothing and catnip for his pet cat.[28]

Churchill joined Roosevelt for the Christmas Eve speech following the lighting of the national Christmas tree outside the White House. In the prime minister's speech, which was broadcast across America, he assured his allies that although far from his family he did not feel an ocean away from home. This simple point of rhetoric was meant to underscore the cultural ties between the two countries. It also highlights the fact that absence during Christmas-time is itself a cultural incongruity. It cannot be overlooked or ignored, even during the rush of wartime preparations and plans.[29]

Several time zones away, in Hong Kong, British troops barely had time to acknowledge Christmas in the frenzy of defending their territory from a Japanese invasion. The military commanders in Hong Kong enjoyed a hurried Christmas dinner cobbled together from canned foods and alcohol before the official surrender to Japanese forces later in the evening. Many of the surviving soldiers and civilians faced a bleak future in the Japanese camps.[30] Subsequent Christmases in these camps were cheerless indeed. No special food or decorations marked the date, and one major general reported that the skeletal men marched through the prison camp, carolling the different barracks, singing with broken hearts.[31]

Song, it seems, is the most portable aspect of Christmas. Irving Berlin penned a song that would capture the hearts of Americans. Bing Crosby's rendition of 'I'll Be Home for Christmas' became a Top Ten hit shortly after its release in 1943, and American soldiers at United Service Organizations (USO) holiday parties almost always requested it. It seems that through song soldiers were able to express their nostalgia for home, and homesick Christmas-keepers' hearts have resonated with the song ever since.

In 1945 many soldiers may have heard that song even while rushing home after years at war. This was a post-war holiday that the nation sank its teeth into. President Harry S. Truman resumed the peacetime lighting of the national Christmas tree, which had remained dark for the war's duration.[32] This jubilant Christmas turned into a four-day holiday, as the president released federal

This postcard, produced for German soldiers in the First World War, sends a 'Christmas Greeting from the Front', 1917.

workers to share Christmas with their families, many having worked through Christmas during the preceding four years of war.[33] The American Army's Operation Santa Claus rushed to process servicemen and women out of the military so they could be home for Christmas. One railway company urged civilians to stay at home so that veterans could reach their destinations. While many obeyed, transport systems around the country were jammed with returning personnel.[34] Some eager veterans hailed taxis when they disembarked in Los Angeles. Amazingly, they found cabbies willing to drive them all the way to distant destinations including Albuquerque, New Mexico; Little Rock, Arkansas; and Long Island, New York. Their drivers gave up their own holidays to honour the veterans' requests and get them home for Christmas.[35] The staggering fare probably helped to ease the pain of their sacrifice.

One discharged American GI went to amazing lengths to reunite with his English bride and their newborn daughter for Christmas 1945. Herbert John Lamoureux was awaiting the paperwork that would allow his wife to join him in Massachusetts, but bureaucracy moved too slowly to bring the young family together for Christmas. So, instead of waiting, he travelled to England without a visa, working in the kitchens of a ship bound for Liverpool. After being denied entry, he jumped off the ship into the icy waters three miles from shore, only to be rescued and arrested by a British patrol. He was incarcerated in France for two weeks, but public outcry gained Lamoureux the chance he needed, and British officials allowed him two days in Liverpool with his wife and newborn – by now it was 10 January – before he went back to Massachusetts to continue his wait alone.[36]

The well-stocked American Christmas party stretched around the world as GIs redirected some of the Army's 680,000 kg (1,500,000 lb) of turkey to the war orphans in Austria, Belgrade, Cairo and Singapore.[37] It was a terribly bleak Christmas for many European countries; each suffered its own emotional loss and shortages of a range of supplies needed for proper Christmas-keeping: Belgium, Germany and Holland lacked the coal needed to warm homes; many of the delicacies of the Danish Christmas feast, such as coffee, chocolate and oranges, could not be had; the French lacked potatoes and fish, except on the black market, and coal was scarce. American troops unearthed 500 boxes of French toys that German forces had intended for Germany, and they distributed these treasures to French children who otherwise had little hope of Christmas presents. British families had coal, but the food on the table that many graciously shared with American GI guests was severely limited by rationing. Toys were also in short supply.[38]

Wars in the twenty-first century continue to keep soldiers away from home over the midwinter holiday. In 2011 both British and New Zealand troops stationed in Afghanistan looked forward to a special meal and extended telephone time on Christmas Day. It is notable that late-December journalism often focuses on what the soldiers miss about home, as if Christmas forces a pause that can only be filled with homesickness or an attempt to crowd out nostalgia with activity and the performance of rituals that rejuvenate the memories of distant home. When outside a war zone, Christmas might mean a day of duty like any other, with some additional efforts by the mess crew to create a Christmas meal for thousands, or it might mean a day of rest and time to watch television.

While governments try to cheer their active military personnel, some people find themselves imprisoned and entirely separated from the support network of family and government. Guards rarely go to any lengths to bring Christmas to captives. Such was the case during the American Civil War. In 1864 Union POWs experienced a truly bleak Christmas hunched beside fires in the Andersonville prison camp, known for its filth, overcrowding and high death rate. One Andersonville POW recorded his Christmas fare: 3 ounces (85 g) of beef and some cornmeal, which the prisoners toasted and soaked in water to create a coffee of sorts. They ate slowly and discussed the Christmas dinners their loved ones would be having, rating the odds of spending another Christmas at home.[39]

The same conversation also engaged hostages in Iran a century later. In November 1979 Iranian students seized employees at the American embassy, and for some the ordeal would last a total of 444 days. One hostage recalls how the students attempted to use

This sketch, titled 'Best Christmas Wishes, from Father, 1915', highlights the importance of the Christmas tree in the German imagination of the period.

Christmas emotionalism to motivate America to action – they wanted the shah returned to face charges. The students filmed the hostages' Christmas messages, and the hostages struggled to find the right balance of Christmas cheer to express to their distant families. During the same season the hostages became the targets of a massive American Christmas card campaign. The thought of the 53 remaining hostages trapped over Christmas roused the American people to send as much mail to Iran as a city of 25,000 would receive in a day, and 85 per cent of those packages, letters and cards were directed to the hostages. Radio stations were behind this endeavour, and the Iranian embassy promised the packages would be delivered. A young journalist became an unofficial postman, ferrying bags of cards to the embassy, where at least some of the mail eventually made it into the hands of the captives.[40]

The emotional draw of enforced separation over Christmas melted the hearts of many. During the hostages' first Christmas in captivity, priests were permitted to join them temporarily to lead them in Christmas services. The following year sympathetic embassies in Tehran sent Christmas presents of chocolate, toiletries and books to the prisoners, thoughtful acts that lifted their spirits.[41] In addition to sympathetic missives, Americans used lights to mark the passage of such a bitter Christmas. The national Christmas tree remained unlit for two years, and in 1980 Americans were encouraged to light an outside Christmas light for only 417 seconds, marking the number of days the hostages had been kept. When the hostages were finally released in late January 1981 and flown to Germany for medical checks, German children came to their rooms and sang Christmas songs, perhaps to make up for the Christmas joy the captives had recently missed.

Ingrid Betancourt is one of the better known of the hostages held by the Revolutionary Armed Forces of Colombia (FARC) in the early years of the twenty-first century. Betancourt, who survived six years of captivity following her capture in 2002, had been a Colombian presidential candidate. Three of her fellow former hostages wrote a book together, and their memories of each Christmas stand out as milestones in a jungle of monotony and deprivation. The

Christmases in captivity were a time to think about distant friends and family, and some hostages fell into a deep sadness during this time. Being away from family sapped the relevance from the holiday, although the FARC did permit limited festivities, including a ration of alcohol. Hostages also created makeshift Christmas lights and a manger scene. Betancourt recalls that listening to Christmas music leading up to Christmas was a self-inflicted torture for the hostages, who had access to a radio. Nonetheless, songs provided one of the most constant forms of celebration in captivity, as hostages with a common culture used Christmas music to bind themselves together in a new, forced family.[42]

Prison inmates have a better idea of when they will rejoin the free community for Christmas, but their holiday is in the meantime also fairly bleak. When celebrities miss Christmas to serve time, tabloids spread the word – the irony of a popular, successful person isolated from friends and family over this most communal occasion demands headlines. However, more than two million people were incarcerated during Christmas 2010 in America alone. In England and Wales, 83,701 prisoners missed their normal Christmas in the same year.[43] Prisons differ: for some, holiday separation is bleak and totally isolated from the consumer-driven rituals of the holiday outside the concertina wire. Others enjoy a decided break from the monotony of incarceration. In 2011 Scottish prisoners benefited from a festive Christmas sponsored by money taxed from inmates' wages. The prison system spent £25,000, or £3.50 per prisoner, on booking bands, comedians and treats for prisoners.[44]

Christian prisoners might find something to celebrate in the religious aspect of the holiday, and chapel attendance grows well beyond normal numbers. Many write about their habit of mentally recreating their childhood Christmases. Prisoners in America might prepare a play for Christmas, enjoy more relaxed rules and schedules, and even refurbish old toys to offer to visiting children. Some low-security prisons allow families to join inmates for the Christmas meal. Those who cannot be with their families have an option of using Christmas to reach out to their children. Prison Fellowship, a large American ministry, runs Angel Tree, a programme founded

10,000,000 MEMBERS
by CHRISTMAS
ON CHRISTMAS EVE
A CANDLE IN EVERY
WINDOW AND
RED CROSS MEMBERS
IN EVERY HOME

The American Red Cross organized drives in the week before Christmas. In the months following this Christmas drive in 1917, funds would have gone towards aiding refugees and providing ambulances and nurses needed for the conflict in Europe.

by a former safe-cracker and bank robber named Mary Kay Beard. While in prison, Beard noticed how inmates hoarded the gifts church groups brought them so that they, in turn, had something to give their children during the brief Christmas visits. Angel Tree offers incarcerated parents a chance to contribute to the Christmas their children are having without them. The programme's goal is to build a relationship between parent and child despite the separation, and to stop the cycle of crime in at-risk families. Mall shoppers might see an Angel Tree listing presents inmates hope someone else will buy for their children, and churches also get involved in providing this type of gift-wrapped Christmas cheer.

Some low-security prisons release certain prisoners for hours, days or weeks over Christmas. In 2012 Ireland offered temporary Christmas release to 160 inmates who were not deemed a threat to the public. As in years past, two failed to return to prison at their appointed times. In an uncommon reversal of the Christmas release, in 2010 a Montana judge sentenced a man to spend the next five Christmases in prison; Daniel Martz, who had attacked and tried to choke a woman, could expect to be incarcerated from 15 December until 1 January for five years straight. The judge hoped that the sentence would keep Martz out of holiday-related mischief.[45]

Television writers often sentence audiences to ponder how it would feel to be separated from family over Christmas, although the high jinks depicted probably bear no similarity to Daniel Martz's experience. A common motif in American television specials has revolved around characters stranded for Christmas. Sitcoms and dramas have used this theme for decades: iconic shows that have included the motif include *The Waltons*, *Magnum PI*, *Full House*, *Golden Girls*, *Home Improvement*, *The Bob Newhart Show* and *The Partridge Family*.[46] The blockbuster series of *Home Alone* films in the 1990s brought the same plot to the big screen. If not stranded by weather or other obstacles, TV characters often feel thwarted by work schedules, imprisonment or wars that keep them away from home. The motif continues as a trite presence in Christmas-themed American television today. In contrast, British television dramas more often have break-ups, tears and, occasionally, body counts as

Christmas-programming motifs. In part the theme of being stranded exemplifies the helplessness people feel in the face of the hectic pace of late twentieth- and twenty-first-century living, but it also expresses a deeper fear of missing out on that idealized, once-a-year experience of Christmas togetherness.

Watching homesick characters is certainly better than finding oneself in the midst of a real-life holiday travel tragedy. The demands of the American Christmas give rise to twice the number of travellers seen around Thanksgiving. Snowy conditions can catch out Christmas-time travellers in airports as they make their way to gatherings with family; with 90 million Americans travelling for Christmas, snow in any one section of the country can cause monumental delays and Christmas-time headaches.[47] Travellers around the world face inconvenience as they struggle to reach home. Tradition demands it of some, and others simply cannot face Christmas alone.

American Christmas specials typically end happily with characters recognizing the importance of family over consumerism; however, in real life happy endings are not guaranteed. Increased alcohol consumption and high expectations, plus additional time with in-laws, means Christmas is a season of both merriment and emotional distress. However, certain problems decrease as the Christmas season peaks. One study researched suicide attempts in eleven countries, finding that there is a decrease during Christmas compared to other days of the year. However, these findings and other similar studies uncovered the fact that attempts spike just after Christmas, climbing to 40 per cent more than on other days.[48] In fact, Christmas has a suppressing effect on suicides, although mental health resources know from studies and experience that they must prepare for a greater need after the holiday. The broken-promise effect may cause these delays. People suffering from depression may hold out hope that the desired event – a vacation or a major holiday – will bring about a change in how they feel. Increased stressors during the holiday, such as alcohol use, family conflicts and unusual schedules, contribute to even greater feelings of depression after the holiday.[49]

A study of Christmas-related depression in young, single adults found that one of the biggest contributors at this time is the perception that everyone else is enjoying themselves. Images and expectations of family togetherness abound, causing an isolated person to feel that they alone lack a loving family. In effect, this makes them homesick for a home they do not have, one that exists only in the mythical version of Christmas that prevails in Western culture.[50] Family doctors are advised to acknowledge unrealistic expectations related to the holiday and to focus patients on the positive aspects of Christmas for their families.[51]

Christmas can certainly deepen a grieving person's feelings of loss. The first Christmas after the death of a loved one represents a harrowing milestone in the grieving process. Loss rocks the home, the heart of Christmas-keeping since the nineteenth century. This ubiquitous experience has been gracefully captured in one of the most famous poems of the Victorian period; Alfred, Lord Tennyson, wrote a monumental poem of sorrow, *In Memoriam*, which uses three Christmases to mark the journey of grief after the death of a young man, Tennyson's friend. The poem earned Tennyson the widowed Queen Victoria's esteem and eventually contributed to his securing the position of Poet Laureate.

Psychologists recommend that grieving people attempt to be flexible over holidays like Christmas. Many aspects of the extended Christmas period are wrapped up in ritual, and these rituals hold memories of those who have passed away. It is no wonder that in re-enacting rituals that were once shared with the departed, the survivor feels emotionally vulnerable. Family members might temporarily schedule new rituals that give survivors a place to experience the holiday without being doused in grief. Others funnel their grief into activity, especially for gift-related rituals. They might donate money to a charity or person in need who in some way resembles the missing loved one.[52] In either case, the bereaved benefit from carefully planning their first holiday season, choosing how they will handle the commercial aspect which may seem so empty, and deciding which traditions they wish temporarily to forego.

How ironic it is that we expect perfection from a calendar event that, because of the very nature of human mortality, must someday see a hole at our family gathering. Reminiscing seems to be a common theme among those who feel isolated from their ideal Christmas. From the bereaved to hostages to Antarctic scientists, when people feel distant from their families at Christmas, they recount their memories, as if recapturing the lost holiday. Even prisoners in solitary confinement mentally relive their past holiday traditions, lovingly lingering over the Christmas table and the tastes that convey belonging and community. For all the attention devoted to gifts, it is the rituals of repetition and identity that people use to sustain themselves when they are away from home at Christmas.

# SIX

# Commercial Christmas

Since medieval times, some Christmas-keepers have celebrated the religious importance of the festival while others have used it as an excuse for drunken carousing. With the domestication of Christmas in the mid-nineteenth century, gift-giving replaced more public, adult-only rituals. Today the commercial preparation for Christmas can keep shoppers distracted for months. The historian Jennifer Rycenga has called Christmas shopping 'a public enactment of one's commitment to the ritual affirmation of personal domestic bliss'.[1] Finely tuned store decorations and piped-in Christmas music turn these commercial spaces into temples of consumerism. Preparing for the holiday by engaging with retailers has become one of the rituals of the secular Christmas.

The notion that Christmas serves as the high holiday of the year has developed out of the secular evolution of the Feast of the Nativity. Church denominations rely on a liturgy that prescribes rites for worship. In these traditions, Eastertide clearly outclasses Christmas as the holy day par excellence. According to that way of thinking, Advent, Christmas Day and Lent are all designed to prepare the worshipper for the real joy, the celebration of Christ's resurrection at Easter. After all, the religious victory of Christ at Easter is the only reason his birth is worth noting. Notably, in the Eastern Church, Easter outshines Christmas in practice as well as on paper. While Easter's resurrection trumps Christmas's birth in Western church liturgy as well, the symbols and commercialism of Christmas have been much easier for the marketplace to inflate, making the midwinter holiday the highlight of the festive year in some parts of the world.

When Christmas shoppers find themselves surrounded by wrapping paper, ribbons and unfinished shopping lists, they can probably thank (or curse) the Romans for starting this tradition; of course, several cultures certainly augmented the social ritual along the way. We do know that Roman citizens offered gifts during their early January festival of Calends, and Christians carried on this tradition with their own midwinter holiday. Shopping lists were not always so long. Homemade gifts sufficed for centuries.

One way to think about it is to recognize that gift-giving did not have to become a paramount element of Christmas, but rather that there was a need to bind individuals together, and Christmas offered a regularly scheduled event for the necessary gift-exchange. Since words so often fail to capture the fullness of human sentiments, we rely on gifts to express what we wish to communicate to loved ones and acquaintances.[2] The ritual of exchanging gifts at Christmas involves a set of complex values that are at work in the intense efforts to find the right gift and package it precisely to express a particular message. One group of social scientists conducted a study during the 1990s to discover that the values that influenced Christmas gift-giving included tradition, edification and social recognition.[3] Giving the same type of gift each year – an updated version of the same idea such as the Christmas Edition Barbie or the newest version of a specific collectible, or even something that has become a stocking stuffer standby – shows the giver attempting to 'freeze Christmas' or perpetually maintain a historical Christmas.[4] Edifying gifts allow givers to try to point the recipient in a new direction, perhaps to suggest a new hobby or expand their life experience in some way. Givers also make decisions based on their desire for social recognition from the receiver, perhaps for the effort that went into a handmade or hard-to-find present; subconsciously the gift is designed to raise the giver in the estimation of the receiver.[5] Scholarship on gift-giving in the Western world over past centuries shows that the drive behind gift-exchange has evolved as the fight for survival has

HARPER'S WEEKLY.

JOURNAL OF CIVILIZATION

VOL. IV.—No. 209.]     NEW YORK, SATURDAY, DECEMBER 29, 1860.     [PRICE FIVE CENTS.

CHRISTMAS DINNER

The meal had long been the focus of Christmas, but here,
on the cover of the Christmas issue of *Harper's Weekly* for 1860,
gift-giving has clearly begun to creep in.

mellowed. Nonetheless, messages for social survival still have a place in the Christmas present.

Little is known about gift-giving during Christmases of the first millennia. Christmas had arrived in England by 597 when St Augustine of Canterbury, sent to Christianize the royalty of Kent, celebrated it by baptizing thousands of people in honour of the day. We know nothing of any gifts he gave or received other than what must have been some very cold dunkings. Christmas is believed to have made its way to Germany in the early ninth century and to Holland a few decades later.[6] Sharing food had been part of pagan feast practices before Christmas came, and for centuries food continued to be the main form of exchange.

Christmas gifts have long served as threads that link those involved in the exchange. For example, on Christmas Day 1067, William the Conqueror presented the pope with much of the plunder his men had taken from England.[7] When they lacked plunder, English kings feasted guests at Christmas to secure alliances. Henry III put on Christmas celebrations for 1,000 knights and peers in 1252 during his daughter's wedding, but the oxen and the funds were provided by the Archbishop of York. Richard II invited ten times as many people to Christmas parties during his reign.[8] Not only did they expect an elaborate table, but royalty had high expectations when it came to the gifts they received. Elizabeth I could anticipate two bolts of cloth from her royal dustman and a small fortune from the Archbishop of Canterbury.[9] Peers, bishops, servants, cooks and pastry chefs all showered Her Majesty with presents fitting their station. The queen counted on these New Year gifts, as they were called, to dress her for the rest of the year. Such gifts sent messages of loyalty, and the queen recorded them most carefully. She also made certain she got more than she gave.

During the sixteenth century in France, Christmas-time gift-exchanges happened on New Year's Day. The powerful bestowed small sums of money, called *étrennes,* on their servants, musicians and the children of friends. Less common were gifts from the weaker to the more powerful, calculated to inspire future benevolence. The other gifts exchanged during the twelve days of Christmas, the

The English illustrator Walter Crane shows children on their way
to church in this design for a Christmas card from 1874.

*aguilanneuf*, passed from artisanal or peasant elders to the youth of
their community. The young men entered neighbouring homes and
sang, then asked to be paid with food or money. The lay musicians
might be appeased with chicken or sausage, but if the homeowner
refused, their message of ill will would last into the New Year and
beyond. The Catholic Church attempted to control, and at times ban,
the gift-giving rituals of France as pagan, and indeed the participants
believed the *aguilanneuf* tradition began with the druids.[10]

As with the French *aguilanneuf*, in less royal households gifts
consisted mainly of foodstuffs. Remember that even in the novel
*A Christmas Carol* (1843), Scrooge sends a turkey, not a basket of
toys, to the Cratchits. The same went for early presents in America,
where colonists might pass along a side of bacon as a Christmas
gift. Before the mid-nineteenth century, the masses saw Christmas
as a time of feasting, not gift-giving.

After Christmas was banned by the English Parliament, the
legalized version of the holiday was not as hale and hearty when
it returned in 1660. Feeding guests resumed as the main form of
gift-exchange, although it is hardly the way we think of presents

today. Cash also worked, depending on the moral fibre of the recipient. In 1705, as the newly installed Lord Keeper of the Courts of Chancery, William Cowper began refusing the usual New Year gifts of money that barristers always brought to the man in his post, hoping for kinder rulings in the New Year. Presents of money and feasting may have lacked the personal touch we expect in gifts today, but they did work to cement social ties between clearly divided classes, as long as the intended recipient did not start acting noble and suggest the gift was a bribe. Industrialization and the advent of the middle class combined in the eighteenth century to give way to a consumer culture. Cultural diffusion helped, as British and American readers learned through books and articles about the household joys of gift-giving that other Europeans already experienced at Christmas.[11]

Although the Victorian Christmas captures the modern imagination, the nineteenth century opened with Christmas on the verge of collapse. *The Times* neglected to mention Christmas at all for nearly half of the years between 1790 and 1835. In 1826 the Lord Mayor of London disliked the ebb he saw in Christmas-keeping, and mandated that shops close on Christmas Day.[12] Further north, one group of Lancashire factory employees voted in 1840 that they would rather have New Year's Day as a holiday from work than Christmas Day.[13] Christmas could have gone either way.

And yet, by the 1850s and certainly by the 1860s, Christmas had surged in popularity throughout England. Not only did it come back fighting, but it was reinvented to carry new messages. For one thing, the various regional holiday traditions became partially if not entirely blotted out by a dominant Christmas narrative proclaimed by the London press. This narrative was one of holiday merchandise and middle-class catharsis, and eventually became child-focused. During the 1840s, gift-exchange broke with the Stuart tradition of patronage – from rich to poor – and became a ritual of giving among equals.[14] The novelty of shop-bought gifts when combined with the increasingly urban population's distance from handicrafts became a boon for the retail industry.[15] Slowly businesspeople began to realize that the sales possibilities were endless.

Some of the trappings of modern Christmas came to life in the nineteenth century. Folk historians collected and sold volumes of Christmas carols. The first printed Christmas card sold 1,000 copies at a shilling apiece following its creation in 1843. It had come about when Henry Cole, busy with other pursuits such as helping to set up the penny post, asked an artist friend, John Horsley, to design a premade Christmas greeting for friends. In 1846 Tom Smith, a London confectioner, developed Christmas crackers from the tissue-paper twists that carried bonbons, and by 1900 his firm was producing thirteen million crackers a year for the English market.[16] Another staple of Christmas decorating, the Christmas tree, was popular by the end of the century in England as well.

The demand for holiday purchases altered the gender roles of the holiday. Before 1880 men were usually represented as the main Christmas shopper for the family, but women quickly took on that role.[17] The historian John Storey has called this reinvented holiday 'a utopian version of industrial capitalism' in which the middle classes could enjoy their wealth and achievements but also temporarily replace competition with goodwill.[18]

After foodstuffs, books were the next traditional gift to develop as part of the British Christmas. As a writer who understood the value of the well-phrased observation, Jane Austen gave her beloved niece Fanny a diary for Christmas in 1804. For those with less imagination, the handsomely bound anthologies known as literary annuals, so popular in the 1820s, were seen as ideal middle-class Christmas gifts in limited circles. By 1850 the 'Christmas book' was not necessarily one about the holiday, but it was certainly intended as a Christmas gift. Reprints of classics and handsomely illustrated table books piled up on booksellers' tables at Christmas-time. All these sales noticeably altered the annual labour cycle of authors and illustrators who rushed to make the November or even early December print dates necessary for maximum profit. Periodicals printed Christmas annuals, cheap paperback anthologies of stories and poems that made for fun holiday reading. Authors like Arthur Conan Doyle, William Makepeace Thackeray and Lewis Carroll all pitched into this frantic December marketplace. Conan Doyle's

The halfpenny post, instituted in Britain in 1870, resulted in an increase
in industrially produced Christmas cards like this one.

*A Study in Scarlet*, which introduced the character of Sherlock Holmes, first appeared for Christmas consumption, and Thackeray produced Christmas books annually during the late 1840s. At first Carroll's publisher had to pacify the touchy author following the speedy pre-Christmas production of *Through the Looking-glass*: 'Why, half the children will be laid up with pure vexation and anguish of spirit. Plum pudding of the delicatest, toys the most elaborate will have not charms. . . . The book must come out for Christmas.' A few years later it would be Carroll badgering his publisher to orchestrate a Christmas release; he had learned the profit of holiday sales to such a degree that *Punch* referred to him as 'the Christmas Carroll'.[19]

Books came to be an expected part of the British Christmas and gift-giving. In 1878 Molly Hughes and her four siblings each gave their father a book for Christmas: 'There he sat, gazing at the pile of five books – too pleased to speak, too pleased to touch them.'[20] Books for children dominated the market, especially following the rise of children's literature in 1870. These commercially produced books solidified the tradition of shop-bought gifts, both in Britain and America.

Instead of books, Queen Victoria opted to offer a gift of food to her troops. As was the case with many monarchs before her, her staff referred to her public presents as New Year gifts. In 1900 she commissioned Cadbury to produce 40,000 tins of chocolate as New Year gifts to send to her troops in South Africa, then in the midst of the Boer War. At home, however, her children received Christmas presents hung on and spread under the Christmas tree. The term 'New Year gifts' did not go out of use until the first decades of the twentieth century. In the United States, in mid-Atlantic American cities, advertisements hocked New Year gifts until they switched to flaunting Christmas gifts around 1870.[21]

Traditional gifts developed rather differently in Continental Europe. In Norway in the nineteenth century, gifts were usually handmade clothes. Surprise presents entered the holiday only after the First World War, and shop-bought gifts became the norm.[22] To the south, the Germans developed a tidy term to describe the feeling that salivating shoppers get when faced with their gift list: *Kauflust*, or the urge to shop. In the 1890s German marketplaces tantalized shoppers with window displays, automated toys, decorated trees and electric lights. The growth of the industrial economy brought mass-produced goods to Christmas consumers. In the 1920s church officials and the Social Democratic Party tried hard to curb this consumer spree by pushing to close shops by 5 p.m. on Christmas Eve, gaining the working man two hours of peace on that day, time that church leaders hoped might be spent at a service.[23]

*Kauflust* fascinates economists and sociologists who also study what they call gift theory. However, gift theory's bleak outlook is not recommended for Christmas-time reading. It is largely about the intangibles we hope to receive as a result of our gifts. Nonetheless, anyone who participates in Christmas gift-exchange has a pretty savvy understanding of the messages that gifts can convey, especially those given outside the core family. For example, when gifts have been previously exchanged, the decision to forego gift-exchange with an acquaintance can signal the end of the friendship. A recipient might feel an unwelcome sense of obligation if a friend has spent more on the gift than expected. Both parties must read their relationship accurately and give accordingly. Since presents are exchanged simultaneously at Christmas, unlike on birthdays, there is little room to revise the gift's message once the exchange has occurred.

Commercially produced gifts now dominate the Christmas stocking, but modern societies have adapted rituals to reintroduce the personal touch otherwise lacking from these presents. When children learn about Santa's mysterious role in gift-giving, the true store-shelf origins of gifts are replaced by a fairy tale.[24] The image of Santa's workshop also provides the fantasy that toys are created using pre-industrial craftsmanship rather than in a factory setting.[25] Gift-givers are more likely to buy luxury items or frivolous gifts at Christmas since this type of item stands out from the routine purchases that recipients tend to make for themselves. Wrapping paper makes this distinction visually as well. It adds a patina of sentiment

This poster by Edward Penfield advertised the Christmas edition
of the American monthly *Harper's Weekly* in 1896. Editors on both
sides of the Atlantic quickly learned that extra leisure time and comfort
reading during the Christmas holidays meant that a Christmas-themed
issue could be counted on to sell well.

and sets the item off from everyday, utilitarian purchases. Similarly, retailers can sell gift-card decorations – stuffed animals, singing envelopes, special cards in holders – because this 'personal' touch is seen to distance the gift card from the commercial cycle.

One way in which Christmas shopping has become ritualized is in its opening each year. In London, Harrods and Selfridges have both begun setting out elaborate Christmas displays in late July. This tactic is partly intended to enthral tourists who might otherwise miss out on this staple of London's Christmas commercial scene. In 2010 the displays appeared in early August, but the success of the event has them creeping progressively earlier, almost to midsummer. Tables of nutcrackers, ornaments, snow globes, wrapping paper and more will only grow as the midwinter holiday approaches.

Over the years, Norway's retailers have also attempted to lengthen the shopping season. Norwegian shoppers get a gift from their government: sales tax is relaxed by half at Christmas-time. One might think this would be reason to stretch the boundaries of the ritual shopping season, but Norwegian shoppers have their limits. In the 1970s Christmas displays went up in late October, but a public outcry pushed the opening of the season to the end of November.[26] Christmas does not seem to suffer in this corner of Scandinavia: in 2000 Norwegian adults gave gifts, on average, to twelve people at Christmas.[27]

In the United States the Friday after Thanksgiving, Black Friday, starts the mad race towards a well-provisioned Christmas. Many employees have this day off, and families have developed traditions in keeping with stores' sales. If the name seems bleak, it is because the Philadelphia police department, which coined it, did not enjoy managing the traffic in Center City on the day after Thanksgiving. By the 1970s the term had spread nationwide. Eager shoppers can now jump onto their computers for online sales that begin the season, and marketing by Amazon and other sites has spread this fad beyond the United States.

Since the early 1990s, Black Friday has been rated as one of the top sales days of the year, occasionally coming in first place. Numbers indicate that the ritual is growing in importance for

American shoppers who are eager to begin the Christmas season of consumerism. In 2009 the National Retail Federation (NRF) estimated that 195 million consumers visited shops and websites during the Black Friday weekend. This number showed an increase of 20 million on the previous year. According to the NRF's survey in 2010, the most popular purchases over this weekend, and a good indicator of popularity over the whole Christmas season, were clothes, toys, entertainment items and electronics.[28]

Retailers publicize doorbuster sales that bring crowds, and occasionally tragedy. Shoppers in 2006 began to exhibit signs of violence, resulting in a few hospitalizations. The death of Jdimytai Damour, a Wal-Mart employee in Long Island, New York, on Black Friday in 2008 demonstrated the brutality of a greedy mob. When the store opened at 5 a.m., the crowd of more than 2,000 customers, many of whom had been waiting through the night, burst through the doors, knocking them off their hinges; Damour was trampled and asphyxiated in the aftermath. Following this classic case of crowd surge and crowd crush, shops have had to implement defensive strategies. Some shopping centres see to it that stores stagger their opening times to lessen the foot traffic. Others remain open all night, but only begin offering discounted prices on specific items at predetermined times.

Yet another safety measure, Cyber Monday, has recently gained popularity and kept bargain hunters out of stores. Cyber Monday, a term first coined in 2005, represents the online sales that occur the first Monday after Black Friday. These sales have quickly become a part of the holiday preparations in the United States, Germany, the UK, Portugal and Canada. Retailers in New Zealand are testing the waters. In 2010 Cyber Monday spiked as the biggest day of the year for online spending, with consumers spending $1,028 billion. Retailers seem to have fully realized their power during the pre-Christmas season, but they may be wielding it unwisely. They have recently coined the term 'Free Shipping Day', which falls around 16 December. It may mean savings, but it certainly lacks the depth and holiness associated with the saints' days that still mark the run-up to Christmas in some cultures.

Between Black Friday, the Saturday before Christmas and any last-minute shopping that occurs on Christmas Eve, American Christmas shoppers in 2010 may have spent an average of $650 each.[29] The numbers are difficult to ascertain for various reasons, and economists debate the means of calculating Christmas sales. The NRF adds all sales in November and December in their total for Christmas purchases, but this includes groceries for both months, and people would be eating even without the holiday.[30] *Scroogenomics* economist Joel Waldfogel contrasts December sales with those in November and January. He found that in 2007, American consumers spent $66 billion, some $4 billion less than the NRF's total.[31] Percentages of sales may give a more manageable picture. Just 8 per cent of the year's shopping days are in December, yet this month boasts 23 per cent of all spending in jewellers, 16 per cent in department stores and 15 per cent in electronic outlets.[32]

Sales bumps occur in December in most largely Christian countries. Despite its reputation for over-consumption, the United States rates below average in the percentage of spending at Christmas-time. Compared to adjacent months, sales in Hungary, Portugal, Brazil, Norway and South Africa spike by 35–50 per cent in December.[33] The U.S. jumps 25 per cent, coming 21st out of the 31 countries analysed. In the opening years of the twenty-first century, the countries with the highest per capita Christmas sales were Norway (the equivalent of U.S.$288 per person); the UK (U.S.$215 per person) and Italy (U.S.$212 per person). America came in at a paltry U.S.$140 per person.[34] Even a country with very few Christians, China, comes in with an average of $4 per person spent on Christmas. This statistic is amazing because Christmas fever has not yet reached the rural areas of China. Because of secular Christmas-shopping rituals, Japan, meanwhile, sees a sales bump of 21 per cent in December.[35]

Individual shoppers may or may not watch their holiday budgets carefully, but overall Christmas sales prove to be highly effective indicators for economists. After all, the year-end sales can represent as much as 30 per cent of a retailer's turnover.[36] At the end of the year, the Hong Kong Trade Development Council puts out a report detailing Christmas sales numbers from all over the world. These statistics prepare Hong Kong tradesmen for the coming year's potential. For example, in 2010 Brazil, Chile and Argentina showed especially strong Christmas sales, suggesting promising markets in these countries for Hong Kong merchandise the ensuing year. Economists can even pinpoint the items that sold well during the global holiday sales, allowing businesspeople to plan accordingly.[37]

One element of Christmas shopping, the gift card, also greatly affects corporate plans. The fad began with the gasoline giant Mobil Oil in 1995, and gift cards have been on the rise ever since. After Christmas 2010, a survey by the International Council of Shopping Centers found that American shoppers had made 14.5 per cent of their Christmas purchases in the form of gift cards. Some studies find that the average Christmas gift card has a value of between $35 and $53.[38] E-gift cards are especially helpful for last-minute shoppers. Statistics show an amazing rush on sales of these cards in the hours before Christmas stockings are hung out – 35 per cent of the holiday e-gift card sales between 6 p.m. Eastern and 8 a.m. Christmas morning.[39] Since 2004 gift cards have become the top-selling item for American Christmas shopping, and the numbers continue to rise.

With the NRF estimating that shoppers spent an average of $145.61 on gift cards as Christmas presents in 2010, it is easy to see how the gift card has become a force with which retailers have to reckon. In 2010 one study predicted that $91 billion would be spent on Christmas gift cards that year. Since more than half of these are redeemed in January, and the credit cannot be counted as revenue until the cards are used to buy things, the Christmas buying blitz rocks the first quarter's economics.[40]

While some might consider them crass and soulless, the popularity of gift cards demonstrates that they fill a need. Givers do not want to waste time agonizing over a gift purchase that might easily result in disappointment or even carefully concealed disgust. Cash still has negative connotations between gift-givers of equal status in the West, but gift cards have become more acceptable, even

Retailers count on the fact that recipients do not always
spend the entire balance put on gift cards.

appearing as gifts between teens. Gift cards have social value, and
are especially useful when the giver is trying to strengthen ties
with a relative with whom they have little involvement.[41] When
marketing experts studied Christmas gift cards and their reception, teen recipients showed themselves to be very adept at reading
meaning in the presentation of a gift card. They recognize that
some givers are settling for an easy gift while others are genuinely
trying to please picky recipients. The economists conducting the
study concluded that gift cards are useful 'in solving gift-selection
dilemmas for givers in a variety of social roles', and especially effect -
ive in giving control of the gift to the recipient.[42] Perhaps this still
smacks of laziness. Nonetheless, the gift card offers a wide safety net
under the tightrope-walk of Christmas present purchases.

The people placing gift cards in Christmas stockings may be distressed to know what happens to them, although retailers probably like the sound of it: on average recipients leave 19 per cent of a gift card's value untouched and unredeemed.[43] In 2005 the hardware franchise Home Depot tallied that year's income from gift-card value unlikely ever to be redeemed at a whopping $52 million.[44] If recipients cannot use their gift card, they might rely on sites like Plastic Jungle to donate or sell it. Even when traditional gifts are exchanged, this buying and giving plumps the pockets of retailers while eliminating value from their products. This may seem like a contradiction, but consider the habits of consumers. When we buy for ourselves, we demand a consumer surplus – the item must be worth more to us than we have paid for it. In the transposed realm of Christmas gifts, the choice to buy and the gift's value to the eventual recipient become disconnected.[45]

The film *Bridget Jones's Diary* (2001) spoofed a common Christmas gift gaffe: parents unfamiliar with their adult children's style and habits buying them embarrassing Christmas-themed sweaters. The recipients would have paid only a small percentage of the sweater's cost, and only if they were willing to pay anything at all. The difference between the donor's purchase price and what the recipient would pay is all lost value. In one survey run by Joel Waldfogel, gift-giving destroyed 13 per cent of the item's value.[46] So, if $66 billion was spent on American gifts in 2007, $12 billion of this spending was lost because recipients undervalued the gift.[47]

One way to reclaim the value of your unwanted gift is to take it back to the retailer after Christmas for an exchange. The culture of exchange has led to another ritual of the commercial season: day-after-Christmas sales. Gift recipients swamp shops again to exchange their unwanted gifts for something more desirable. Others rush to check out the newly marked-down prices as soon as Christmas has passed. In the UK online sales begin on Christmas Day, and an estimated 4.8 million people tear themselves away from social events for the solitary experience of filling online shopping carts. Britons spent £131 million on Christmas Day in 2009, up from £102 million in 2008.[48] Notably, these online sales are not returns, but new purchases made by people thrilled to extend the shopping rituals of the Christmas season.

The child-centred nature of Christmas often prises open wallets and contributes significantly to sales figures. Before the mid-nineteenth century, this focus was largely lacking from the German and British Christmas. A romantic view of childhood began affecting literature and parenting habits around this time and, as a result, Christmas got a makeover. Germany saw the change first. Starting in 1809, a frequently reprinted article by Samuel Taylor Coleridge detailed German Christmas gifts he saw on a trip to Ratzeburg, and this description or ones like it probably motivated British parents to choose a child-centred Christmas.[49] Coleridge's report focuses on the emotion of the Christmas scene that binds parents and children together:

> There is a Christmas custom here which pleased and interested me. The children make little presents to their parents, and to each other; and the parents to the children. . . . Where I witnessed this scene [of gift-exchange] there were eight or nine children, and the eldest daughter and the mother wept aloud for joy and tenderness; and the tears ran down the face of the father, and he clasped all his children so tight to his breast, it seemed as if he did it to stifle the sob that was rising within him. I was very much affected.[50]

In the 1840s the writer William Howitt was able to compare German and British Christmases, stating that British children were isolated from much of the festivity while their German counterparts received the lion's share of the Christmas attention.[51] Periodicals exposed British parents to European customs at a moment when middle-class parenting was evolving. Suddenly parents wanted to bring an elaborate Christmas into their homes so that they could recreate an idealized Christmas tableau with their children; those children grew up wishing to continue the cycle in their own families.[52]

One reason for the fascination with the German Christmas was that Germany was a relatively close, largely Protestant country with an active Christmas schedule. The candle-decked trees and the tableaux they created gave authors something to write about, and Victorian readers latched onto the expansion of Christmas gifts from previous standbys like food and books to a wealth of toys, especially German-made ones.[53] From the mid-century until the start of the First World War, German toys dominated the British market, so much so that in 1913, 81.5 per cent of toys in Britain were German imports.[54] Ironically, just as the Victorians fetishized the German Christmas, today's celebrants claim a pastiche of the Victorian Christmas as a way of accessing what they see as a home-centred, simpler holiday.

Toys had also become a feature of the late nineteenth-century American Christmas. During America's involvement in the First World War, the child-friendly Christmas suddenly faced a patriotic obstacle. The Council of National Defense hoped to maximize bond sales during Christmas 1918 by banning toys that year. The toy manufacturers of America were understandably concerned about the Christmas-morning disappointment American children would feel, and so they brought a compelling argument and a bag of toys to a special meeting with the Council: 'Deprive youngsters of toys, especially educational toys, and the country will lose a generation of doctors, engineers, and scientists.'[55] The toymakers then wowed their audience with miniature submarines, trains and puzzles. In the end, children's Christmas stockings were saved. Today toy options seem endless. Manufacturers jockey to capture the attention of children in the weeks before Christmas. One study researched how effective television marketing is by contrasting Swedish children's Christmas lists with those of British children. The survey reviewed the difference between the letters children wrote to Father Christmas to see how pre-Christmas advertising affects children under seven and their recall of brand names. Swedish laws forbid commercials aimed at children, but this is clearly not the case in the UK. Based on the youngsters' requests to Father Christmas, brand recognition fails to work smoothly on this age group; however, the

Christmas forces an uncomfortable juxtaposition of plenty and the greater awareness of want, as in 'Christmas Eve', a pen and watercolour sketch by the German artist Ludwig Richter, 1874.

frequency of child-centred advertising does cause children to make greater demands on Father Christmas.[56]

Yet another influence on the changing heart of the British, Canadian and American Christmases was the feminization of the holiday. Media and shopping pressure taught women the 'Christmas imperative', which, according to the academic Leslie Bella, burdened women with the responsibility of maintaining Christmas traditions. The American creators of the 'Unplug the Christmas Machine' workshops call women the 'Christmas Magicians'.[57] Ethnographers have followed women's roles in gift-exchanges. The English word 'gift' comes from the Common Teutonic word meaning 'bride price', but in Old High German it could also mean 'poison'.[58] Women who are worn out preparing gifts that convey appropriate messages may find something toxic in the ritual.

Meanwhile, others turn shopping into an event. Christmas tourism can widen the shopping spectrum of holiday consumers. The German National Tourist Office currently promotes trips to Germany to visit Christmas markets with this advice: 'If you're tired of commercialism taking over this holiday period and would like to get right away for a real traditional Christmas you might consider heading to Germany, where gifts are not mass-produced but craftwork of real quality.' Tourists and Germans alike swarm pedestrian zones to shop for nutcrackers, bratwurst, greenery such as holly, speciality gifts and food, all while absorbing a festive mood that mixes seasonal merriment with commercial bliss. Customers stay warm and sociable amid the bustle by patronizing hugely popular *Glühwein* stands, where they can buy mulled wine and other hot drinks. Much has changed since Christmas markets sprang up in the fourteenth century. Today an estimated 2,500 Christmas markets employ 188,000 people during the month leading up to Christmas. Analysts cannot be sure of the profits in this type of diverse enterprise, but they estimate that the markets rake in between €3 billion and €5 billion each year.[59]

The 1980s began to see the growing popularity of German-style Christmas markets in the UK. They now take place in Bristol, Manchester, Leeds, Winchester, Edinburgh and York.[60] Shoppers can enjoy German-themed or local, organically raised foodstuffs while listening to carol-singers and browsing through the work of artisans and sweet-makers. Cultural analysts see this as a desire to access a seemingly less commercial, less modern form of Christmas consumerism. The nineteenth-century notion that Germans own a purer Christmas continues to spur Britons to imitate them.[61]

Among the many factions within the world of Christmas, there is the strife between commercial industry, which wants Christmas-keepers to buy more and celebrate in bigger, more expensive ways, and voices that challenge celebrants to find a simple Christmas. There is in fact a long tradition of criticizing the way others keep Christmas. After all, in medieval Europe people often complained about the rowdy Christmas-keeping of others, and the same concerns obviously led to laws against Christmas carousing in colonial America. As Christmas became more domesticated and more child-focused, commercialism emerged as the new Christmas demon. Some have organized around this concept, like the Society for the Prevention of Useless Giving (SPUG, *c.* 1912), which worked to free American employees, especially poorly paid shop girls, from having to buy gifts for their supervisors. SPUG leaders charged members 10 cents to join the society and encouraged members to wear their pins and boycott factory collections for administrator gifts.[62]

Some defenders of Christmas have tinkered with rebranding the holiday. The Evangelical Alliance in London runs a website called 'Simplify', which offers tips about how to de-hassle Christmas. In 2005 a whole town's worth of churches in Lancashire chose to avoid the word 'Christmas' and made an effort to use 'Feast of the Nativity' instead. Anglican, Catholic and Methodist ministers had met in September to discuss the relentless partying and commercialism of Christmas. By changing the name to emphasize the birth of Christ, they felt they could redirect celebrants back to the religious origins of the holiday.[63]

Many groups have taken up the call against what they see as the evils of Christmas commercialism. In 2010 the Bonifatiuswerk of German Catholics called for Santa-free zones and a return to

A popular part of German Christmas markets are the stalls selling
*Glühwein*, a combination of spices, red wine, citrus and sugar.
Christmas Market in Strasbourg, France, 2010.

St Nicholas. This church aid organization feels that the bishop offers a kindlier, less greedy representation of the holiday. The public is certainly aware of the subtle cultural connotations of these Christmas figures, as we will see in the next chapter.

# SEVEN

# Characters of Christmas

Despite the wild approval of Santa seen during American Thanksgiving and Christmas parades, the global image of Santa brings mixed reactions. Children gleefully anticipate his arrival, but cultural purists and scholars might bemoan his ubiquitous domination of pre-Santa Claus Christmas characters. Some families refuse Santa entry in an effort to keep their faith at the centre of the holiday. In other cultures, such as Japan and China, Santa's arrival ousted no one, and he is inextricably tied with sales and the bounty associated with Christmas. Santa detractors from cultures with long Christmas histories might prefer to fight against what they see as the Americanization and commercialization of their local Christmas traditions. Santa seems to be firmly entrenched in the modern Christmas, but this has not always been the case. In northern Europe, demons and dangerous characters populated midwinter festival traditions for centuries. Christianity eventually spread a cult of St Nicholas, whose origins mark him as distinct and separate from Santa Claus, despite the modern merger of these two figures.

St Nicholas lends legitimacy to Christmas parades and events in many countries today. Most of what we know of the real man is based on legends surrounding a fourth-century bishop of Myra in Turkey. The infant Nicholas is said to have started his religious devotions early by refusing breast milk during fast days. The more famous legends associated with the saint include his three gifts of dowry money wrapped up and tossed through a window to save an impoverished nobleman from selling his three virgin daughters

As a bishop from the 4th century, Nicholas would not have worn the standard robes we expect to see on Catholic bishops today.

into slavery or prostitution. As a pilgrim to the Holy Lands, he prophesied an impending storm, and then revived from death a sailor who had fallen from the mast. On the homeward journey, God sent a huge storm that disabled the rudder and foiled the plans of a dishonest captain who had planned to delay Nicholas's return to Myra; divine intervention then sent the rudderless boat straight to the saint's desired destination.[1] As a result of these and other miracles, Nicholas eventually became the patron saint of boatmen, fishermen, shipwrights, sailors and pirates. Russians, Sicilians, newlyweds, old maids and notaries can also appeal to the indiscriminating saint.

The attendance records of a historical church council meeting offer the main evidence for Nicholas's actual existence.[2] Bishop Nicholas must have travelled the relatively short distance from Myra to Nicaea to join Catholic bishops called to the First Council of

Nicaea to establish a universal date for Easter and the divinity of Christ. Nicholas is supposed to have slapped the face of Arius, the Alexandrian bishop who, history records, led the debate against Christ's divine identity.

After his death, the saint became a highly prized commodity. In 1087, with Myra in Muslim hands, the Catholics of Bari, Italy, thought that relocating the saint's relics to their own city might attract blessings, pilgrims and profits. Where his true remains currently lie is a matter for debate, since Venetians also claimed to have removed the relics, and the monks of Myra declared that they never handed the bones over to anyone. The bones in Bari are traditionally held to be the remains of Nicholas, although a few of his atoms might forever reside in the New World, since a piece of this skeleton was passed on to a Greek Orthodox church in New York City before its utter destruction on 11 September 2001.[3]

By the twelfth century, St Nicholas's popularity within the Church outshone that of every saint and canonized figure but the Virgin Mary.[4] The cult of Nicholas travelled throughout the European Continent and became caught up in existing gift-giving rituals. Twelfth-century French nuns gave gifts to children in honour of St Nicholas, and Nicholas markets became a midwinter commercial event in many towns. The cult was also used to keep children in line, since the threat of St Nicholas's correcting rod was a large part of his identity.[5] In England, with Elizabeth I's accession in 1558 and the Protestant Reformation, St Nicholas began to withdraw as he became seen as Catholic anathema. Elsewhere Nicholas-related costumes were censored or banned, as in the case of Arnhem, in the Netherlands, where biscuits baked in the shape of Nicholas were outlawed.[6] European communities drew upon old traditions of the Wild Man or pre-Christian god figure. They created other, scarier midwinter gift-bringers armed with the whip or rod, such as the Krampus of Central Europe, Hans Trapp of Alsace and the Belsnickel of Germany.

Meanwhile the Protestant Reformation had little effect on Nicholas's identity in his home country of Turkey, yet things were changing there too. The Ottomans reigned and fell, and eventually the Greek Christians were expelled in 1922. Three decades later the overwhelmingly Muslim Turks decided to maximize interest in their Christian saint. The figure they chose to market was a blend of St Nicholas and Santa Claus. A statue of the bishop St Nicholas eventually stood in the town square of Myra, now known as Demre, from 2000 until 2005. At that point Demre replaced the clearly Christian figure with a statue of the American Santa Claus, his arm raised and holding a hand bell. While the Salvation Army may have been tickled by the commendation, this revision did not last long. In 2008 a new sculpture captured the anachronistic image the Turks wish to sell of Nicholas: a Turkish man in traditional dress holding the hand of a child. Over 60 tour buses filled mainly with Russian Christian pilgrims make their way to Demre, where they can tour St Nicholas Church, recently renamed the Father Christmas Museum.

Western countries have also been altering their engagement with St Nicholas, although his cult continues to be strong in certain quarters. In 1970 the Roman Catholic Church downgraded him from a major saint to one whose veneration was merely voluntary.[7] In 2006 Vienna began the more stringent enforcement of a decade-old policy of banning St Nicholas from visiting kindergartens in the city. The white-bearded figure is simply too scary, proponents argued. Austria also supports an anti-Santa movement, which tries to keep the American icon out of the Austrian Christmas.

Scary or not, St Nicholas continues to be a dominant character in the Netherlands. Here the saint and his sidekick Zwarte Piet, or Black Peter, dock in a ship from Spain in the middle of November to take advantage of this very important season. He begins by meeting the mayor of Amsterdam, and continues with a three-week round of visiting schools, hospitals and other public venues. The fun ends with small gifts placed in children's shoes in time for St Nicholas Day, 6 December. Christmas Day, then, is reserved for holiday fare and church services.

The Santa of the Macy's Day parade in New York City and the bishop of Salzburg's St Nicholas Day spectacle might be surprised to learn that they are considered near relatives. The red suit, the white

A damaged statue of St Nicholas built *c.* 1870 still watches over the ruins of a neo-Gothic church destroyed in the bombing of Hamburg, Germany, in 1943. The site is now a memorial.

beard and the gifts link these two historic figures. Nonetheless, they stand for completely different cultural values. The historian Phyllis Siefker has argued that Christmas celebrants in search of historical context are too quick to link these bearded men. Perhaps the Dutch did not import the Turkish St Nicholas with them into the New World. The first Dutch settlers were, after all, reformed to the point that they rejected the Catholic tradition of saints. Also, records suggest that Santa predated St Nicholas's arrival in the New World.[8] In fact, Siefker and others make a strong case for Santa's deeper connection to the Wild Man of Europe.

A hairy beast figure of the woods, this Wild Man personified mysterious natural forces. He was known by various names throughout Europe: Pan in Greece; Cernunnos in England; Orcus in the Pyrenees; the Jass in Switzerland. Horned, grotesque and in possession of phallic symbols, the god represented the fertility that farming cultures desperately needed. Adherents believed that he

This woodcut of 1566 after a design by Pieter Brueghel the Elder shows the German Wild Man, a figure who contributed to the development of Santa Claus.

must be killed so he could be reborn to bring further prosperity. Consequently Irish shamans executed him, or an animal representing him, every seven years, and the French and Scandinavians carried out their rituals every nine years. The rites coincided with the harvest and midwinter feasting.[9]

Would it bother modern parents to discover that the fat man for whom they set out snacks is more directly related to the German Pelznichol or 'Furry Nicholas', also called Belsnickel and Bellschniggle? This hairy figure, brought to the United States by German settlers, dressed in furs and skins, and was far more likely to be covered in soot than the spotless Turkish saint.[10] A Philadelphia newspaper in 1827 recorded that a grimy Belsnickel travelled down chimneys in the night carrying a bell, a whip and goodies for the stockings prepared below.[11]

The transition from Wild Man to cheery Santa is a difficult one to follow, but some clues exist. One of the figure's other names, Kris Kringle, was in vogue by the 1840s and may stem from the Pennsylvania Dutch word *Grisht-kindle*, meaning Belsnickel's presents, or the word *Christkindlein*, for the Christ Child, the more religious bringer of holiday treats.[12] During the holiday the Pennsylvanian Germans welcomed Belsnickel, a descendant of the Wild Men, and poems and books for children began to capture the essence of a fur-clad gift-giver. The famous poem first published as 'A Visit from St Nicholas' and later known as ''Twas the Night before Christmas' appeared in a New York newspaper in 1823. The figure there has the name of the Turkish saint, but none of the religious qualities. He even dresses like an untidy Wild Man: 'He was dress'd all in fur, from his head to his foot, and his clothes were all tarnish'd with ashes and soot.' Early black-and-white representations tend to depict Santa with the blotchy nose of a drunk. Indeed, when the artist Thomas Nast designed the Santa Claus images for *Harper's Weekly* starting in 1863, he drew on his childhood memories of the furry, elfish Bavarian Pelznichol.[13] The image has been stable for some time now, and even in Singapore and Australia Santa ignores the heat of a midsummer Christmas and can frequently be seen fully clothed for cold weather, often accompanied by his reindeer.

Santa grew in stature and cleaned off his soot over the decades until he was well established as the American gift-giver, although he did keep some of the fur, which now trims his suit. This transformation was perhaps the result of a conspiracy of poets and artists who wished to dissociate Christmas's newest character from the wild street debauchery of labouring classes, which disturbed Christmas worship and worried the gentry.[14] Santa was further domesticated by marriage, and Mrs Claus entered the legend during the 1880s.[15]

Almost as soon as he was established as a Christmas character, Santa began helping to sell a number of products, from coal to jewellery, from soap to fizzy drinks. In 1931 Coca-Cola famously borrowed Santa's image to sell its beverage, by then denuded of its coca, to children. Haddon Sundblom designed this hyper-commercial Santa drinking the product, since laws still forbade advertisers from showing children consuming it.[16] Such an image was also intended to boost winter sales of the drink.[17] Sundblom continued producing Santa ads for Coke until 1964, and they became a memorable visual element of the American Christmas.[18] Incidentally,

Pepsi's campaign in the summer of 2011 tried to show that in summer Santa drinks Pepsi.

Rudolph, 'the most famous reindeer of all', only joined Santa's troupe following a campaign for the Montgomery Ward department store in Chicago in 1939. The advertising editor, Robert Lewis May, designed the story of the outcast fawn for a holiday flyer that made it into the hands of millions of consumers. Ten years later Rudolph's story appeared in a song sung by Gene Autry. That was all it took to entrench this staple character into popular culture.[19]

French Christmas celebrants have witnessed a revolution of Christmas characters in the decades since the Second World War. Before the war, the Nativity scene served as the focal point of Christmas. Following the Marshall Plan, which brought American interests and cultural icons to France, the clergy stepped up to police the Americanization of French culture. The minor character of Père Noël was becoming identified with the American Santa. Clerics in Dijon took vengeance on a Père Noël effigy in 1951, hoping to redirect French celebrants away from a commercial holiday and back towards a Christmas centred solely on Christ's birth. Despite this twentieth-century persecution, Père Noël continues to celebrate Christmas in France. In some regions, he is expected to visit twice during the Christmas season: once on 6 December and again on Christmas Eve.

So the Wild Man of Europe crossed the ocean, stole the Anglicized name for the Dutch *Sinter Claes* or St Nicholas, became associated with American commercialism, and began his uncharted cultural domination of the world from there. Today Santa provides some of the ritual structure to the American Christmas. During the weeks leading up to the holiday, children can visit Santa at malls, where he sits on a throne dressed splendidly in red and white. Children pop up onto his lap (or merely stand beside him, in highly litigious cities) and tell him what they would like for Christmas. A helper elf might snap a photograph; indeed, photography outfits often organize these profitable annual tableaux. Once this important communication has been made, children can wait for

Christmas Eve, when they put out cookies and milk for Santa and carrots for his reindeer. Poor Santa might hanker after the heartier beer and mince pies Australians set out for Father Christmas.

Santa's route is no longer clouded in secrecy. The North American Aerospace Defence Command allows volunteers to report the merry elf's progress. The tradition began in 1955 with a typo and a compassionate, imaginative colonel. That Christmas Eve a Sears department store advertisement promoting calls to Santa inadvertently listed the telephone number of the Colorado Springs' Continental Air Defense (CONAD) Command Center. During the Cold War, this programme acted as a sentry for Soviet missile attacks. The colonel on duty that night could not patch the eager children through to Santa, but he did ask his staff to answer the busy phones with details of the suited man's current location. The tradition continued, and today volunteers inform millions of children about Santa's progress through a website and social media.[20] By watching the North American Aerospace Defense Command (NORAD) reports online, children can be sure to be in bed before

In Denmark, the red- or grey-clad Christmas gnome (*nisse*) plays mischievous tricks on Christmas-keepers. Families prepare a bowl of rice pudding to placate the *nisse* on Christmas Eve.

Santa arrives in their town, at which point he comes down the chimney to fill their stockings and scatter presents under the tree. After all this activity, Santa returns to his home to rest and take stock of next year's events.

As for the location of Santa's home, however, the exact coordinates remain clouded in controversy. In his famous illustrations of Santa, Nast eventually chose to place his home at the North Pole. Perhaps envisioning the fight for Santa's citizenship, Nast felt the North Pole could be claimed by no one, and offered a nearly central location for northern hemisphere fans of Santa.[21] Today American children trust that Santa crafts his lists in the North Pole, but enterprising folk all over the world beg to differ. Since 2007, when a Swedish firm mentioned that Kyrgyzstan would be the most central location for a European Santa, that country has jumped on the idea of marketing itself as the new North Pole. Federal employees organized a Santa Festival and an international Santa mailbox. The Soviet regime had imported the gift-giver Ded Moroz to Kyrgyzstan, but now the country chooses to market itself as an international tourist destination by adopting Santa Claus as its most generous citizen.[22]

Santa's Finnish home is more controversial than the one in Kyrgyzstan. The Sami, a formerly nomadic group, live in the northern reaches of Finland, Sweden and Norway. While some Sami have integrated with their countries' dominant cultures, a remnant still raise reindeer for meat and milk and dress in their distinctive clothing, down to the curved shoes. The Santa Claus Tourist Centre in Rovaniemi, Finland, mixes Sami culture with Anglo-American Christmas culture, commercializing the Sami and cheapening their rituals. Here tourists can meet Santa and his reindeer. During the 1980s the Finns of Lapland successfully stole Santa from Oslo, Norway, where British children had formerly been sending their gift lists, largely because of the annual gift of an enormous Christmas tree to thank Britain for its help during the Second World War. An international campaign brought in more than half a million letters a year to Rovaniemi, and tourists followed.[23] Samis have protested outside this theme park to object to the usurping of their cultural image. Some fear that the commercial reduction of Sami culture to Christmas kitsch will put off Sami teenagers from embracing their own rich heritage.

Despite Rovaniemi's popularity with letter writers, Drøbak in Norway has staked its claim as Santa's birthplace. The town has operated Santa's Own Post Office since 1990, and email applications are also accepted. In America, regional post offices bring in volunteer 'elves' during December to manage Santa's mail, most of which is addressed to his home at the North Pole. North Pole, Alaska, prides itself on its Christmas identity and has been handling letters to Santa since 1954. On the other side of the continent, North Pole, New York, manages incoming letters too, and it also attracts tourists with

Thomas Nast's rotund Santa from 1881, the most famous of the Santa images he contributed to *Harper's Weekly* between 1863 and 1886.

its alpine flavour, rides, shows and resident Santa. It does not require its guests to be very good at geography.

In America, too many Santas can lead to conflict. The Amalgamated Order of Real Bearded Santas (AORBS) invites men with real beards and at least one experience of playing Santa to join their club, which numbers in the hundreds. Panels at the order's conventions cover beard maintenance and reindeer facts, and members seem to have lots of fun. The order has been most famous recently for its internal political squabbling and eventual split stemming from individual profiteering over the Santa image.

With a real beard or not, sometimes a single Santa stands out from the crowd for his tireless philanthropic efforts. A plaque in Newtown, New South Wales, commemorates the work of Syd 'Doc' Cunningham, better known by the name Black Santa, which he registered. Starting in the 1960s, Cunningham created a simple Santa costume out of red overalls and pyjamas before bringing Christmas gifts to destitute children in the west. Cunningham went on to earn the 1982 Australia and New Zealand Army Corps (ANZAC) of the Year award, which honours selfless compassion towards one's community, and the 1987 Aboriginal of the Year award for his tireless efforts on behalf of the poor. Before his death in 1999, he would stand outside a market, collecting money for the poor with the help of a sign that read, 'Wellington Aboriginal Children, we need your help for a bush Xmas.' For more than 30 years Aboriginal children looked forward to his delivery of gifts by helicopter at Christmas-time.[24]

No matter where they originate, a certain suspension of disbelief is required in relation to these gift-givers. While parents are usually quick to correct children's belief in monsters and other pretend characters, they encourage the belief in Christmas gift-bringers. The importance, sociologists think, is in the way adults modify the story to cater to the values held by their family.[25] The Santa figure is the secular nexus of materialism and benevolence.

Children progress through six stages of belief in figures like Santa before they come to accept that this Christmas character is a myth.[26] Many psychologists have looked into how children make

Thomas Nast created this montage of Santa and Civil War-era
Christmas vignettes for an issue of *Harper's Weekly* in 1865.

this transition, and the research finds that children change little over
the years. A series of questions about belief in Santa Claus was posed
to school students in Lincoln, Nebraska, in 1896 and again in 1979,
and the findings showed that the twentieth-century population was
about six months older on average than their great-grandparents
had been at the point at which they discovered that Santa was a
culture-wide hoax.

But why do parents perpetuate the lie of the gift-bringer?
Parents often exhaust themselves and overextend their credit to provide gifts for their children, and then they deflect any gratitude the
children might feel by attributing the effort and expense to an
absent figure. Gift theorist Jacques T. Godbout has some pretty
bleak theories about this. Parents might be releasing children from
feeling 'too onerous a debt'.[27] Or they might be attempting to show
a love so pure that no gratitude or emotional payment is required.
Godbout also suggests that the grandfatherly figure of Santa represents the ancestor, a dislocated image in Western society. He is a
link with past generations, and parents may wish to incorporate
themselves into this myth to manage the way they will be seen after
they die.[28]

Older gift-givers still carry sacks filled with presents all over Europe, although some of these characters have been influenced by the return of the European Wild Man from the Atlantic shores. Now he dresses in red, has been tamed by children and answers to Santa. Many of Western Europe's regional gift-giving figures, such as Finland's Joulupukki and Denmark's *nisse*, have lost their distinctive qualities as they have evolved to resemble the American Santa Claus. For example, in Norway, *julenisse*, tall elves wearing ankle-length robes, are occasionally replaced by Santa Claus, although the *julenisse* are the central attraction at community celebrations that run until the middle of January.[29] Norwegians also have female *nisse* with braids to keep the male *nisse* company. *Julenisse* made of largely natural materials decorate Norwegian homes during Christmas-time, and the larger ones are more likely to have a distinctly Santa-esque look. There does not seem to be much resentment about this gradual shift, perhaps because the look of the *julenisse* has evolved continuously through the years.

Rather than being a descendant of St Nicholas, the English Father Christmas sprang up separately as a personification of Christmas and an English version of the Wild Man. Father Christmas was originally associated with meat and drink and a jolly Yuletide, but not with gift-giving. The first record appeared in the mid-fifteenth century in a carol, and he came to be an introductory character in mumming plays.[30] Ben Jonson created a club-wielding Father Christmas character in a Christmas masque of 1616.[31] The Puritans tried to stamp out Father Christmas, but he survived to be somewhat augmented by Victorians newly invested with the significance of Christmas. The John Leech drawing of the Ghost of Christmas Present for Dickens's *A Christmas Carol* captures the Father Christmas who, decades later, during the 1870s, became the bringer of gifts to children. He lost the crown he had earlier worn at times, and by the 1880s he was popping down chimneys and generally imitating Santa Claus.[32]

The name Santa has become interchangeable with Father Christmas, although 'Santa' is used almost exclusively in America. Santa always wears trousers and a hat with a tassel, while Father

Christmas might don a robe with a hood. In the New World Father Christmas has something of an antique feel. He seems more at home in the woods than in a toy-production hub. Regardless of connotation, the assumption that these two names refer to the same person undermines the depth of each figure's long history. They may have been nearly the same character since about 1870, but before that Santa Claus was a fairly new creation, and Father Christmas had an edgier, more hedonistic meaning. Children may not worry about the distinction between these names as they fall asleep on Christmas Eve, but adults may appreciate the differences of culture that become too easily blurred by the red-robed figure selling just about anything.

The thirteen Icelandic Yule Lads, roguish descendants of trolls, begin visiting children in the twelve days leading up to Christmas. They used to be associated with a cat monster that ate children who had not yet received new clothes, but today they have followed

Originally the mischievous *nisse* was male, but since Christmas has evolved to focus on family, the tradition has evolved to provide the *nisse* with a wife and children of his own.

Each of the traditional Icelandic Yule Lads has a penchant for a particular prank.

Santa's style and tempered their mischief. Now they might be depicted wearing red rather than their medieval Icelandic garb, and the presents they bring certainly help endear them to children.[33]

One Christmas visitor was intentionally marketed to be distinct from Santa. Ded Moroz, or Father Frost, hails from Russia. There he travels with his lovely snow-maiden granddaughter, Snegurochka, probably the least repulsive of the gift-givers' companions in Europe. Ded Moroz initially took cover in 1917 when Lenin declared him to be in league with the churches and Christianity was outlawed. The long-robed figure's connections to the pre-Christian rituals eventually saved him, and in 1948 he was allowed to continue his gift-bearing journeys if he followed orders. Stalin required Ded Moroz to wear blue robes so as to be visually distinct from the western Santa, and he had to work during the New Year celebrations, not at Christmas. Zarya, a governmental employment agency, handled Ded Moroz's appearances after that; Stalin's government had reinstated this Christmas character as an employee of the regime. Now that Russia has embraced capitalism, Ded Moroz is free to wear the deep red, ankle-length robes he seems to prefer.

Some Christmas characters cannot possibly be mistaken for Santa Claus. These are the demon figures that often accompany the benevolent old men who deposit gifts throughout Europe. The jovial robed gift-givers once brandished weapons of punishment as well, but now that side of their character has nearly been forgotten. Gruesome characters who threaten punishment have evolved as a way of policing child behaviour. The most visually menacing of these figures is, without a doubt, the demonic-looking alpine Krampus.

Krampus, or the Krampus, arrives in Austria on St Nicholas Eve, 5 December, along with his merrier companion and master. Krampus wears chains on his wrists and carries birch twigs in a bundle, a phallic symbol and reminder of his possible connection to witch coven initiation rituals.[34] Krampus hands out the birch sticks, which look like brooms, to houses where children might need some encouragement to behave throughout the year.[35] Whether a consequence of the European fertility besom associated with witches' brooms or not, the birch may also be the key to seeing Krampus as St Nicholas's

The Krampus is an especially terrifying Christmas character, but the events of *Krampuslaufen*, or Krampus runs, draw large crowds.

darker, violent side. A Dutch myth holds that St Nicholas returned from the dead to punish a bishop who forbade the singing of the saint's responses, and the violent punishment was a near-fatal birch beating.[36]

Where St Nicholas is tame and gentle, Krampus is wild and terrifying. When they participate in the Nicholas play or *Nikolospiel* together, Krampus steals the show.[37] In Hollersbach, Austria, a wild parade of many Krampuses, all dressed in thick furry costumes, demon-faced masks and gravity-defying horns, stirs the crowds of onlookers each year during the *Krampuslauf*, or Krampus run. The Krampuses lope down the night-time streets lit by the eerie glow of contained fires, periodically whacking onlookers with their birch bundles. Some of these wild figures are tame enough to draw the bishop St Nicholas's sleigh while the saint blesses the crowd from beneath his towering bishop's hat and immense white beard.

The Dutch St Nicholas, Sinterklaas, enjoys the companionship of Zwarte Piet, or many Zwarte Pieten. Typically a group of young, white women dress in medieval male attire with white ruffed collars and black wigs, blacken their faces with paint, and cavort around St Nicholas when he appears to meet children. Zwarte Piet translates as Black Peter, and it was another name for the Devil during medieval times. This is why the character still wears blackface today, although the image has sparked some racial controversy. Terrified by Zwarte Piet in her childhood, Mieke Bal has written about how the Dutch Christmas custom is 'deeply problematic'.[38] Attempts have been made to market Zwarte Piet differently. In 2006 the Dutch media presented a new narrative about how St Nicholas travelled through the rainbow. As a result, the Piets sometimes wear a rainbow of colours, not just black. However, this tactic has been tried before and failed. One alteration to the narrative has developed over the years: the Piets have lost their taint of Hell. Now they toss sweets and biscuits to children at St Nicholas events, or down the chimney straight into children's shoes.[39]

In eastern parts of France, Le Père Fouettard, the whipping Father who accompanies St Nicholas, holds the stick or sack for carrying off children. He appears unkempt and with some degree of blackface. Čert (Devil) and Anděl (Angel) accompany St Nicholas on his rounds of the streets in Prague in the Czech Republic, or, outside the city, into the homes of village children who benefit from a more personal encounter with the three companions. Čert's job is to threaten to carry bad children off to hell.

Some gift-givers have been female, like the Befana of Italy, who comes down chimneys on the eve of the Epiphany. In France Tante Arie, a witch with goose feet and iron teeth, enters through windows and leaves gifts or birch rods, depending on the child's behaviour. The Germans added Frau Holle to their list of Christmas characters, and in Haute-Saône in eastern France female fairies known as *trotte-vieilles* might either offer gifts or threaten to eat children.[40] In Norway the *lussi*, a terrifying witch, policed tardy Christmas decorators who were not ready in time for the winter solstice. She was also said to kidnap disobedient children by coming down the chimney after them.[41] The Norse *oskorei* also terrorized farmers at Christmas-time; homeowners had to protect their farms against these troublemakers. The *oskorei* especially liked to carry off Christmas food and ale. The *lussi* and the *oskorei* are now relegated to legend and do not appear in current Norse customs. The *lussi* did, however, leave her mark in the Scandinavian devotion to St Lucia. Today in Scandinavian countries, 13 December is St Lucia's Day, the start of the Christmas season. Girls wear white dresses and candle wreaths to commemorate the Italian martyr. After her conversion and commitment to a virgin devotion to God, Lucia refused to marry. Local Roman forces tortured her to death, but divine intervention prevented the fire they set from consuming her body. Now, flame is used to mark her day. Since the date and name coincided with pre-Christian rituals, the Swedish Church easily transitioned the population into this holiday, and it was not shaken by the Reformation.

The form of today's St Lucia celebration has been in place for two centuries. The Advent holiday was transmitted from Sweden to Norway in the 1950s, where it became popular for a while, though now it is a shrinking custom there, largely relegated to schools and day-care centres.[42] The Caribbean island of St Lucia celebrates its

National Day in conjunction with St Lucia's Day, and the festivities are clearly tied to an early Christmas festival, with emphasis on the Christmas tree. In parts of Italy near where St Lucia was born, it is said that she brings gifts or coal to children in the night, and if anyone tries to see her, she will throw ashes in their eyes.

And where among all these costumed characters does Jesus Christ fit in? It was only in the early seventeenth century that the Protestant Reformation exiled St Nicholas in favour of the *Christ-kindl, das Christkind* or the Christ Child, who now brought gifts on Christmas Eve. Similarly, *le petit Jesus* gained attention in Catholic countries, usually impersonated by a young teenage girl dressed in white. Parts of Austria, Germany, the Czech Republic, Liechtenstein, Brazil, Venezuela and Louisiana are also among the regions where the Christ Child still serves as a gift-giver, although the globalization of the contrasting Santa image does impact on the tradition's strength. The *Christkind* is not entirely divorced from the commercial

Traditionally each farmstead had its own *nisse*, but around the start of the 19th century the *nisse* began to take on the characteristics of Santa Claus.

aspect of Christmas, since each year a child is chosen to appear as the *Christkind* on the opening night of urban Christmas markets.

The shepherds of the gospel story are given attention in some Christmas celebrations. In parts of France Christmas Eve means dusting off traditional shepherd costumes. Celebrants then process with a farm cart jingling with bells and led by a ram. Inside, a lamb represents the Christ Child. The Shepherds' Festival ends when the procession of costumed worshippers arrives at the church and hands the lamb over to the priest.

In Spain, the gift-givers are the three kings, who wait until Epiphany Eve (5 January) to bring their presents, just as they did centuries ago in Judea. These kings – Caspar, Balthazar and Melchior – appear in parades wherever Spanish culture brought its influence. The Philippines and much of Latin America celebrate with a parade, as does New York's Harlem. The Harlem parade celebrates the city's Latino population and entertains children with puppets, street performers and real camels. The camel really steals the show in Syria, since it takes the credit for delivering gifts. Syrian children learn that the youngest camel to visit the Baby Jesus was healed and given immortality by the Saviour. The camel spends its time delivering gifts on New Year's Day, or it might mark children's wrists with a black smear if they have been naughty.[43]

The symbol that called the Magi, the star, shines brightest in Poland. The all-important meatless Christmas Eve feast cannot begin until a child has sighted the first star in the sky. Afterwards Gwiazdor, the Starman, brings gifts and teases children about their behaviour. He may quiz them about religion or ask them to sing songs. Gwiazdor wears long robes decorated with stars, and carries a staff topped by a star. Starboys accompany him, and these same boys can be seen on Christmas Day, which is largely devoted to visiting family and feasting on ham or other meat dishes.

If celebrants are looking for an alternative to the religious meta-narrative of Christmas, the academic Richard Belk has argued that they can choose between Santa and Scrooge.[44] As Scrooge scholar Paul Davis has said, 'Scrooge is alive, to begin with.'[45] The curmudgeonly miser's heart-warming conversion story has taken on a life

By the early 19th century, Santa had fully invaded the culture of the American Christmas. Metal Santa chocolate mould, *c.* 1920.

of its own, one that its creator could never have imagined. Dickens made so depressingly little from the original publication of his short book that he would probably despair at the profits other people have made and continue to make on what was supposed to be his own cash cow. The novel appeared for sale just one week before Christmas, and pirated copies and unauthorized theatre productions soon allowed the story to spread further than the official print run could manage. The characters became a much-loved Christmas tradition, and Dickens went on to write four more Christmas books in the same emotional vein before turning his holiday energies to the periodicals he edited.

Scrooge's story is the subtext for television specials, Hollywood films and advertisements every year. *Carol* aficionados can barely keep up with the related reincarnations of the novella. The famous miser has been impersonated by Scrooge McDuck, Rowan Atkinson, Beavis (of *Beavis and Butt-head*), Martin Lawrence, Cruella de Vil, Cicely Tyson, Susan Lucci, Vanessa Williams, Kelsey Grammer,

Tori Spelling, Jack Palance, Patrick Stewart, Fred Flintstone, Michael Caine and a host of others. *Carol* expert Fred Guida has suggested that a major new film or television adaptation of the book arrives every fifteen to twenty years, but that does not stop producers from trying every other year as well.[46] And the reason? As Dickens himself knew, there is money to be made in *A Christmas Carol*, mostly because the target audience yearns for it. Author Robert Louis Stevenson had a strong reaction to reading Dickens's Christmas novels; he wrote that he felt 'so good after them and would do anything, yes and shall do anything, to make it a little better for people. I wish I could lose no time; I want to go out and comfort some one.'[47] Stories exist of American factory owners giving their employees a day off at Christmas after reading Dickens's tale. Empathizing with Scrooge offers an emotional catharsis to an audience who, like the ultimate miser himself, wraps itself in a capitalistic economy.

The miser's lessons continue to resonate within the commercial Christmas of the West. Some of the elements in Scrooge's conversion include a shift in focus from the individual to the family and a lesson about rejecting selfishness and embracing brotherhood. The Christmas modelled in *A Christmas Carol* may soothe class tensions by creating a limited timeframe for social inversions.[48] Furthermore, Scrooge learns to enjoy spending lavishly, and this image harmonizes with the popular consumer-led Christmas of the present century. Readers and film-goers alike look forward to Scrooge's spending spree at the end of the tale. This, after all, is an iconic endorsement of the Christmas shopping that skates the thin ice of materialistic generosity.

Scrooge, of course, has an opportunity to meet an incarnation of Father Christmas in the Ghost of Christmas Present. This character merrily introduces Scrooge to the needs of those around him. The gift-bringers of Christmas serve us in a similar, if more introspective, way. They reveal what a culture needs Christmas to offer at a particular time: an approving model of adult debauchery; a reformed, child-focused elf; a holy saint who tolerates the company of a demonic rule-enforcer; a trendy globalized figure who encourages commercial extravagance. That evolution makes for a wonderfully twisted map of global transmission and cultural transformation. Perhaps, as Santa relaxes with his cup of cocoa and Mrs Claus at his side, an endless list of children's demands in his hand, his eye twinkles as he remembers that he was once a Wild Man of Europe.

# EIGHT

# The Imported Global Christmas

A visual display of the global Christmas would result in a vast diagram of cultural transfer. The earliest Christmas, it must be allowed, was celebrated quietly on an unknown date in Bethlehem. The event went unrecognized until the development of powerful urban churches, as in Rome and Antioch, in the fourth century. From there the knowledge of Christmas travelled with missionaries throughout Europe. In time, these Christianized northern peoples included Christmas habits – many of them tied to pre-Christian rituals – in their developing sense of cultural identity. Eventually emigrants would carry the torch of Christmas to their destinations around the world; their holiday light would burn all the brighter because they saw it as a vital aspect of their membership of the community back home, one from which they would be psychologically reluctant to withdraw. Missionaries transported Christmas from Christian societies in Europe to islands dotting the Pacific, African outposts and inland Asian missions. More recently, the global media has continued that work, albeit in a far less spiritual manner.

Without a doubt, there is a global fascination with the German and English Christmases. Both nations had seen Christmas evolving to meet their needs. These desirable versions began to develop in the early decades of the nineteenth century. Nonetheless, today they are held to be somehow more authentic than other Advent rituals. Much of this has to do with how immigrants reminisced about the home life at Christmas, but it also relates to nineteenth-century coverage of Christmas in the colonies. Let us start with the closest geographic connection. As has been mentioned, even in England, the German Christmas is touted as the more genuine experience, an ongoing perception dating from the early nineteenth century. The German holiday shone out as a bright light of domesticity, and without fully probing why this resonated with them culturally, the British looked to Germany as they couched their own developing cultural needs in what seemed to be a more rooted tradition.[1] Similarly, Americans learned to idealize the English Christmas through printed descriptions. Early Victorian Christmas novels flourished in America too, largely because of the lack of copyright laws. American publishers could print the work of English novelists without paying them a penny, to the detriment of American writers who inconveniently demanded payment. A generation earlier Americans had been influenced by Washington Irving's Christmas writings, especially the English country Christmas scenes in *The Sketch Book of Geoffrey Crayon, Gent.*, in which class harmony and benevolence characterize the day. This same eighteenth-century Christmas served as the template for celebrations in the American South.

Today the Victorian Christmas lives on in frequent productions of *A Christmas Carol* and the Victorian-style kitsch to be found in Christmas cards, ornaments and decorations. Americans can consume the Victorian Christmas viscerally by attending the Dickens Christmas Fair, which has been held in San Francisco for more than three decades. There San Franciscans can sample British food and folk music while browsing shops run by salespeople who have donned Victorian garb and accents. Nevada City, California, offers a similar Victorian Christmas fair, mainly emphasizing shopping opportunities and costumed enthusiasts. Towns brand their Christmas markets as Victorian to draw on a nostalgic enthusiasm for Dickens's Christmas. Some even import Dickens himself. During the month leading up to Christmas, Dickens's great-great-grandson Gerald Charles Dickens tours the United States, bringing his genetic authenticity to audiences eager to access the Victorian Christmas.

For years Gerald Charles Dickens has toured the United States in the weeks leading up to Christmas, offering one-man performances of *A Christmas Carol* reminiscent of the readings his great-great-grandfather gave more than a century earlier.

Americans reading the same pirated periodical articles as their English cousins in the nineteenth century picked up a passion for the German Christmas too, but Americans also had the example set by German immigrants. The German settlers in Pennsylvania began celebrating Christmas in raucous ways long before their Quaker and Presbyterian neighbours accepted the holiday; Germans seemed to own the festival, and the perception persists. In recent decades German Christmas markets have popped up in many cities around the world, including Philadelphia, Pennsylvania; Chicago, Illinois; Kitchener, Ontario; Ljubljana, Slovenia; Bath, England; Karuizawa, Japan; and Melbourne, Australia.

The German/English traditions seem to have developed a momentum that could not be slowed. By Christmas 1886 Parisians had adopted the Christmas tree and its decorations, and they even experimented with plum pudding, which a Paris correspondent for the *Daily Telegraph* described as tasting like gingerbread porridge.[2]

While holiday recipes transported easily, holiday weather did not. Colonists and Europeans fetishized snowy Christmases and taught more recent inductees to Christmas to do the same. Charles Dickens had included snow-covered Christmases past and present in his *A Christmas Carol*, perhaps a reflection of the snowier winters of the early nineteenth century when England experienced the effects of the Little Ice Age. This was the period from about the mid-sixteenth century until the mid-nineteenth century, when temperatures dropped in the northern hemisphere. Especially cold winters were reported in 1650, 1750 and 1850. Lower temperatures meant that rivers that never freeze today could support ice fairs, like the Thames Frost Fairs in London, the last of which took place in 1814.

So snow became an iconic aspect of the holiday, even in climates where it rarely occurs in December. For example, London seldom sees snow at Christmas; lowland England can boast less than one white Christmas every ten years, according to the meteorological averages. Snowy sets in Christmas films contribute to the perception, as does the nostalgia that Christmas used to be snowier and winters used to be colder.[3] As a result, Christmas cards in Britain, New Zealand and Australia often show snowy winter scenes. Sometimes Christmas-keepers even get creative. In Minnamurra, New South Wales, the fire department has created detergent 'snow' at Christmas-time to entertain delighted, bubble-covered children in swimsuits.[4]

Of course, some parts of North America are far more likely to receive snow on or around Christmas, and early settlers in Canada boasted of their perfect Christmas climate. Climate change may eventually affect this snowy Christmas certainty; 2011 saw significantly less snow than usual, and climatologists see a pattern. Sarnia, Ontario, once had a 75 per cent chance of a white Christmas, but today the city's odds have dropped to just a 33 per cent chance.[5]

We do not know what the weather was like in Canada at Christmas 1643, but that year inspired a special Canadian contribution to the holiday. Father Jean de Brébeuf, a Jesuit missionary to the Huron, created a Christmas song known as '*Jesous Ahatonhia*' or the 'Huron Carol' to help bridge the gap between his religious culture and that of the indigenous Canadians. His song replaces elements of the Nativity with images more familiar to the Hurons. Baby Jesus is wrapped in rabbit skins and born in a bark lodge, and hunters rather than shepherds come to see him. Chiefs bearing gifts of pelts replace the Magi of European tradition, as the song explains how Gitchi Manitou, the Indian name for God, arranged his son's birth. The Huron accepted this song in their own tongue. Two decades later another Jesuit reported overhearing a dying Huron girl sing the song as she passed into a peaceful sleep on Christmas Eve, the night before she died. Since that time, people across Canada have picked up the refrain of the 'Huron Carol' as a way of celebrating Christmas.[6]

In New Mexico, Native American traditions also date back centuries. Santa Fe and the surrounding pueblos serve as a uniquely southwestern Christmas destination. Centuries-old Spanish religious plays bring audiences to the churches of Santa Fe, the state's capital.[7] Outside the city, fortunate visitors come to view the pueblo dances. These are Native American religious ceremonies, not performances; while elders open the events to eager tourists, they ask observers to refrain from photographing or filming the ceremony. Pueblo inhabitants bring out their folding chairs to watch the dancers, some of whom have had to compete for their place. Dancers wear colourful cloaks, headdresses and fringed leggings. Feathers and bells may embellish the outfits as the dancers take part in Deer Dances, Matachine Dances or Christmas Dances. In San Felipe, Santa Ana and Tesuque pueblos, the dances begin following Midnight Mass on Christmas Eve. In the Deer Dance celebrants act out a deer hunt with some dancers wearing antlers and holding sticks in their hands to imitate the front legs of deer. The Matachine Dance, a blend of Spanish and Native American cultures, is a series of choreographed pieces with stock characters: a king, a girl, two clowns, a bull and soldiers. Some fans plan a Christmas Day that will take in several of these events at the various pueblos such as Taos, Zia, Santo Domingo and Tesuque.

The indigenous people of Hawaii had an altogether different experience absorbing Christmas. An English captain celebrated the first Christmas in Hawaii in 1786 by ordering a special dinner and

The piñata continues to be associated with Christmas
as well as birthdays. This little girl takes aim in Mexico
in the first decades of the 20th century.

punch for his men, but this happened on the deck of his ship,
anchored in the harbour of Waimea Bay of the Sandwich Islands, as
they were then called. In 1817 another English crew faced Christmas at sea, but these sailors were invited to join the chiefs for a feast
in honour of the birth of the guests' saviour. In 1820, when a ship

carrying the first team of Protestant missionaries arrived in Hawaii, the indigenous culture was at a religious crossroads. Kamehameha the Great had died, and his wives and son discontinued the *kapu* system of polytheistic worship. Into this religious upheaval the missionaries brought their gospel, and they quickly worked out a written version of the Hawaiian language. The New England churches that sent these missionaries were avoiding Christmas themselves, so the holiday went largely unnoticed in Hawaii until the 1840s.

The Chief's Children's School, which was responsible for the education of Alexander Liholiho, later Kamahameha IV, began celebrating Christmas with cake and a release from studies, and the future king and his brothers greatly enjoyed the tradition. Later, as king, Kamehameha IV declared that 25 December would be known as Hawaii's day of thanksgiving. In so doing, he was following the advice of Protestant missionaries who disagreed with Christmas, but he marked the date as a special one, and citizens were welcome to celebrate it for whatever reason they desired. Some attended church; others patronized circuses and subscription balls where they danced quadrilles, waltzes and polkas. Shopping in late December had already been on the rise. Perhaps the king recalled the joy he felt at the holiday as a child, because six years later in 1862 he welcomed Christmas as a national Hawaiian holiday. He had the Anglican mission decorated with native cypress boughs and the Calvinist church decorated with a Christmas tree. The king joined his Anglican bishop in a procession through Honolulu for the midnight service, and a multitude of the king's subjects lined up to watch the torch-lit procession and enjoy the fireworks.[8]

That ubiquitous holiday greeting, 'Merry Christmas', has a Hawaiian version. Because Hawaiian does not include the /r/ or /s/ phonemes, and also because Hawaiian syllables cannot end in a consonant, early Christmas-keepers on Hawaii created their own version: 'Mele Kalikimaka'.[9] Bing Crosby and the Andrews sisters made this greeting famous through the song of that name in 1950, so that many people throughout the world have learned to wish others a 'Merry Christmas' in Hawaiian.

Today Hawaiians and tourists alike flock to the Honolulu City Lights celebration held at the Honolulu city hall. Here a tall Christmas tree lights the night sky and the live entertainment taking place nearby. Santa wears shorts and rides an outrigger rather than a sleigh. During President Obama's term in office, Hawaiian Christmases have also included news coverage of this native son's return for family holiday gatherings.

On the other side of the International Date Line, Spanish missionaries introduced Filipino converts to Christmas in the 1500s after Ferdinand Magellan brought the archipelago to Spain's attention. Many of the islands' customs come from Spain and the West; however, the islands also show a diversity of Christmas customs that spring from the Filipinos themselves. For example, the colourful, decorative *paról*, or bamboo star lantern, represents Christmas in the Philippines. These have traditionally been made by stretching Japanese paper over a bamboo frame. Originally they lit the way to early-morning Masses. Today the star frames might be covered in any decorative materials – shells, feathers, lights or anything that can be attached. To Filipinos, the *paról* represents community, faith and the Star of Bethlehem.[10] In the mid-twentieth century Filipinos began tweaking American Christmas symbols such as the blue-eyed Santa and his snow-covered sleigh. The new, thinner Filipino Santa wears a bamboo hat, cotton clothing and sandals and rides a water buffalo to deliver presents.[11]

Elements of the European Christmas have filtered across the globe in intriguing ways. St Kitts and Nevis imported the traditional English mumming play to their Christmas festivities, although the process of transmission shows interesting textual journeys. According to Peter Millington, the 'West Indian plays are like Mummers' plays from England, only more so.'[12] Millington proves that the adult mummers on these islands had developed their play not from the oral tradition of the British Isles, but from a censored, child-friendly version that a Victorian novelist repackaged and sold in the 1880s. Juliana Horatio Ewing regularly sold novellas for Christmas publication, and her *The Peace Egg and a Christmas Mumming Play* of 1887 contained a bowdlerized mumming play suitable for children.

The plot shows a series of combat scenes between characters like St George and the Dragon, St Patrick and the Black Prince of Paradine, and St George and Slasher. A Doctor character occasionally appears to cure fallen combatants, but the play is generally thin on plot.[13] This version of the play was in use by West Indian mummers by the 1930s and continued for at least 30 years. Today the 'mummies', as they are called on St Kitts, are better known for the traditional 'Bull Play', a blend of British and East Indian heritage.

Until the twentieth century, oral communication was the most prolific way to transmit Christmas customs. Missionaries instructed Marshall Islanders in the celebration of Christmas when they arrived in the 1850s, but these early visitors could never have guessed how the Christian inhabitants of one beleaguered atoll would adapt a syncretic Christmas to meet their cultural needs. Following the Second World War, the inhabitants of Enewetak were forced to leave their tiny ancestral atoll when the American military carried out nuclear tests on it from 1948 until 1958. The displaced inhabitants found a cold reception on their new atoll, where long-time

Traditional *párols* are made of rice paper and electric lights. Popular since the 1930s, they are a major symbol of Christmas in the Philippines. One city, San Fernando, hosts a Giant Lantern Festival with oversized *párols*.

residents saw them as rough, unenlightened people. The Enewetak people were permitted to return to their own, much-altered atoll in the 1970s, although it was not declared safe until 1980. In the midst of all this upheaval, they developed Kurijmoj, their prolonged Christmas, as a method of proving their great worth. For the people of Enewetak, it also allows for a significant performance of the population's communal identity.[14]

Like the European holiday, Kurijmoj celebrates the birth of Christ, but it more significantly focuses on the coming of Christianity to the Marshall Islands and the islanders' perception of love learned from Christ.[15] Unlike its European counterpart, Kurijmoj does not leach earlier and earlier into the year based on consumer trends; rather, it brazenly dictates that preparations for the holiday start as early as March. Throughout the Marshall Islands, Kurijmoj is a marathon of a Christmas celebration consuming the greater part of the calendar year, although the actual official celebration lasts for four months, from September until mid-January. For several weeks from mid-January to mid-March, islanders focus on other concerns but, once Easter passes, they begin to make plans for the next Kurijmoj. Men raise pigs for the feast, women begin preparing pandanus-leaf crafts, and breadfruit is harvested and fermented for *bwiro*, a typical Christmas gift.[16]

Marshall Islanders form *jepta*, performance groups that sing and dance in competition with one another as the main entertainment on Christmas Day, known in the Marshall Islands as Twenty-fifth Day. These songfest rituals date back to the 1940s, and the people use them to declare their membership of a club but also of their island culture. Clubs begin serious practice in September. Despite months of preparation, 24 December often turns into a day of busy toil as celebrants ready food and gifts. On Twenty-fifth Day the celebration begins promptly at 6 a.m., and club mates and kin exchange food baskets weighing 11–18 kg (25–40 lb) with the hope of overwhelming their friends with their generosity.[17] The *jepta* begin performing in the local church at 10 a.m., and the community celebration continues there until nightfall. In the days following 25 December, the entire community turns out for volleyball and softball games as well as additional church services until the close of this highly anticipated season in mid-January.

In some Chinese cities, Christmas preparations also dictate the annual labour market, but only because factories continuously fill orders for Western Christmas consumerism. While the Christmas shops in Rothenburg, Germany, welcome Chinese tourists with open arms, German merchants sometimes wonder if their products are being carried eastwards to be replicated in a Chinese factory.[18] Certainly there is a market for replicas in China. In Yiwu's Futian Market, Christmas items sparkle from the shelves of 7,000 shops that serve commercial merchants rather than individual consumers. Christmas decorations are popped out of 3,000 Chinese factories, and more than u.s.$900 million worth of Christmas tinsel was exported in 2003. Producers of all this glitter do not care to educate themselves about the background or religious origins of Christmas; indeed, one Chinese factory owner admitted to knowing nothing about Christmas except its commercial relationship to the thousands of fat, red-suited men his factory produces. His hardworking, often barefoot employees could not know any more either, although they see the profit in keeping the machines going.[19]

The products that roll off these conveyor belts reach Europe and America by way of huge cargo vessels like the Danish-built *Emma Maersk*, which is a quarter of a mile long and can hold 11,000 metal shipping containers. Suppliers fill these 6-m (20-ft) containers with Christmas crackers, toys and decorations destined for export and, while environmentalists decry their carbon footprint, Christmas demands in Europe and America keep them moving. In 2006 the *Emma Maersk* delivered its Christmas cargo to Suffolk and eventually returned to China full of British waste illegally marked for recycling.[20]

Increasingly, holiday items are finding a place in China's domestic market. The secular reinvention of Christmas in nineteenth-century America and England allowed it to become an acceptable import even among atheist regimes and countries with few Christians.[21] British-held Hong Kong had celebrated Christmas as a public holiday, but Christmas has not been a traditional holiday

At an amusement park in Hohhot, Inner Mongolia,
a boy boards a Santa ride on a hot August day.

for mainland Chinese citizens. Yet urban dwellers have recently joined the global family of Christmas-keepers. Retail groups like the Hong Kong Trade Development Council watch Christmas sales in China very closely, mostly because they recognize the profit to be had if all of China begins buying Christmas presents.

Chinese retailers have every reason to spread Christmas joy, and financial monitoring organizations tend to believe that these retailers have actually influenced sales and holiday habits simply by decorating for Christmas.[22] The Christmas avalanche has really picked up in the last two decades. In Nanjing, 2002 saw some of the larger stores begin decorating in early December, but smaller retailers waited until late December. Salespeople might wear Santa Claus suits while they serve shoppers, and expatriates recall Chinese friends asking them for gift-giving advice. Twenty years ago Christmas was absent from shops and streets, but now it seems that Christmas is here to stay in China's retail sector.

The Chinese who celebrate Christmas tend to be young: most were born since the 1980s. They find the Western holiday a sophisticated alternative to China's traditional festivals, although most know nothing about what Christians commemorate at Christmas. Christian churches cannot legally preach to anyone under eighteen years of age, Bibles cannot be published or distributed without governmental approval and the Great Firewall of China restricts what the Chinese can read on the Internet. With much of Christmas's history shrouded by communism's control, some citizens have an eerie feeling about Christmas, supposing that it must have an evil or mystical origin.[23]

Nonetheless, a small percentage of the population has explored its religious significance. As early as 1997 an upswing in Christmas marketing brought curious visitors to Christmas services in registered churches. One church in Beijing that usually serves only 300 saw 30,000 visitors for Christmas worship. In 2008, 1,500 people assembled for Midnight Mass at Beijing's Church of the Immaculate Conception, and more crowded outside the building to watch on oversized screens.[24]

A group of doctoral students began an anti-Christmas movement in advance of the holiday in 2006. The students posted their plea on a website, encouraging their countrymen to resist the invasion of this symbol of Western culture. Instead, they hoped the Chinese would oppose Western influences and return to Confucianism, and they blamed the government's laxity for letting Santa into the country. Newspapers doubted their petition would do much good since Christmas and Valentine's Day rituals have grown in China, especially among the younger generations, so that they actually dominate the traditional Spring Festival.[25]

Chinese urban hotels cater to Christmas jollity by offering American meals and entertainment. Customers recently paid $150 to dine on Christmas Eve. The management might schedule acrobats, singers and kung fu performers.[26] The reasoning behind the glitzy entertainment, it seems, is that those organizing the earliest Christmas dinners felt that Chinese customers would be bored if the evening's fare consisted simply of turkey, vegetables and a knife and fork. Entertainment was deemed necessary to bring Chinese to restaurants and hotels at Christmas.

with a holiday that would suit a workforce now separated from the old rice-producing culture of the past. Christmas offered urban families new traditions that were child- and retail-centred, something they could negotiate away from their ancestors' rice fields. The holiday came to celebrate modernity, idealized affluence and the family.[31]

Within a few short decades the Japanese added a romantic dimension to the family-centredness of Christmas. Today Christmas Eve serves as the Japanese's second Valentine's Day, and it is given over to sex and presents. It has even been called a hotel-holiday, a great contrast to the hearth-hugging folks celebrating in the Western world. Lovers vie for bookings at Tokyo hotels where high prices reflect the commercial endorsement of the tradition. In 2007 the Mandarin Oriental Hotel in Tokyo offered a butler, champagne and a limo to go with booked rooms. The holiday suite came with a Christmas tree trimmed with diamond necklaces that guests could keep, but few were willing to invest that much in Christmas romance.[32] Those who failed to reserve hotel rooms might wait in line for space in a hotel that rents rooms by the hour. Japan's love hotel industry allows guest to speed up the registration process; customers simply swipe their card through a machine which gives them a key card, and they pay only for the time spent in the room – much like a parking space. The room decor is usually more eccentric than at a typical low-budget hotel chain. Beds might sport special lighting or be placed inside a classic Cadillac.[33]

Christmas in Japan has such a strong association with passion that one hotel in Osaka has branded itself a year-round Christmas love hotel. The Hotel Chapel Christmas welcomes customers with a friendly Santa head and a Christmas tree in the lobby. Since they are paying by the hour, lovers need to find their rooms quickly. They pay at a machine and then board the elevator, which spouts Christmas carols. At their floor, Christmas lights twinkle like a trail of breadcrumbs to point them to their room, complete with red and green decor.[34]

Women receive jewellery, sometimes from several different men, and they may pick out a gift for their boyfriends in return. In the 1990s trendy Japanese men bought jewellery from Tiffany's for the women in their lives. In recent decades Japanese women have developed a fad for knitting Christmas sweaters for their boyfriends, and those who can't knit find someone to do it for them.[35] These rituals stem from how the Japanese have seen Christmas celebrated in Western cinema since the middle of the twentieth century.[36] The hierarchical nature of gift-giving during the Japanese Christmas is more a part of the national tradition. Men know that they are expected to give more than women, and this is a holiday in which superiors are seen to give lavishly to inferiors. During other holidays, like New Year, inferiors give unreciprocated gifts to their superiors, as in the case of a student offering a present to a teacher. Valentine's Day sees women showering their male friends and colleagues with gifts of chocolate as an obligation gift, one that men do not reciprocate. The February holiday has been on the rise for a few decades too, and chocolate confectioners certainly promote its continuance.

Yokohama has recently begun hosting a traditional German Christmas market that emphasizes the family at Christmas. A tree shines in the middle of the market, and while the Germans running the stalls might complain that the locale lacks a Christmassy chill in the air, the Japanese customers feel they have stumbled upon a perfect holiday tableau.

Japanese Christmas parties welcome everyone. *Bonenkai*, or end-of-year parties, offer copious amounts of alcohol, but only to the men and professional women, such as geishas and entertainers, who are in attendance. Meanwhile, office Christmas parties provide an alternative space where female colleagues feel comfortable mingling with their co-workers.[37] Families with small children might choose to celebrate Christmas, but they give up the practice when their children get older.[38] Christmas for Japanese children means a gift – perhaps a book or video game – and a family dinner at home.[39] Since most homes lack a hearth, young Japanese children hang stockings on the pipe that is used to heat the bathtub stove.[40] Christmas trees are displayed in public spaces rather than in individual homes, and some can be quite elaborate. In 2007 one Japanese aquarium rigged a Christmas tree linked to a copper wire in a fish tank, and when the electric eel's body touched the wire, the energy it gave off lit up the tree.[41]

Those not romancing the night away might be standing in line to buy KFC for their children. The character associated with that franchise looks enough like the Western Santa Claus that parents willingly wait hours in line to provide their children with this fried treat.[42] In Tokyo the chain sells a holiday meal special that costs U.S.$5, and its popularity makes December a very profitable month for KFC. For families looking to indulge beyond fried chicken, a department store offers a meal of capons stuffed with black truffles, *foie gras*, sausage and chestnuts imported from France, bearing an $850 price tag.[43]

One unique image that dominates the Japanese Christmas is the strawberry-topped Christmas cake. Initially a reaction to Second World War sugar rationing, the Christmas cake also contains visual symbolism harking back to traditional Japanese culture. The Japanese term *yo* signifies European and American things, and *gashi* means sweets. Yo-gashi came to represent Western affluence in a period following Japan's most extreme sugar rationing. In 1946 the average Japanese citizen consumed just 0.2 kg (7 oz) of sugar; following the American occupation, that amount skyrocketed to 29.29 kg (64 lb 17 oz) per person in 1973. *Yo-gashi* symbolized status and affluence, two ideas that the Japanese considered as American as Christmas.[44] Not only did it satisfy the Japanese sweet tooth, but the Christmas cake also offered visual symbols of prosperity. On traditional holidays, pounded rice moulded into round shapes, called *mocha*, was used. The rounded shape captured the Japanese idea of harmony. Furthermore, the uncommon, more refined white rice used for *mochi* symbolized luxury, and the white Christmas cake offered a new sweet version of these old holiday dishes. The fact that bakers could refrigerate the whipped cream used to ice the cakes also impressed consumers, since this symbolized modern technology and luxury. The strawberries mounded on top remind the Japanese of the traditional meaning of red: the colour that wards off evil spirits. The combination of red and white also features in Japanese weddings and other ceremonies.[45] Today the holiday treat continues to be provided by bakeries rather than made at home.

So a Japanese Christmas typically includes what is now a tradition: a sponge cake covered in whipped cream and strawberries. Families can find variations on this theme, but the white and red cake is the most prevalent. Commuting parents often make two stops to bring these shop-bought delights – KFC and the Christmas cake – to the table.

As in China, Christmas draws the largely non-Christian population to the few cathedrals, where they enjoy the atmosphere of holiday celebration. One citizen of Tokyo explained that scheduling a Christmas visit to a cathedral is seen as trendy and romantic.[46] The attendance at a church service might be just one stop in an evening of café hopping and hotel romance.

The over-the-top commercialism of the Japanese Christmas is simply not viable for most of West Africa. Citizens of Sierra Leone, one of the ten poorest countries in the world, celebrate a very simple Christmas. Child labourers have a day's break from their work on palm plantations, and the main event of the community celebration is the dancing. The recent civil war has destabilized much in the small sub-Saharan country. As recently as 2007 Christmas lights sold poorly because there was no reliable electricity supply, even in the capital, Freetown. The power supply has improved somewhat, and even grim poverty does not dim the Christmas enthusiasm of Sierra Leoners who focus on simple pleasures. Recently the Muslim president, Alhaji Tejan Kabbah, offered a Christmas Day speech reminding his citizens to celebrate Christmas as a time of sharing and giving.

Several countries on the west coast of Africa celebrate Christmas with masquerades. These celebrations in Mali, Sierra Leone, Gambia and Nigeria show a mix of pre-Christian traditions. Rock paintings show that masquerades have long been a part of West African culture; however, anthropologists can only guess at the remote origins of this tradition. Today some adult dancers conceal their faces, wear gravity-defying headdresses and sport costumes composed of long, dried natural fibres such as grasses. The effect can be that of a mesmerizingly agile haystack. In Nigeria, Christmas masqueraders cover themselves in greenery and woven reed designs, their faces further covered by woven nets and topped with a tall ball of more plant fibres. Another design features striped clothing decorated with tassels, but the massive head covering, a wooden frame extending several feet in all directions, once again steals the show. Singers and drummers supply the beat, and the masqueraders dance. Traditionally the maskers' goal is to invite spirits to interact with the mortal realm.[47]

Nigerian celebrants head home to their family's village of origin to see these masquerades and attend church. The children often receive sunglasses as a special accessory. On Christmas Eve and after Christmas church services, villagers gather to watch dance performances outside. Nigerian Igbo masqueraders are called Mmwo, which is pronounced 'moor'. Mmwo remains mysterious, and male dancers are appointed by elders to remember ancestors by interacting with their spirits in this manner. A special Mmwo is reserved for Christmas Day, New Year's Day and the death or crowning of a king. This Ijele Mmwo is shaped like a haystack and covered with dolls, vibrant colours and tassels.[48]

Citizens of Ghana honour midwives during Christmas, a nod to a local legend they have about the midwife Anna and how she helped to deliver baby Jesus and then save him from Herod's wrath.[49] Ghana news sources regularly report how many babies have been born on Christmas Day at various city hospitals, how many were natural births and the names of the midwives involved.

Some West African countries have been heavily influenced by European and American Christmas habits. Senegal, a largely Muslim country, has seen a rise in Christmas-keeping as a result of the television coverage of Christian practices. Both the 5 per cent of the population that are Christian and some of their Muslim neighbours have begun exchanging gifts.[50]

Guinea-Bissau has a rich tradition of Christmas-keeping adapted from its Portuguese connections. Part of their tradition is commercial, as in the imported *bacalao*, or dried cod, that must come from Scandinavia. Prices for the fish skyrocket in the weeks before

The Lighting of the Snowmen has been an annual tradition in Sonoma, California, for over a decade. Residents come to enjoy traditional Christmas pastimes like decorating gingerbread and visiting Santa Claus.

Christmas, but only a small portion of the very poor population can participate in this ritual. The large Catholic population celebrates with mass and gifts, and their Muslim neighbours join them for street parties, celebrating Christmas with little religious tension.

Protestant Liberia enjoys a quiet, family-orientated Christmas with church services and small gatherings. This is how many Liberians were spending their time in 1989, during what has come to be known as the Christmas Eve Invasion, when armed rebels led by Charles Taylor entered the country to overthrow Samuel Doe, who was himself in place following an earlier coup. The insurgents eventually captured and killed Doe in September of the following year, setting up Taylor as the next dictator in charge of Liberia. Following the eras of those dictators and their civil wars, democratic Liberia is now working to rebuild its infrastructure. Today children receive gifts of apples, symbols of love in Liberia, and little else owing to the overwhelming poverty.

While Christmas has evidently embarked on a leaderless, drifting global takeover, local cultural needs and financial restrictions will thwart any universal Christmas for the foreseeable future. When nations find a need for Christmas, they adopt it as their own. The malleability of the holiday is, after all, what has allowed it to thrive as an official holiday for nearly 1,800 years.

# NINE
# Public Christmas

Despite its long history, Christmas has not always been recognized by modern states. Christmas had been an acknowledged holiday in England since before continuous records really began, and certainly before the establishment of the Bank of England. The Bank Holidays Act of 1871 officially established Boxing Day, but Christmas, while it might be referred to colloquially as a bank holiday, does not actually hold that title. Instead, like Good Friday and any Sunday, it is a traditional day of rest. In America, it took 60 years after Independence for the first state, Alabama, legally to recognize Christmas as a holiday. The rest of the states and territories slowly followed suit, and it became a national holiday in 1870.

Christmas started out as a fairly public holiday, only to retreat into the domestic space in the nineteenth century. Before that, when societies were more agrarian, out-of-doors carousing characterized Christmas.[1] Men participated in mumming by dressing up in disguises – smocks or shirts covered in rags or ribbons – and walking from house to house to trade entertainment for beer or money. Remnants of these rites persisted into the nineteenth century in England, and Thomas Hardy depicted a Christmas mumming play in his novel *The Return of the Native*, partially to celebrate the culture of his childhood. Typically Father Christmas introduced the play, in which St George fought a Saracen or Slasher between speeches by other minor characters in a drama generally lacking in plot.[2]

The alcohol-fuelled social components of mumming have made it a popular tradition all over the northern hemisphere. It has been a favourite Christmas-time custom in Scandinavia since at least 1500. Young people dressed up as animals or the Devil and took part in a subconscious exploration of fear associated with the longest nights of the year, the time when ghosts were imagined to appear. In Sweden, celebrants would say they were going 'Yule ghosting'. Similarly, inhabitants of the Faroe Islands enjoyed the raucous parading. There it has been called 'going Gryla', after the local name for a many-tailed female troll who would carry off children.[3] In Norway mumming is known as *Julebukking*, and people wearing disguises still knock on their neighbours' doors and find a welcoming invitation to partake of food and drink. Mumming customs in nineteenth-century Russia, like the one Tolstoy describes in *War and Peace*, are thought to be related to pre-Christian rituals of dressing like spirits during festivals. Young Russians might dress as goats, horses, bears or beggars, visiting homes and expecting holiday hospitality.[4]

Mumming traditions spread from the Old World to the new. As we have already seen, some citizens tried legislation to outlaw or otherwise control the holiday chaos. Mumming evolved to create much-loved rituals in Newfoundland, where Jannies, as the mummers there are called, make house visits, and hosts try to identify their guests. The masks and evening merriment give a feel of Halloween and Christmas combined. Newfoundland mummers might cross-dress and hide their true figures, and cover their faces in plastic masks or pillowcases. Small, tightly knit Newfoundland communities tend to harbour some fear of outsiders, and in the mumming ritual, insiders get a chance to impersonate the feared strangers and simulate their imagined threat to the community.[5]

Philadelphia, which is the home of the famous New Year Mummer's Parade, developed this cultural highlight as an attempt to control Christmas merrymaking through legal means. The eighteenth-century Quakers of Pennsylvania had tried to curb the roaming groups of Christmas Belsnickels and mummers by arresting them. The habit does sound annoying: large groups of young masked men would burst in on householders, refusing to leave until they had been given beer, cakes or at the very least money to supply the required viands. The Pennsylvania House of Representatives passed a law in 1801 to punish Christmas masqueraders with up to three months in prison and a hefty fine of $50 to $1,000. The ban hardly stuck, since Philadelphia had to police gun-carrying Christmas Eve masqueraders, as well as noisemakers. In the end, the costumed celebrants switched to New Year's Eve, and the city acquiesced by officially permitting New Year's Day parades starting in 1901. Today mummers in elaborately feathered costumes entertain crowds and a national television audience on New Year's Day. The thousands of banjo-strumming, strutting mummers come from working-class, largely union backgrounds. Many of those stunning mummers could be found working on the docks or fitting pipes the rest of the year. The practice that is cherished today was also banned in Boston and Newfoundland in the mid-nineteenth century.[6]

Enslaved people in the West Indies and one small region of North Carolina where Caribbean slaves had been transplanted turned the increased mobility they enjoyed during Christmas into a parading ritual. Like mummers, men who participated would dress in costumes. These included women's clothing, whiteface, animal costumes or rags. A similar practice is known as Junkanoo in the Bahamas, though the origin of the word has been much debated. In Jamaica, where the event is known as John Canoe, parades flourished in the early nineteenth century; the John Canoe dancer would wear a house-shaped headdress topped with porcelain dolls or puppets, and the whole cap was so large that he had to hold it on with both hands. Celebrants travelled with music and approached white people asking for money in return for performances. A Jamaican law of the 1920s required John Canoe groups to obtain a licence, and the timing of the strolling companies was strictly limited. These John Kooner, Jonkonnu or John Canoe parades also took the performers into the homes of the slave owners and their neighbours. Some children of slave owners recorded this as the most festive element of their holiday.

Today Nassau boasts the largest John Canoe parade in the Bahamas. Clubs create elaborate feathered, themed costumes and dance down the streets. The warm weather allows dancers to show much more skin than in similar mumming traditions in colder climes. Nassau residents kindly staged a Junkanoo for the James Bond film *Thunderball* (1965). The Jonkonnu of Jamaica has lost much of its earlier popularity, but some groups can be booked for cultural events. In Jamaica, specific characters and mumming scripts developed in the eighteenth century, and some groups still maintain these traditions.

Something about Christmas still pulls people into the streets, especially musicians who hope for gifts of money or food. In Calabria and the Abruzzi in Italy, bagpipers leave their mountain homes and travel from house to house. The itinerant musicians play hymns in front of the *presépio*, or Nativity mangers, that can be found in nearly every house, and homeowners thank them with gifts of food or money.[7] In Puerto Rico the tradition is undertaken by adults dressed as the three kings. They sing *aquinaldos*, very old carols, and play guitars in the hope of receiving a gift from the homeowners.[8]

Some house-to-house traditions eschew alcohol and feature children instead. In Greece, children carry out a Christmas tradition today that is much like the pre-twentieth-century mumming of America and England and the Belsnickeling of Germany and colonial America. They carol from door to door, expecting sweets or money, which they are allowed to keep. So many of Greece's older traditions have been replaced by the global Christmas performance that it is remarkable that this one remains.[9] In Romania, too, schoolchildren entertain homeowners with Christmas songs, poetry and stories. Sometimes they carry a lighted paper star held aloft on a stick, a traditional Christmas icon.[10]

One of the dangers to present-day Christmas party-goers that medieval carousers did not face is the threat posed by drunk drivers. During the last period for which information is available in the United States, 2001–5, some 40 per cent of vehicular fatalities caused between Christmas and New Year in America were linked to intoxicated drivers. During the rest of December the figure shrinks to 28 per cent. Impaired drivers cause an average of 45 fatalities on Christmas Day and 54 on New Year's Day, while other days of the year see an average of 36 deaths from drunk drivers.[11]

The office Christmas party may be the rowdy occasion that replaces the house-to-house mumming of the past. These events encourage employees to overlook the usual office formalities. In the UK, high expectations for the office Christmas party have spawned an entire industry. Companies like Office Christmas organize memorable holiday parties. Economic conditions since 2008 have caused this party tradition to take something of a hit. The BBC, for example, once paid £50 per person towards the Christmas party fund, but by 2009 that figure had dropped to nil. Event-planning companies that counted on the Christmas party industry – formerly worth £1 billion a year – face drastic cutbacks themselves as a result.[12]

One of the most popular Christmas decorations for office and municipal spaces is the humble Christmas tree. The evergreen tree that decorated medieval Christmases evolved and spread during the nineteenth century. It is an often-repeated myth that Prince Albert brought the Christmas tree to Britain. German immigrants to England as well as Hanoverian members of the royal family had decorated with Christmas trees in the decades before Prince Albert's

Early Christmas-tree retailers faced some scorn, but it soon became clear that the industry would bring in profits. Today Christmas-tree agriculture is a serious industry.

This image of the royal family's Christmas tree at Windsor Castle
appeared in the *Illustrated London News* in 1848 and helped to
popularize the Christmas-tree tradition.

famous table-top tree. Nevertheless, the prince reinforced the trend when he set one up in Windsor in 1841. The *Illustrated London News* engraving of domesticated Christmas bounty followed in 1848, and the middle classes were smitten.

The Christmas tree is an icon for one of Christmas's more recent evolutionary shifts. In America and Britain between 1840 and 1860, the holiday gradually transformed from a public one to one centred in the home. The household had recently changed from a place of manufacture and commerce to one of leisure and renewal. The idealism of Christmas fitted the new perception of home perfectly, and the evergreen tree became a focal point for this domesticated holiday.[13]

Historians have found evidence of Christmas-tree sales from this period, such as an enterprising logger who brought Christmas trees to New York City to sell on the sidewalk in 1851. His wife had laughed at the plan to sell trees at a time when they seemed free for the taking. They were both shocked at his financial success. Fifty years later, at the turn of the century, it was estimated that 20 to 25 per cent of Americans brought Christmas trees into their homes.[14]

One Chicago family became a valued part of the Christmas tree tradition, although it cost them dearly. The Schuenemann brothers loaded their fishing schooner with Christmas trees and sailed across Lake Michigan from Manistique, Michigan, to Chicago starting around 1887. They sold trees from the Clark Street Bridge and became a staple sight at Christmas-time. However, the older brother and his trees went down in a storm in 1898, and although the younger brother continued the enterprise, he too died in a storm, along with seventeen crew members, while bringing Christmas trees to the people of Chicago. After that disaster in 1912, his wife and daughters continued selling trees in this manner, but Christmas must have been a difficult holiday for them to enjoy.[15]

The massive deforestation resulting from the Christmas-tree tradition caused President Theodore Roosevelt some alarm. The early years of the twentieth century actually saw a shortage of trees in some markets, and inhabitants of New York City were told that only people with children should vie for the available trees.[16] Those harvesting trees had not yet begun planting seedlings; instead, they would buy the rights to cut roadside trees. To people who saw the results from the road, it seemed as though America's forests were in danger indeed. The president forbade the use of any Christmas tree in the White House, but his sons ignored him, secreting a tree in a cupboard. When their father found out and reprimanded them, the boys sought the advice of a leading conservationist, Gifford Pinchot, their father's friend and advisor. Pinchot assured the president and his smirking sons that Christmas-tree harvests could in fact improve the health of forests. Thereafter, the boys were allowed their own private tree, although the White House maintained its official anti-tree stance.

The tradition eventually gave way to a responsible agricultural industry, one that Theodore Roosevelt's famous cousin (fifth cousin, actually) Franklin D. Roosevelt took up. In fact, F.D.R. listed his occupation as tree farmer on official documents such as his voting registration. Even during the Second World War, F.D.R.'s secretary arranged for the president's Christmas trees in his hometown to be harvested at Hyde Park and sold by a chain store in New York City.[17]

This crop offers more than just holiday cheer; one acre of Christmas trees produces enough oxygen for eighteen people.[18] In America, Christmas trees are professionally harvested in nearly every state, although Oregon tops the chart with over six million trees harvested and sold in 2007. North Carolina, Michigan and Pennsylvania follow. A third of all real tree sales in America happen at Choose Your Own farms, where families enjoy the tradition of trailing through an evergreen farm to find and cut the perfect tree. Once their own Christmas presents are put away, American tree farmers begin planting 40 million seedlings each spring in preparation for Christmases to come. They need to be prepared; 81 per cent of Americans now use trees to celebrate Christmas.[19]

In Hawaii celebrants either buy a Norfolk Island pine or queue up to claim more iconic species of pine trees when the refrigerated shipment of Christmas trees arrives from the mainland shortly after Thanksgiving. When people do not have access to evergreens or fake evergreens, they improvise trees. In San Juan la Laguna, Guatemalan villagers build an iconic evergreen-shaped tower entirely out of recycled soda bottles and aluminium cans. Bright equatorial sun glints off the 'tree', a testament to the creativity of the holiday spirit. In Europe, Denmark leads the way in Christmas-tree growing. Despite the seeming ubiquity of the tinselled tree, the market is anything but stable; the European industry has been evolving even during this century. Until 2005 the European Union subsidized Christmas-tree farming, but that came to an end, forcing 15 per cent of Danish tree growers to give up the industry between 2005 and 2007. This has meant higher prices for German, British and Dutch Christmas-keepers who buy Danish trees. Ironically, Eastern Europe's growing wealth has recently led to an increasing demand for high-end trees produced in Germany and Denmark.[20]

While it might add controversy to the pastime, the hunt for that perfect tree should become increasingly easier as tree farmers turn to cloned Christmas trees. This step should bump up the percentage of seedlings that grow into lovely, well-shaped trees. Previously between 60 and 70 per cent turned out suitably shaped for household use; cloned varieties tend to reach 95 per cent perfection.[21]

The artificial tree may seem like a late twentieth-century evolution, but people have been looking for easy ways to store trees for over a century. A whole cottage industry evolved in Germany in the late ninteenth century to create feather trees. Manufacturers attached dyed quills to a trunk and boasted of their product's easy, flat storage. Others kept dead trees for years, swathing empty branches with cotton for a snow-covered effect.[22] In the 1990s, sales of artificial trees began to overtake sales of real trees in the United States.[23] That trend may now be receding, and the war between real and artificial continues. The National Christmas Tree Association has every reason to emphasize the renewable resource of real Christmas trees. Their poll of 2010 shows that u.s. consumers bought 27 million farm-grown Christmas trees and 8.2 million artificial trees that year.[24]

An artificial tree would never do for iconic public spaces. One famous American tree, which lights up Rockefeller Center in New York City, has been a tradition since 1939. The tree that proudly stood in that spot in 2001, harvested in New Jersey, weighed 8 tons. At the end of the season, the branches are ground into mulch and sold to benefit the Boy Scouts of America, and the trunk is modelled into obstacle jumps for the American Equestrian Team's practice.[25] Ever since 1923 the White House lawn has been the backdrop for the National Tree.[26] Over the years conservationists asked for a live tree, and so the National Christmas Tree has been repeatedly replanted at the Ellipse in sight of the Washington Monument. The tree's lonely situation offers it no protection from the elements, and it frequently needs to be replaced. Presidents typically make a Christmas address during the lighting of the tree, although Ronald Reagan skipped this tradition for eight years following an unrelated assassination attempt. Presidents have also used the lights of the National Tree to express political agendas. For example, in 1979, under Jimmy Carter, this was the tree that remained unlit in remembrance of the American hostages held in Iran.[27]

The National Christmas Tree Association runs a contest for its members each year, and the winner presents a tree from his or her farm to the presidential family for use in the Blue Room as the official White House tree.[28] Ever since Jacqueline Kennedy chose a *Nutcracker Suite* theme in 1961, the First Lady has typically suggested a motif for decorating the tree. The Blue Room tree is often one of twenty or thirty trees to decorate the White House each Christmas.

No doubt some of the glass ornaments decking those presidential trees have travelled from Germany. The ubiquitous glass Christmas-tree ornament sprang from a cottage industry of glassblowers in Lauscha in the Thuringian mountains. Starting in the 1840s, glass-blowers added these baubles to their inventory and, by the 1930s, some 2,000 homes produced most of the glass ornaments decorating trees in Europe and America. The craftsmen of Lauscha had discovered how to silver the insides of glass bubbles and make various shapes using moulds. Woolworths sent buyers from America, and Lauscha benefitted from a reliable demand. Following the Second World War, the Lauscha workers found themselves citizens of East Germany, isolated from their American market. Thereafter, the precious glass ornaments had to be smuggled out under the fence. With this obstacle in place, the industry declined. Today American tourists to Germany might still bring home samples of these ornaments, but they are most likely not made in Lauscha.[29] Christmas trees themselves can be highly significant gifts. The grateful people of Norway have made a present of a Christmas tree to London every year since 1947. The tradition began during the Second World War, when Norwegian commandos brought a Norwegian Christmas tree to King Haakon VII in exile in London.[30] Following the war, the tradition took on a new meaning – one of gratitude. The lighting of this public tree in Trafalgar Square at the start of December is a ritual opening of the Christmas season. Crowds pack the square to see the lighting of the traditional Norwegian decorations, vertical lines of light bulbs.

Back in Norway, Christmas trees express patriotism. Evergreens are decorated with Norwegian flags because the Christmas tree's arrival in Norway coincided with an upsurge in nationalistic feeling there.[31] Following the Nazi occupation, patriotism further guaranteed the formerly outlawed flag's place on the tree.[32] Like the Danes, Norwegians also like red and white, heart-shaped baskets – said to have been invented by Hans Christian Andersen – and straw decorations. Before Christianity came, Norwegian families warded off ghosts and midwinter demons, the *oskorei*, by sleeping all together on straw-covered floors. The straw insulated the sleepers and warded off the demons, and the Church encouraged the continuance of the tradition as a celebration of Christ's birth.[33] Now straw ornaments contend with glass and plastic ones to grace the Christmas tree.

One of the most common straw ornaments in Scandinavia is that of the Yule goat, or *Julbock*. Two centuries ago the goat was a spirit that checked to make sure houses were preparing for Christmas appropriately, and later it combined with the global idea of a gift-bringer. In Denmark and Norway the goat became the helper of the *nisse* or Christmas elves. In Finland the goat is called Joulupukki, and, interestingly, this term was stretched to refer to the Finnish Santa figure. Throughout Scandinavia the goat now mainly exists as small, hand-sized straw ornaments on or below

Christmas trees, but originated as the mythical animals Thor hitched to his chariot.[34]

The Yule goat inspired Scandinavians to build outdoor statues out of straw, a building material that is particularly prone to flame. Gävla, a city on the Baltic Sea north of Stockholm, lays claim to the most famous, but also most accident-prone Yule goat. The merchants of the Swedish city have built a straw goat annually since 1966, except for the years when the inescapable arson attacks on their civic contribution frustrated them to the point of despair. They would prefer that arsonists leave their expensive Christmas icon alone, but vandals seem to see the straw goat as an inviting target, regardless of the guards who have been stationed to defend it. Webcams and flame-retardant technology gave the merchants new hope, and the tradition lives on. In 2012 the donated Yule goat cost $30,000 to build and stood 13 m (43 ft) high. The 3.6-ton straw figure survived for ten days before vandals once again hopped the fence and speedily set it on fire with an injection of highly combustible liquid.[35] Each year the drama unfolds. In 2009 the vandals hacked into the webcam feed just before they burned the goat. If the goat survives its gruelling stint in the public square, as it occasionally does, the merchants place it in storage for the following year. Whether it burns or not, the Gävla goat can be seen as a symbol of the amazing fluidity of Christmas icons.

Like the Norwegian spruce in Trafalgar Square, Christmas trees can represent friendship between countries, but also a call for peace between militants. In 2010, 200 military personnel collaborated to decorate a 24-m (80-ft) Christmas tree in a Colombian jungle. The purpose of Operation Christmas was to send a message of peace to guerrillas who are far from home. Strategists hoped that when guerrillas walked past the tree and sensors turned on its 2,000 lights, they would feel homesick and rush home for Christmas.[36]

One especially charged example of Christmas decorating is the employment of Christmas decorations on the demilitarized Korean border as a provocative response to North Korean aggression. The South Korean display took a seven-year break following a warming of Korean relations in 2004, but the lights went back up in 2010

The Gävle Christmas Goat of 2006, treated with fireproofing solvent, was only the eleventh of its type to survive into the new year. It was eventually dismantled.

after a South Korean island was targeted and four people were killed. The evangelical Full Gospel Church of South Korea decorates a 30.5-m (100-ft) tower with Christmas lights and an enormous crucifix, beaming a symbol of the Christian Christmas and religious freedom to a nearby North Korean city. The message certainly angers the regime in North Korea, since it displays a symbol of opulence and working electricity that might tempt North Korean citizens. Pyongyang has protested at the Christian symbolism and threatened to retaliate. In 2011 the lights were cancelled in deference to the passing of North Korea's Kim Jong-il.

The lights that decorate that highly politicized Korean Christmas tower represent a truly American contribution to the holiday. On New Year's Eve in 1879 Thomas Edison entertained thousands of people with the display of his early light bulb. Three years later a friend of Edison's used his invention to decorate a Christmas tree. The wealthy of newly electrified New York City followed suit, although they had to hire someone to wire each string of lights.

While lights have gone through many evolutions – including bubble lights, flashing lights and lights shaped like chilli peppers – they continue to dominate the decor of any Christmas tree.[37]

A different light gives the American southwest its own Christmas flair. Illuminations known as *farolitos* outline buildings in and around Santa Fe, New Mexico. These paper bags held down with sand and lit with simple candles create a lovely scene, a tradition passed down from Spain. Records show that the same type of decoration lit up a church in Toledo, Spain, in 1595.[38] Today *farolitos* create lines of warm light outlining churches, homes, walkways and public buildings.

But someone has to pay for the sand, candles, bags, light bulbs and electricity to light up public spaces. Government-supported decorations come with a price tag. For example, in 2010 Christmas trees, lights and the electricity to keep them going cost Newcastle-under-Lyme Borough Council in Staffordshire almost £100,000. Budget cuts have sliced plans for future festive decorations in half.[39]

Canadians are probably not thinking of the utility costs when they celebrate with Christmas lights. The prime minister pushes an enormous green button early in December to bring electricity to some 300,000 lights strung around municipal buildings. Historic buildings, museums and government offices all shine in the midwinter darkness until Epiphany. The opening celebration gives the prime minister an opportunity symbolically to lead the nation in Christmas decorating and pass on a holiday message to the crowd of 20,000 that gathers to mark the event. Provincial and territorial authorities plan similar celebrations to bring people into public spaces and initiate the national celebration of Christmas. The month-long lighting programme is also marketed to draw tourists to Ottawa.

While many governments financially support Christmas festivities, in the Philippines the law of the land actually legislates for Christmas cheer. Ferdinand Marcos instituted this law in the 1970s: 'WHEREAS, the Christmas season is an opportune time for society to show its concern for the plight of the working masses so they may properly celebrate Christmas and New Year.' The law requires employers to pay employees a thirteenth-month paycheque so that 'the working masses . . . may properly celebrate Christmas and New Year.' Some employees additionally receive a Christmas bonus.[40]

Whether or not you benefit from a state-mandated bonus, you probably look at display windows a little differently at Christmastime. Nineteenth-century media descriptions of Christmas lingered over the produce market displays; eventually, industrially produced toys and gifts began to fill shop windows. These miniature showrooms have become elaborate customer magnets in some urban centres. Veteran display designer Simon Doonan calls the New York City ritual 'part side-show, part diorama, part street-theatre'. As people gather on the street to ogle the displays, the stores that spend tens of thousands of dollars on them hope that they will lure customers inside.[41] In New York City the tradition began in the 1920s, when stores built large display windows. The extreme nature of decorating truly got going in 1938, when Lord & Taylor threw down the gauntlet for all of Fifth Avenue to see. It is an artist's proving ground, and well-known figures like Andy Warhol and Maurice Sendak started out as window artists.[42] Macy's windows have recreated scenes from *Miracle on 34th Street*; Bergdorf Goodman once went with the theme 'divas and goddesses'; in 1997 Lord & Taylor created amazing scenes from *A Christmas Carol*. The detail and creativity are stunning: one designer made wallpaper out of 40,000 Twinings English Breakfast tea bags. This level of craftsmanship brings fans back year after year to gawk at the free show and is a testament to American holiday commercialism.[43]

The London department store Selfridges unveils its Christmas windows in mid-October, and families make a tradition of viewing them. The number of window-shoppers jumps by 30 per cent during the Christmas season. Members of the creative, production and styling teams work together on the year-long project of crafting the identical, stunning displays that appear simultaneously at different branches.[44] Similarly, in Australia, Myers Stores have drawn crowds to their Christmas windows since 1956. The more than one million people who come to see the storybook- or theatre-themed displays begin milling around the unveiled windows in early November.[45]

Belgian shops decorate their windows with manger scenes crafted out of the wares they sell, so window-shoppers might see dioramas constructed from butter, neckties or chocolates. Manger scenes also draw visitors in Chile, where homeowners leave their doors open so that visitors can visit their *pesebre*, or Nativity scene, and pay homage to the Christ Child. In Burkina Faso children build manger scenes at the entrance to their compounds and visitors commend the children's work with small gifts of money left in a bowl. The children use paper or mud bricks, and decorate with whatever they have to hand – Styrofoam packing peanuts, metal shards or plastic objects.[46]

In more prosperous America there are more options for Christmas decorations. In fact, the desire to decorate has engendered companies to fill the need. One chain of Christmas decorators serves a clientele of 40,000, decorating the exteriors of their homes or their office lobbies. Their customers seem to take Christmas decorating very seriously. The owners of a mansion in Atlanta paid $24,000 for their professional Christmas makeover.[47]

If you grumble about how others decorate for the holiday, you might just want to consider going into politics. In 2002 the Moscow mayor, Yury Luzhkov, created a local law that requires shopfronts to contain Christmas decorations by 1 December or face a fine. The mayor was a little more lenient towards his colleagues, permitting public offices to delay decorating until 15 December. One spokesperson for the mayor explained: 'People who, for example, operate a store, must understand that it is not their house but a kind of public place. After all, their mission is to please consumers and to keep them in good spirits.'[48]

Mayor Luzhkov and his defensive employee accept that the holiday has an aspect of community-building about it, especially when it comes to civic celebrations.[49] Small towns and big cities welcome the Christmas shopping season, which has developed over the twentieth century into a civil religion, a time when local governments sponsor the celebration of civic community. Mayors, public school bands, fire departments, public monies, royalty, presidents and prime ministers have clear and active roles in the celebration of Christmas.

In the United States, presidential Christmas parties have been a tradition since the time of the second president. Presidents have been involved in hosting children and benefiting charities for most of the country's history, long before President Ulysses S. Grant signed the bill into law that turned Christmas into a national holiday in 1870. President Theodore Roosevelt's Christmas customs, whether or not they included Christmas trees, involved adding a short Christmas Eve sermon to the worship service he attended in New York. If anything, the twenty-first century has only increased the social demands of the presidential family. In 2009 Michelle Obama's East Wing Social Office planned to host more than 50,000 people at the White House during a full season of seventeen holiday parties and eleven open houses. In addition to White House events, the presidential couple lend their names to charity functions such as Christmas in Washington, a televised fundraiser for the National Children's Medical Center.[50]

Monarchs and politicians have extra duties during Advent. The king of Spain always gives a Christmas Eve speech, and Britain's monarch has broadcast a Christmas speech since 1932. Monarchs in Sweden, the Netherlands, Belgium and Luxembourg similarly sit in front of decorated Christmas trees, national flags or roaring fires as they reach out to their subjects. The Canadian prime minister, the Australian prime minister, the Samoan head of state and leaders around the world offer Christmas messages that generally express sentiments of peace and togetherness, often including personal vignettes and hopes for the future. These communications express more than Christmas wishes; they are usually designed to impart a message of stability and sometimes a challenge for national unity or national improvement.

Some countries have come late to the civic approach to Christmas events, for obvious reasons. The first-ever public Christmas to be celebrated in Baghdad was organized by the Iraqi Interior Ministry in 2008. Military snipers looked down from surrounding rooftops as ministry personnel mixed with the crowd and sought to improve their image. The ministry was decorated with an enormous poster of Jesus and plenty of Iraqi flags, as well as featuring an assembly of ethnically diverse children. Diversity was clearly the main ingredient of the celebration, since few of the attendees were Christian, and the military band stuck to martial tunes.[51]

In Turku, Finland, an annual tradition has unified the country for centuries. Every Christmas Eve at noon the country pauses to listen to or watch the broadcast of the Declaration of Christmas Peace. The text of the brief declaration suggests a reaction to rowdy partying rather than warfare, since celebrants are cautioned to avoid illegal and improper behaviour. Families gather in the square for the lively performance of a time-honoured ritual. The event includes a performance of the hymn 'A Mighty Fortress is Our God' and the national anthem. Apart from in 1939, the Finnish declaration has rung out from Turku's town hall or square since medieval times.

Many Christmas-keepers absent themselves from home and television viewing at Christmas to serve food in soup kitchens. Since the rowdy Stewart Christmas, the season has been one set aside to feast the poor. Today charity at midwinter takes countless forms, many of them allowing the celebrant to engage with the needs of his or her community.

While shoppers rush around stores, the bell-ringing of the Salvation Army reminds them of the benevolence of Christmas. The evangelical organization targets the intersection of public space – the pavement – and the commercial temples of Christmas shopping. The Army's red kettle first appeared when a creative captain put one out to collect money for Christmas meals for the poor in 1891 in San Francisco. Today 25,000 bell-ringers drag out their kettles each year to collect money, which goes towards meals, Christmas gifts, rent payments, rehabilitation centres and disaster relief. In 2008, the red kettles brought in u.s.$130 million. A single day of bad weather, like the one the American northeast saw in 2009, can cost the Red Kettle Christmas Fundraising Campaign $5 million.[52]

The start of the twentieth century saw the birth of the Christmas stamp, a tiny gift that combined with Christmas goodwill to drastically reduce the occurrence of tuberculosis. A Danish postal clerk, Einar Holboell, dreamed up the idea while stamping mounds of Christmas cards in 1903. The next year, with the support of King Christian and prominent philanthropists, the Christmas seals programme got underway. That first year alone the equivalent of U.S.$18,000 was raised by selling a stamp decorated with the portrait of Queen Louise and marked with the word *Julen*, or Christmas. This initial Cinderella stamp idea allowed people to pay just 0.02 Danish kroner for a stamp and affix it beside their regular postage. The stamps themselves had no value as postage, but they did transmit the message of Christmas goodwill from household to household and from Denmark to the rest of Europe and the United States.

One of the most public ways to declare your acceptance of Christmas is to send missives to all your friends assuring them that you are in the holiday spirit. Christmas cards originated in England. As we have seen, Sir Henry Cole, a founder of the Victoria & Albert Museum, commissioned John Horsley to design a card for sale in 1843. Workers hand-tinted 1,000 cards and they were sold for 1 shilling each. With so much profit at stake, the tradition could not be limited to Britain. In 1874 a German immigrant to America, Louis Prang, began printing cards in Massachusetts. Ten years later his print run was in the millions.[53]

After more than 150 years of Christmas-card sending, the tradition has recently been declining. One American marketing firm found in 2005 that among the shrinking pool of consumers who buy cards, 77 per cent bought Christmas cards. In 2009 that number had dipped to 62 per cent.[54] According to the Greeting Card Association, which keeps track of UK card sales, in 2008 British consumers bought 678.9 million Christmas cards, which represents 45 per cent of greeting cards sold that year. The psychologist Cary Cooper has called Christmas cards 'a form of social networking'.[55] In the twenty-first century, other forms of networking may replace the Christmas card. Members of Generation Y tend to avoid mailing responses such as thank-you notes, and Facebook offers a different sort of connection. Many users of Facebook might wonder why they should send a Christmas card when their online friends have up-to-the-minute knowledge of them and their families, including their Christmas sentiments.

Henry Cole commissioned John Callcott Horsley to design this
first commercially printed Christmas card in 1843.

In countries where Christmas is legal and Christmas-keepers
are abundant, Christmas must be negotiated in the community and
at home. Some Christmas-keepers have vital roles in each sphere.
Being raised in this environment eases the transition from one to
the other; nonetheless, Christmas-keepers recognize the differences
between the two and respond in subtle ways to their private and
public Christmases.

TEN

# Christmas and the Church

O n Christmas Eve in 1951, clergymen hanged and burned an effigy of Father Christmas on the railings of Dijon Cathedral. Furthermore, the priests carried out their efforts in the sight of 250 Sunday School children who had been gathered so that they might learn about the danger of being seduced by the secular symbol of Christmas. Claude Lévi-Strauss made this event infamous by writing about it in an essay; the anthropologist linked Father Christmas to the ancient needs expressed through the Roman Saturnalia. Lévi-Strauss believed that the priests were right to feel threatened by Father Christmas, claiming that he is the most vibrant figure of modern paganism.[1] While the mock execution in 1951 did nothing to curb the growth of Father Christmas around the world, it does represent the conflict between the Church's wish to own Christmas and the uncontrollable growth of the global, secular Christmas.

Savvy churches shy away from burning Father Christmas in front of schoolchildren today. However, Christian groups do continue to struggle to express their message of reverence for the Nativity within cultures that emphasize other themes of Christmas. Some Christians living within these cultures choose to draw stark lines between their Christmas and the one taking place in the public sphere. For example, groups of evangelical American Christians reject Santa Claus entirely, wishing to focus only on Baby Jesus during the Advent season. Others go further and excise the Christmas tree from their celebrations, citing its possible link to Teutonic pagan practices. These families might decorate with a Jesse tree instead; this is a type of Advent calendar that grew out of the prophecy in the book of Isaiah that the Messiah would come from the line of David, Jesse's son. Such decisions tend to be made on an individual basis rather than handed down by Church authorities. However, organized Christian bodies face similar pressures. Do they reach out to secular society during the time when they seem to have the most in common with it, or do they draw lines of difference to mark the holiness of a Christ-centred celebration? This chapter will cover the way in which Christian churches handle Christmas festivities, and how their adherents struggle to balance the messages of the Church with the messages of the media and popular culture.

Finding that balance has been a centuries-long conundrum for churches. The same rowdy behaviour that had annoyed the seventeenth-century Puritans continued to cause consternation among Anglicans in subsequent centuries. Anglicans, however, sought to reinvent the holiday with religious significance. In the eighteenth century, many Anglican churches offered communion only at Easter, Whitsun, Michaelmas and Christmas, encouragement for the faithful to attend on Christmas morning. Anglicans made their way to Christmas services throughout the Victorian period as well, although the church attendance of Dissenters was not always so steady. Nonetheless, by the turn of the century one *Saturday Review* journalist guessed that nearly every Englishman who went to church on Sundays also attended on Christmas Day.[2]

Once the Puritans put to rest their war on Christmas, church services became the norm for most American Christians on Christmas Day, but it was a fairly slow transition. Calvinist denominations were slowest to accept the holiday. Presbyterian ministers of around 1800 might have called it a form of corruption tied to popery, superstitious and anti-Christian. Judging by the tone of their tirades, many would happily have joined the Dijon Catholics in burning Santa – that is if they could have stomached the sight of him and if they could have tolerated sharing a task with Catholic clergy. Congregationalists also decried Christmas. One Congregationalist pastor claimed that if Christ wanted his flock to celebrate

Christmas, 'he would have at least let us [know] the day'.³ But a few years later, in 1782, this same clergyman joined his Rhode Island neighbours in celebrating Christmas. It seems that the American Presbyterians, Baptists, Congregationalists and others had generally softened in their strict stance on Christmas by the 1850s. Quakers may have held out the longest; in the final decades of the nine-teenth century, some Quaker families adopted the secular but not the religious aspects of Christmas. Meeting houses might be locked and lifeless on Christmas Day, but many of their members were celebrating by their own hearths.⁴

The American Sunday School Movement, a multi-denomin-ational Protestant outreach ministry, hesitated to accept Christmas formally, no matter how many Sunday School teachers saw the benefit of decorating a tree to attract and entertain their juvenile students. At first the movement ignored Christmas, partially because the American denominations were, in the early nineteenth century, in deep disagreement about the validity of the holiday. The national curriculum intentionally overlooked the Nativity story until 1881, but it offered a non-Christmas alternative until the turn of the century in case the manger offended any personnel.⁵ During the first quarter of the twentieth century, almost all the denomin-ations gave way to recognizable modern Christmas habits: the children's pageant, carols and a church service with a meditation on the Nativity.

Of course, along with the Anglicans, a few other denominations embraced the Nativity fully even from the start. The Episcopalians of the American South enjoyed their version of the Britlish Christmas. The Moravians were another Christmas-loving church, as were the Lutherans.

The perception of Christmas's religious significance altered dur-ing the Victorian period. At first, and for a long time, the holiday had largely been tied to atonement, meaning that Christmas was a reminder to act with benevolence and magnanimity in an effort to be worthy of the joys of the holiday. Periodicals called readers to action, and good works became a focal element of an Englishman's preparations for the day. The Victorian scholar Neil Armstrong has argued that the nineteenth century saw a switch from this emphasis on atonement to one of incarnation, redirecting Victorians' interest from their own roles in society to the personhood and, more importantly, the childhood of Christ. Such a switch, Armstrong believes, caused the theological realignment that allowed Victorians to invent the child-centredness of Christmas.[6]

Not everyone liked the nineteenth century's revision of Christmas. In Germany, Catholic clergymen took issue with the loss of the contemplative Advent season. Gifts and Advent jollity were criticized as Protestantism sneaking into the Catholic celebration. The myth that Martin Luther created the first decorated Christmas tree probably did nothing to endear that tradition to the Catholic authorities. The adoption of family-centred rituals kept Catholics away from Christmas Mass, and German clergy were slow to accept these changes to the nature of the holiday in the popular imagination.[7]

The tension between the faith-based celebration of the Nativity and the consumer-driven expression of Christmas has existed since the holiday began to focus on the shrine of the hearth and children in the nineteenth century. Christmas-keeping Protestants who had embraced Santa Claus began to see him as a usurper of Christ's place at the centre of the holiday. The Christmas scholar Leigh Eric Schmidt argues that this tension is in part owing to the puritanical denial of Christmas; since the Presbyterians, Baptists, Quakers and others sought to ignore the existence of Christmas, the holiday grew up in America largely without any deep religious support. Instead, it was cast solely into the secular sphere, where it has thrived.[8]

Protestants who tentatively embraced Christmas in the nineteenth or twentieth centuries initially did so with little religious fervour, choosing secular celebration rather than profaning their beliefs about the religious validity of Christmas.[9] A Methodist publication of the 1880s, for example, warned against finding any Biblical authenticity in Christmas, which it touted as too Roman Catholic for taste, but the pamphlet did encourage Methodists to use the day for family reunions and merry togetherness.[10] At the same time, other formerly anti-Christmas denominations were struggling to insert religious significance into the holiday.

The first decades of the twentieth century saw American Christians struggling with the popularity of Christmas consumerism now that they wanted the religious side of the holiday to dominate. The Milwaukee Archconfraternity of Christian Mothers, a Catholic group, first campaigned with the slogan 'Put Christ back into Christmas' in 1949. The movement spread beyond Wisconsin's borders, and Catholic and Protestant organizations backed parades and movements in cities all over the country.[11] Ironically, store owners sponsored the local initiatives, and typically they agreed to use the slogan and portray Nativity scenes in their windows. This is exactly what happened in Evanston, Illinois, in 1951. As a result, according to Schmidt, the cry for a Christ-centred Christmas actually served as a benediction for the holiday's rampant consumerism.[12] The shops benefited from the appearance of focusing on religion even as they profited from the secular gift rituals of the holiday.

The Knights of Columbus picked up the cause in the 1960s, revising the slogan to the now familiar 'Keep Christ in Christmas'. This fraternal organization prepares billboards, Christmas cards and radio and television commercials to remind Christians to celebrate in a religious way. Spokesmen for the organization have stated that they are not interested in pressurizing non-Christians to put Christ into their Christmas. The Knights of Columbus have also have fought legal battles to maintain Nativity scenes in public spaces. In the Action Steps for their campaign, the Knights challenge members to display Nativity scenes in their gardens, and they suggest acts of service that will help one to seek a Christ-like spirit during the holiday: send a care package to a deployed soldier, sing carols at a nursing home, mend a broken relationship.[13] Today a separate group, Authentic Christian Living, maintains a Facebook page devoted to keeping Christ in Christmas. Another Protestant ministry, Focus on the Family, encourages Christians to read scripture during Advent, to bake a birthday cake for Jesus and to make a list of birthday presents for him that take the form of acts of service and generosity towards others. These more conservative

Christian groups welcome rituals that mark the religious nature of the holiday.

Of course, one of the most formal and visible ways in which Christians participate in the religious nature of Christmas is by gathering at church services devoted to highlighting the scriptural basis of the Nativity. For Roman Catholics, Christmas Day is a holy day of obligation. This means that Catholics will fill the pews for Christmas Eve services or Midnight Mass only to return to them a few hours later for Christmas Day services.

News reports usually comment on whether or not national leaders attend church at Christmas. As the head of the Anglican Church, the Queen attends an Anglican church service at Christmas. For the last few decades the British royal family has celebrated Christmas Day with a short walk to St Mary Magdalene's church on the Queen's estate in Sandringham, Norfolk. Up to 3,000 onlookers might leave their homes in the early hours of Christmas Day to join the crowd that watches the royals make their public promenade. The Queen's children and grandchildren generally join her as she pauses to greet people and accept their bouquets.

It is not unusual for Protestant churches to add additional activities and services to their roster during Advent: perhaps a children's Christmas pageant, carol-singing visits to members unable to leave their homes, and usually a Christmas Eve service that vibrates with a frisson of joy and expectation and often ends with a dimming of the lights as each person holds a lit candle to sing the closing hymn. This service originated in a programme of scripture readings followed by carols that was created by English cleric Edward White Benson in 1880. It went on to be used in British churches with ties to colleges. Back then the carol service occurred before students left for their Christmas break, but in 1918 Eric Milner-White adopted it at King's College, Cambridge, for a Christmas Eve service.[14] Like many good ideas, this one made its way across the Atlantic, and today it forms the basis of most mainstream American Protestants' idea of Christmas at church. British churches schedule Christmas Day services and offer communion, but most American Protestant churches remain empty unless Christmas falls on a Sunday. In fact, knowing that many Americans prefer to spend Christmas Day at home with family, some churches reduce the number of services on Christmas Sundays. Nine per cent of Protestant American churches have recently cancelled Christmas Sunday worship, according to one 2011 survey of 1,000 pastors.[15] One Tulsa mega-church named Church on the Move chose to cancel Sunday service in 2011 following a busy schedule of pre-Christmas services and events, largely to give their thousands of volunteers and staff members a day to be with their families. This fairly controversial move makes headlines every Sunday Christmas, an event that is due to happen six times between 2013 and 2050.

The Amish have found a solution to the conflict between the desire to worship Christ and the sacred American tradition of being with family at Christmas. This subgroup of the Mennonites, which rejects modern conveniences, often celebrates two Christmas Days. The first is spent in religious solemnity with the household; on Second Christmas the Amish visit others in their community. Horse-drawn Amish buggies throng the roads of Pennsylvania, New York, Ohio and Indiana, a sign that they are in the mood for visiting. Sometimes up to 40 buggies fill the farmyards of a house, the men chatting indolently outside in the cold while dozens of women work to prepare an enormous meal inside. The Amish exchange cards and both homemade and shop-bought gifts at Christmas, but they avoid Christmas trees, Santa Claus and of course any electronic decorations.[16]

In some ways, Christmas Eve fulfils the same role as the Amish First Christmas for non-Amish American Protestants. The modern Christmas Eve service is designed to be welcoming to Christians who may enter the church only on Christmas Eve and at Easter, worshippers sometimes referred to as CE, or Christmas-Easter Christians. No matter how often they fill the pews, those who attend the Christmas Eve service experience a fulfilling tradition of beloved Christmas carols, community and candlelight. To children, this special expectation may partly be driven by the knowledge that their presents are finally within reach, but adults attempt to pause in this hour to honour the God that continued his play for salvation by sending a baby to Bethlehem.

Some Christians do more than meditate about Christmas in Bethlehem; they plan a holiday pilgrimage. The magical quality of Christmas in the Holy Land brings in thousands of holiday pilgrims each year. For reasons of denominational territorialism, aspects of Christmas in Christ's birthplace have gone unchanged for centuries. Bethlehem offered the setting for the Nativity and the events of the first Christmas, and one could argue that this tiny Judean town exported Christmas to the rest of the world. Today Bethlehem is situated in the West Bank, and when the Christian pilgrims make their way to the Church of the Nativity on Christmas Eve, they must brave numerous checkpoints to enter, just as Palestinians endure them upon exiting.

The twenty-first century began with muted Christmas celebrations in Bethlehem, following a Palestinian uprising that scared away tourists who would usually patronize the gift shops. In 2009

Amish buggies gather for Christmas dinner. It is not uncommon to see upwards of 30 men in black hats waiting around outside while the women prepare a meal in a very crowded kitchen.

The original basilica on the site of the Church of the Nativity is traditionally said to have been built by St Helena in AD 339. Today the interior continues to be maintained by three sets of clerics who must abide by the 19th-century Status Quo, a guideline regarding who has authority over different sections of the structure.

the number of Christmas tourists in the Holy Land had dropped to 50,000; however, by 2010 crowds of over 100,000 had returned, which certainly helped the little town which depends almost entirely on tourism.[17] Tourists especially come at Christmas to see the site where Christ allegedly drew his first breath. A church first rose over the humble cave in 339, and since then many alterations have been made to commemorate the spot. Habitual Christmas-card senders might be surprised to learn that church leaders have long defended a cave stable rather than the humble lean-to structure so often depicted beneath the sparkling star. Under the Church of the Nativity lies the Grotto of the Nativity, a 40- × 10-ft (12- × 3-m) space containing an altar to mark the location of Christ's birth. For centuries censers have hung over the spot, now covered in marble, and a fourteen-point silver star surrounds a hole that allows one to touch the bedrock that may have been present at the birth.

With tension, if not security, eased outside the Church of the Nativity, it might seem appropriate to find the interior a place of peace and calm. This is not always the case for the men who maintain the building. The Greek Orthodox Patriarchate of Jerusalem oversees the Basilica of the Nativity, and the Roman Catholic Church runs the adjoining Church of St Catherine. Furthermore, Orthodox Armenian clerics also care for sections of the complex, which contains a monastery for each sect. After centuries of disputes and a general failure to get along, the ruling Ottoman sultans ordered all the clerics of the different denominations to continue to manage only the parts of the building they had always managed. This even governs who walks down which aisle, who cleans which areas and who stores equipment where. As a result, the priests have developed an extremely territorial approach to church management.

Sometimes the strict lines of ownership lead to turmoil. On 28 December 2011, between the Western and Eastern celebrations of Christmas, the Armenian and Orthodox monks who oversee parts of the church property began a brawl. The Greeks were cleaning some chandeliers in an Armenian section of the church, and a ladder ended up in disputed territory. No one was injured in the melee, suggesting that the monks showed restraint even when smacking each other with brooms, but Palestinian police were needed to calm the scene. Four years earlier seven monks had been hurt after a fight sparked by that year's Christmas clean-up.[18]

The different Christian sects claim diverse sites for their Christmas rites just as they schedule various dates for their celebrations. Roman Catholics hold services on 24 December in St Catherine's Church. Participants in the ceremony follow the Latin Patriarch of Jerusalem as he processes from the church, through the Basilica of the Nativity and into the grotto beneath it. Here he lays a wooden figure of the baby Christ on the birth spot. Churchgoers have to obtain tickets, albeit free ones, to attend the evening service, Midnight Mass and the Masses held in the grotto.

The Protestants, meanwhile, bus in celebrants from Jerusalem for Christmas Eve services in Shepherds' Field and the Basilica of the Nativity. Tour groups can book caves located in Shepherds' Field in which to celebrate Christmas Eve services. The Orthodox Christians – Copts, Ethiopians, Romanians and Greeks – hold their outdoor procession and multiple services in the Church of the Nativity on 6 January, and Armenians round off the season with their Christmas celebrations on 16 January.

While Christians' hearts are drawn to Bethlehem throughout Advent, their eyes might be turned towards Rome on Christmas Eve. In the mid-nineteenth century, tourists and Roman Catholics queued up to celebrate a Christmas Eve Mass with the pope in the Sistine Chapel; then they thronged St Peter's to join him for High Mass on Christmas Day. There was a dress code for the service: men had to wear formal evening dress coats, and women could wear only black with a simple veil covering their heads.[19] The dress code has changed considerably, but the popularity of this Christmas destination continues. In 1944 a newly liberated Rome celebrated a joyful Midnight Mass on Christmas Eve, the first for some time. American GIs crowded on top of the confessional booths to secure a clear view of the goings-on. Today things are far more regulated; those hoping to attend in person must secure tickets for the Midnight Mass, but the rest of the world can tune in. These Christmas services have been broadcast throughout the world since 1974. In 2010 Pope Benedict began streaming his Christmas Eve Mass online. In 2011 this streaming service carried his message bemoaning Christmas commercialism to viewers around the world. Furthermore, the timing of the so-called Midnight Mass has recently moved to 10 p.m. to ease the pope's schedule during a very busy time of year.

Many of the Catholics watching the pope's Christmas Eve Mass participate in their own local church's Advent activities. Advent, the period encompassing the four Sundays before Christmas, is for Catholics a time of preparation. The Catholic Church begins Advent with the Sunday nearest to the close of November and includes four Sundays leading up to Christmas Day, also known as the Nativity of the Lord. The name of the season comes from the Latin words *advenio* and *adventus*, 'to come to' and 'arrival'.[20]

The Catholic Church and High Church Protestants seek to avoid the secularization of Christmas by keeping Advent as its own season – one that is devoid of the merriment of carols and clearly distinct from the long pre-season party of the secular Christmas. Liturgy and homilies encourage a longing frame of mind: parishes are taught to use this time to wait on the coming of Jesus rather than to prepare for the hoopla of Christmas. Gaudete Sunday, the third Sunday in Advent, takes a joyous theme. The name comes from the Latin word for 'rejoice', which appears in the reading for that Mass, Philippians 4:4: 'Rejoice in the Lord always: and again I say rejoice.' The liturgical readings for Gaudete brighten compared to the sombre tone of the first two Advent Sundays.

The Catholic Church has a special set of Advent hymns that focus the congregation on this waiting period. These include 'O Come, O Come, Emmanuel', also well known by Protestants, and others such as 'On Jordan's Bank' and 'When the King Shall Come Again'. These Christmas carols are not the ones that fill the airwaves during the secular Advent season, but they do fit the Church's liturgical agenda. Lutherans and Episcopalians similarly delay joyful Christmas carols.

It is not until Christmas Eve that Christmas begins in earnest for Catholics, and many families traditionally postpone decorating their tree until the period of waiting for Christmas ends with the holiday's true arrival. Vespers on 24 December marks the switch from Advent to Christmastide, the second period in the liturgical calendar of the Catholic Church; this time of celebration lasts until Epiphany. Traditionally decorations will remain in place until then, although following the liturgical calendar causes Christians to be out of step with the holiday habits of their secular neighbours.

Protestants may share their liturgy with the Catholic Church, but their Advent wreath holds different symbolism. Catholics highlight the rose-coloured Gaudete candle to be lit on the third Sunday of Advent. Protestant churches might identify each candle with an element of the Christmas celebration: hope, peace, joy, love and, on Christmas Eve, the Christ candle. Readings and meditations during Advent Sunday services explore these themes.

The Catholic Midnight Mass is certainly not limited to the service at St Peter's in Rome. In fact, it serves as the centrepiece of

Christmas ritual in many regions. In France, celebrants attend a Midnight Mass, and then enjoy a meal called *reveillon*, either at home or at restaurants that stay open all night.

Filipinos attend not one but nine consecutive Christmas Masses, and these are scheduled early in the morning, at four a.m. Depending on the size of the community, the sound of bells, fireworks or the local priest's knock at the door call celebrants to Misa de Gallo, or Mass of the Rooster, on 16 December. The sequence continues for nine days in all, allowing celebrants to make a sacrifice in honour of Christ's birth. Street vendors station themselves near the church, and delicious smells waft through the pews, promising a hearty meal once the Mass has ended. Then family and friends chat over piping-hot dishes of sweetened sticky rice and cups of tea or thick hot chocolate.[21]

In Norway, Christmas is the busiest time for parish churches. Norwegians tend to travel over the Easter holiday, but at Christmas-time families attend the Christmas Eve afternoon service that began after the Second World War. Most of these attendees do not go to church the rest of the year – Norway has the lowest proportion of church attendance in Europe. The state church of Norway, which is Lutheran, offers a family-friendly time for the Christmas Eve service, which is packed as families renew their once-yearly tradition.[22]

There are clusters of Moravians in America, Tanzania, England, Germany and elsewhere. The Protestant Moravian beliefs originated with John Huss's heretical divergence from the Roman Catholic Church in the fifteenth century. His followers grew, and in the eighteenth century they developed a Love Feast tradition. Today they hold a Christmas Love Feast for the children or one for the whole congregation. During today's Love Feasts, American Moravians prepare special coffee and serve it with sweet, buttery buns to people sitting in the pews. It may sound like a tasty version of communion, but it is not a sacrament. In the Caribbean, tea is on the menu, and African Moravians enjoy a meal of peanuts. Following the simple repast, the congregation may hear a sermon or enjoy the amazing choral presentations of this highly musical denomination.

They end by passing the light of the Christ candle from taper to taper through the candlelit pews. The Eastern Orthodox Church adheres to a 40-day Nativity Fast. During this time, healthy individuals avoid wine and most meats, although fish and wine may be consumed at weekends during the period. The elderly and nursing mothers are exempted from these requirements, although they can also share in a fast from greed and anger. Christmas Eve, a day on which no solid food may be eaten, ends when the first star is seen in the sky and the Christmas feasting can begin. The Eastern Orthodox Church celebrates Jesus's baptism, not the coming of the Magi, on Epiphany, which is like a second Christmas in importance. During the service for Epiphany, priests bless water and sprinkle it throughout the church before distributing the leftover water to be taken home in plastic bottles. Animals, homes and offices receive a sprinkling with the water as well.[23]

Of course, not everyone is in church on Christmas Day, and of those who are, many pause only briefly before resuming the commercial aspects of Christmas. In 2008 the number of Britons making a Christmas Day purchase online overtook the number who attended a Christmas Day church service. The estimated 5.24 million shoppers were enticed by Boxing Day specials that began on Christmas Day. In comparison, 4.5 million Britons attended church on Christmas Day that year.[24]

As a group unlikely to join those church services, neo-pagans find other ways to make merry in late December. In the 2001 British census, just over 42,000 people identified themselves as pagan.[25] One survey in 2008 found 1.2 million neo-pagans in the U.S.[26] While they do not decorate with Nativities, some pagans accept aspects of Christmas. Their main holiday of the season is Yule, a name for the winter solstice derived from Scandinavian tradition. That night might find covens out holding prayer walks around mazes or re-enacting a ceremonial fight between the oak and the holly tree. The solstice, the longest night of the year, represents the victory of light over darkness and the promise of lengthening days and summer's warmth. Neo-pagans celebrate this with lights, so bonfires or fireworks feature in the pagan Yule.

Christians in cold climates are less likely to celebrate outdoors in December, unless they are taking part in a live Nativity scene. The legend of the first crèche or Nativity scene attributes it to St Francis of Assisi and dates it to 1223. The saint is credited with erecting a scene that would show the inhabitants of Grecio, Italy, how the location of Christ's birth might have looked. St Bonaventure wrote about the event, assuring all that St Francis had obtained the pope's approval for this innovative re-enactment before collecting the live animals needed to add authenticity. The illiterate observers were greatly moved by the tableau, which introduced them to the narrative of Christ's birth in a new and tactile way that has dominated many church Christmases in the ensuing centuries. Today in Catholic Nativity scenes, the manger remains empty until Christmas Eve, at which time a statue or doll representing Jesus finally completes the scene.

In Spain, the scene of the Nativity captures Christmas enthusiasm. Antique Nativity scenes are a common decoration in the homes of Spanish families. Churches organize live Nativities, with real people standing still to create famous tableaux from the Bible accounts of Christ's birth. In some places celebrants act out the Nativity.[27] Churches in America might organize a live Nativity, too, and here church members dress in approximations of Judean outfits made of tin foil, polyester and bathrobes, braving whatever their local weather serves up in late December. Those with access to farm animals draft in sheep and donkeys to join the performance. Guests walk or drive through the displays.

In Central and South America there are vibrant Nativity rituals based on traditions imported from Spain. Las Posadas started in Spain, but today is a more notable ritual in Guatemala, Mexico and the American southwest. For nine nights in a row, starting on 14 December and ending on Christmas Eve, community or church groups re-enact Mary and Joseph's search for shelter as described in Luke's gospel. Children either dress as Mary and Joseph or carry statues of the holy parents from house to house. They sing songs at each door as they ask for *posada* or lodgings, but are rejected until they reach their final destination of the night, which welcomes them in for a party. Sometimes neighbours organize the festive schedule for their children, but in some cities like Santa Fe, New Mexico, the churches team up for the re-enactment.

In Guatemala this journey to Bethlehem happens inside the home. Villagers devote one entire room of their house to a creative diorama that changes each day to mark the events leading up to Christ's birth. The family moves the figures towards the Bethlehem stable each day, until all finally arrive in time for the virgin birth. At first plastic figures of Mary and Joseph move down the road, and later the shepherds follow in their wake, each figure moving a few inches each day during December. After the hours of effort that go into creating these scenes, homeowners welcome their neighbours and even strangers in to view the results.

At the heart of the Nativity scene is the Baby Jesus. Churches and families have developed a reverence for the Baby Jesus, the vulnerable image of God incarnate that continues to form the twenty-first-century Church's religious centre at Christmas-time. Christian children colour pictures and act out scenes carrying dolls representing Baby Jesus. The term 'Baby Jesus' is an accessible version of Christ, one with which children can readily empathize. This infant is, of course, deified, but he is more vulnerable than the grown-up, miracle-performing Christ who calmed storms and drove out demons. Church materials and children's books with a Nativity theme offer Baby Jesus as a distinct character, temporarily de-emphasizing the adult Christ.

Baby Jesus is a less divisive figure than the adult Jesus. Who can argue with a helpless infant? The child does not verbalize an exclusive path to Christian salvation, although he is the very symbol of it. He lies passively in his manger crib. Cards and picture books do not show him fussing; he is serene even as a newborn. The Catholic tradition of assembling a Nativity scene but leaving the manger empty throughout Advent emphasizes the wait for that final piece of the puzzle. This is part of what the mid-twentieth-century priests of Dijon wished to convey when they singed a Santa suit. The dramatic act of killing Father Christmas must have blurred their message for the intended audience, but the priest who dreamed up the scheme had a reason. He hoped to communicate what to him was a beautiful truth. It is not Christmas until Baby Jesus can take his rightful place at the centre of the church celebration.

# Conclusion

As a child growing up in suburban America, I saw Christmas as the highlight of the year. Even now, when the 25th of any given month rolls around, my grandmother and mother cannot help but remark on how many months are left before Christmas. The business of adult life has lessened the expectation of Christmas somewhat, but still the countdown runs year-round. That expectation now involves creating our family's version of Christmas for my own small children. They relish the ritual of decorating the tree, taking part in a Christmas pageant and sprinkling coloured sugar on cut-out butter cookies. Each family treasures its own version of the celebration and, as they spin through their own annual expression of Christmas, it can be nearly impossible to see the holiday's global impact, the bigger picture that prevents anyone from owning it.

Each year the symphony of Christmas deepens its balance of sound, but, because there is so much history to the centuries of Christmas, Christmas-keepers cannot possibly juggle all the memories and rituals that have accumulated over the years. Some, like the echo of old Christmas carols long forgotten, pass away from common use, while new songs find a place in the soundtrack of the holiday. When we step back from our own experience of Christmas to appreciate the patina of the centuries, certain elements demand attention.

While purists would probably like to imagine that the power of Christmas defies politics, this is woefully inaccurate. Furthermore, the ubiquitous nature of Christmas in many cultures makes this an

The Belsnickel, a rather terrifying Pennsylvania German Christmas figure, contributed to the amalgamated Santa. This one still roams a Pennsylvania German museum at Christmas-time.

ideal battleground between world views. Already Western nations have seen the potent religious aspect of Christmas diminish, at least under the publicly funded spotlight of the secular sphere. Adherents can still easily find the Christian heart of Christmas, but it is not worn prominently on the holiday's sleeve.

In the homes and hearts of faithful Christians, Christmas will always be about the birth of Christ, the first step in his progress to the Cross three decades later. Christians may struggle to keep that focus during a blizzard of obligations and social outings, but the core of their faith is wrapped up in the holiday. If anything, Christmas may continue its transition into an entity with a split personality: highly meaningful for the Christian faith in some places, and an enormous secular party in others.

The linguistics that have grown up around Christmas since the late twentieth century attest to this split. While this is less common in Great Britain, some American celebrants heartily wish friends and neighbours 'Happy Holidays'. Others see this congratulatory phrase as an attack on the Christian heart of Christmas or, on the emotional level, at the Christmas of their childhood when it was perfectly acceptable to claim Christmas publically. The 'Happy Holidays' sentiment incorporates all late December events, levelling each to an uninspiring, vague blip. Of course proponents of the phrase embrace it because it allows them to express their cultural relativism, graciously encouraging their audience in whatever December party plans he or she has in mind. What one atheist blogger has called a 'crazy Orwellian avoidance of the term "Christmas"' does raise hackles in certain quarters.[1] Some listen carefully to public figures, noting which have the courage to identify Christmas. They blog furiously when entities like Google run a 'Happy Holidays' banner on their site on Christmas Day. Others bristle when Christmas, which highlights one faith tradition only, receives extra attention.

While there is no going back, it seems dull to lump Christmas together with Kwanza, and those two together with the pagan Yule, and all three with the Jewish Hanukkah, even if the speaker is throwing in the New Year for good measure. Each of these holidays has a history and story of its own that deserves to be honoured by recognizing its existence.

Despite the best efforts of politically correct censors, it will surely be impossible for Christmas to retain a connection with its antecedents and also become an entirely politically neutral holiday. Perhaps if a future political state were able to cut off the historical root of Christmas and censor the holiday's multifaceted nature, the tradition might then be controllable, but it would no longer be Christmas. The history of Christmas – the sense of tradition in which it is steeped – is integral to the holiday's value and meaning.

While celebrants cannot all know that history entirely, they do relish the sense of durability that comes with Christmas.

The future of Christmas is as bright as a city's worth of LED decorations, but only because the holiday will continue to evolve to meet celebrants' needs. The sacred aura of Christmas depends on its seeming timelessness, but a hundred years from now the holiday will have changed enormously. As informed Christmas-keepers know, the holiday refuses to be held by any bonds. It belongs to all. Cultural and personal needs drive the ongoing evolution of Christmas, from bawdy Krampus-themed cards to rainbow-coloured reinventions of Schwartz Piet. The holiday compels publishing schedules in the West, toy manufacturing in China and food production in the Marshall Islands. It causes more money to be spent than some small countries have at their disposal. It offers peace. Ironically, it brings about the height of commercialism as well as quiet reflection on a tiny child. In all this contradiction, one thing is certain: Christmas will continue.

# References

## ONE: The Original Christmas

1  Alden Mosshammer, *The Easter Computus and the Origins of the Christian Era* (New York, 2008), p. 9.
2  W. F. Dawson, *Christmas: Its Origin and Associations* (London, 1902), pp. 13–14.
3  Leon F. Scheerer, 'Did Augustus Order a Census?', *Christian Education*, xxx/4 (December 1947), p. 331.
4  Ibid., p. 332.
5  Paul L. Maier, *In the Fullness of Time: A Historian Looks at Christmas, Easter, and the Early Church* (Grand Rapids, MI, 1991), p. 8.
6  Scheerer, 'Did Augustus Order a Census?', p. 332.
7  Michael E. Bakich, 'What was the Star of Bethlehem?', *Astronomy*, XXXVII/1 (2010), p. 36.
8  *The Gospel of Luke: Revised Standard Version* (San Francisco, 2001), p. 23.
9  Craig A. Evans, ed., *The Bible Background Commentary: Matthew–Luke* (Colorado Springs, CO, 2003), p. 49.
10  Maier, *In the Fullness of Time*, p. 4.
11  Walter Brandmuller, *Light and Shadows: Defending Church History Amid Faith, Facts and Legends* (San Francisco, 2009), p. 89.
12  'When a Virgin Gave Birth', Matthew 1 – IVP New Testament Commentaries, www.biblegateway.com (25 August 2013).
13  Maier, *In the Fullness of Time*, pp. 17 and 16.
14  'When a Virgin Gave Birth'.
15  Ibid.
16  Maier, *In the Fullness of Time*, p. 22.
17  David Noel Freedman, Allen C. Iyers and Astrid Biles Beck, eds, *Eerdmans' Dictionary of the Bible* (Grand Rapids, MI, 2000), p. 580.

18 Paul Barnett, *Jesus and the Rise of Early Christianity: A History of New Testament Times* (Downers Grove, IL, 1999), p. 34.

19 Mark A. Chancey, *Greco-Roman Culture and the Galilee of Jesus* (Cambridge, 2005), pp. 47–8.

20 Gordon Franz, 'Oh Little Town of Bethlehem', www.biblearchaeology.org, 7 December 2008.

21 Ray Summers and E. Jerry Vardman, eds, *Chronos, Kairos, Christos Two* (Macon, GA, 1998).

22 Maier, *In the Fullness of Time*, p. 14.

23 Ibid., p. 44.

24 Stephen C. Carlson, 'The Accommodations of Joseph and Mary in Bethlehem Κατάλυμα in Luke 2.7', *New Testament Studies*, LVI/3 (2010), pp. 328–9.

25 Richard C. Trexler, *The Journey of the Magi: Meanings in History of a Christian Story* (Princeton, NJ, 1997), pp. 35, 72.

26 Ibid., p. 75.

27 Ibid., p. 102.

28 Ibid., p. 38.

29 Maier, *In the Fullness of Time*, pp. 70–71.

30 Solomon Zeitlin, 'Herod, A Malevolent Maniac', *Jewish Quarterly Review*, LIV/1 (July 1963), p. 1.

31 Ibid., p. 3.

32 Ehud Nezer, *The Architecture of Herod, The Great Builder* (Grand Rapids, MI, 2006), p. 5.

33 Ibid., p. 10.

34 Ibid., p. 12.

35 Ibid., p. 15.

36 Peter Richardson, *Herod, King of the Jews and Friend of Rome* (Minneapolis, MN, 1999), p. 19.

37 Nezer, *Architecture of Herod*, p. 16.

38 Richard T. France, 'Herod and the Children of Bethlehem', *Novum Testamentum*, XXI/2 (April 1979), p. 114.

39 Ibid., p. 115.

40 Summers and Vardman, *Chronos, Kairos*, p. 179.

41 Richardson, *Herod, King of the Jews*, p. 18.

42 Ibid., p. 21.

43 Herbert Lockyer, ed., *All the Angels in the Bible: A Complete Exploration of the Nature and Ministry of Angels* (Peabody, MA, 1995), p. 3.

44 Ibid., p. 29.

## TWO: Early Celebrations and Customs

1 Susan K. Roll, *Toward the Origins of Christmas* (Kampen, Netherlands, 1995), p. 174.
2 Frederick Cornwallis Conybeare, 'The History of Christmas', *American Journal of Theology*, III/1 (1899), p. 1.
3 Beryl Rawson, *Children and Childhood in Roman Italy* (New York, 2003), p. 135.
4 Michael E. Bakich, 'What Was the Star of Bethlehem?', *Astronomy*, XXXVII/1 (2010), p. 37.
5 Ibid., p. 38.
6 Ibid., p. 34.
7 Joseph F. Kelly, *The Origins of Christmas* (Collegeville, MN, 2004), p. 64.
8 Ibid., p. 59.
9 Ibid., p. 60.
10 Ibid., p. 63.
11 Greg Tobin, *Holy Holidays!: The Catholic Origins of Celebration* (New York, 2011), p. 14.
12 Alexander Murray, 'Medieval Christmas', *History Today*, XXXVI/12 (1986), p. 33.
13 Penn L. Restad, *Christmas in America: A History* (New York, 1996), p. 5.
14 Margaret Baker, *Discovering Christmas Customs and Folklore: A Guide to Seasonal Rites*, 3rd edn (Risborough, 2007), p. 7.
15 Bakich, 'What Was the Star?', p. 34.
16 Murray, 'Medieval Christmas', p. 32.
17 Alexander Tille, *Yule and Christmas: Their Place in the Germanic Year* (London, 1899), p. 123.
18 Kathleen Stokker, *Keeping Christmas: Yuletide Traditions in Norway and the New Land* (St Paul, MN, 2000), p. 6.
19 Ibid., p. 8.
20 Ibid., pp. 12–13.
21 Karen Louise Jolly, *Tradition and Diversity: Christianity in a World Context to 1500* (New York, 1997), p. 205.
22 Joe Perry, *Christmas in Germany: A Cultural History* (Chapel Hill, NC, 2010), p. 15.
23 Richard Fletcher, *The Barbarian Conversion: From Paganism to Christianity* (Los Angeles, 1999), pp. 255–6.
24 Prosper Guéranger, *The Liturgical Year: Advent* (Dublin, 1870), p. 26.
25 James W. McKinnon, *The Advent Project: The Later-Seventh-Century Creation of the Roman Mass Proper* (Berkeley and Los Angeles, 2000), p. 147.

26 Ronald Hutton, *The Stations of the Sun: A History of the Ritual Year in Britain* (Oxford and New York, 1996), p. 11.

27 Ibid., p. 3.

28 Restad, *Christmas in America*, p. 6.

29 Ibid., p. 7.

30 R. Chambers, ed., *Chambers Book of Days* (London, 1864). See www.thebookofdays.com, accessed 10 September 2012.

31 Iørn Piø, 'Christmas Traditions in Scandinavia', in *Custom, Culture and Community in the Later Middle Ages: A Symposium*, ed. Thomas Pettitt and Leif Søndergaard (Odense, Denmark, 1994), pp. 61–2.

32 Neil MacKenzie, 'Boy into Bishop', *History Today*, XXXVII/12 (1987), p. 10.

33 Ibid., p. 11.

34 Daniel Diehl and Mark P. Donnelly, *Medieval Celebrations* (Mechanicsburg, PA, 2011), p. 23.

35 MacKenzie, 'Boy into Bishop', p. 12.

36 Piø, 'Christmas Traditions in Scandinavia', p. 63.

37 MacKenzie, 'Boy into Bishop', p. 14.

38 Ibid.

39 Hutton, *Stations of the Sun*, p. 105.

40 Thomas Hervey, *The Book of Christmas* (London, 1836), p. 59.

41 Peter Klein, 'The Poppyhead at Ludlow: Boy Bishop and Lord of Misrule?' *Transactions of the Shropshire Archaeological and Historical Society*, LXXIV (1994), p. 80.

42 Ibid.

43 Hutton, *Stations of the Sun*, p. 106.

44 Olga Horner, 'Christmas at the Inns of Court', in *Festive Drama: Papers from the Sixth Triennial Colloquium of the International Society for the Study of Medieval Theatre, Lancaster*, ed. Meg Twycross (Woodbridge, 1996), p. 45.

45 Ibid., p. 42.

46 Clifford Davidson, *Festivals and Plays in Medieval Britain* (Burlington, VT, 2007), p. 18.

47 Daniel J. Foley, *The Christmas Tree* (Detroit, MI, 1999), p. 42.

48 Ibid., p. 47.

THREE: Christmas in Art and Culture

1 Joe Perry, *Christmas in Germany: A Cultural History* (Chapel Hill, NC, 2010), p. 253.

2 Ibid.

3 Ibid.
4 Gertrud Schiller, *Iconography of Christian Art*, trans. Janet Seligman (Greenwich, CT, 1971), vol. I, p. 26.
5 Ibid., p. 59.
6 Ibid., p. 60.
7 Ibid., p. 64.
8 Ibid., p. 74.
9 Ibid., pp. 76–7.
10 Ibid., p. 88.
11 Roger Dobson, 'Is Painting Earliest Portrayal of Down's Syndrome?', *British Medical Journal*, international edn (18 January 2003), p. 126.
12 Nicholas Genes, 'Down's Syndrome Through the Ages', www.medgadget.com, 18 November 2005.
13 Keith Harrison, trans., *Sir Gawain and the Green Knight* (Oxford, 2008), p. 4.
14 Jean Louise Carrière, 'Sir Gawain and the Green Knight as a Christmas Poem', *Comitatus: A Journal of Medieval and Renaissance Studies*, I/I (1970), p. 37.
15 Clement A. Miles, *Christmas in Ritual and Tradition, Christian and Pagan* (London, 1912), p. 47.
16 Ibid., pp. 50–80.
17 Ibid., pp. 80–81.
18 William Sandys, ed., *Christmas Carols, Ancient and Modern* (London, 1833), p. li.
19 Tara Moore, *Victorian Christmas in Print* (New York, 2009), p. 121.
20 Richard W. O'Donnell, 'Will the Real Christmas Poet Please Stand Up?', *American History*, XXXIX (February 2005), p. 18.
21 Ibid., p. 18.
22 William Waits, *The Modern Christmas in America: A Cultural History of Gift Giving* (New York, 1994), n.p.
23 Ibid.
24 Kerry Larson, ed., *The Cambridge Companion to Nineteenth-century American Poetry* (Cambridge, 2011), p. 106.
25 Thomas Hardy, 'The Oxen', in *Poet's Choice*, ed. Edward Hirsch (Orlando, 2006), p. 48.
26 Paul Ferris, *Dylan Thomas: The Biography* (Washington, DC, 2000), pp. 204–5.
27 Dylan Thomas, 'Memories of Christmas', *On the Air with Dylan Thomas: The Broadcasts* (New York, 1991), p. 22.
28 Ibid.
29 Philip Nel, *Dr Seuss: American Icon* (New York, 2006), pp. 118–19.

30 Dr Seuss, *How the Grinch Stole Christmas* (New York, 1957), n.p.
31 Nel, *Dr Seuss*, pp. 130–31.
32 'Dr Seuss's How the Grinch Stole Christmas', http://abc.go.com, 15 November 2013.
33 Moore, *Victorian Christmas*, p. 9.
34 James Munson, 'The Old English Christmas of Washington Irving', *Contemporary Review* CCLXV/1547 (December 1994), pp. 324–6.
35 Washington Irving, *The Sketch Book of Geoffrey Crayon, Gent* (Philadelphia, PA, 1871), p. 303.
36 Moore, *Victorian Christmas*, p. 82.
37 John Michael Varese, 'Why *A Christmas Carol* was a Flop for Dickens', *The Guardian* (22 December 2009).
38 Moore, *Victorian Christmas*, p. 20.
39 Ibid., p. 19.
40 Ibid., p. 147.
41 Ibid., p. 149.
42 Ronald M. Clancy, *Sacred Christmas Music: The Stories Behind the Most Beloved Songs of Devotion* (New York, 2008), p. 68.
43 Ibid., p. 77.
44 Eric Westervelt, 'A Church, an Oratorio and an Enduring Tradition', www.npr.org, 22 December 2011.
45 Clancy, *Sacred Christmas Music*, p. 85.
46 Ibid., p. 86.
47 Ibid., pp. 36–7.
48 Alexander Murray, 'Medieval Christmas', *History Today*, XXXVI/12 (1986), p. 38.
49 Barry Cooper, 'Christmas Carols', in *Christmas, Ideology and Popular Culture*, ed. Sheila Whitely (Edinburgh, 2008), p. 90.
50 Clancy, *Sacred Christmas Music*, pp. 92–3.
51 Max Cryer, *Love Me Tender: The Stories behind the World's Favourite Songs* (Auckland, 2006), p. 126.
52 Theron Brown and Hezekiah Butterworth, *The Story of the Hymns and Tunes* (New York, 1906), p. 464.
53 Nancy Smith Thomas, *Moravian Christmas in the South* (Winston-Salem, NC, 2007), p. 121.
54 Henry Beauchamp Walters, *Church Bells* (London, 1908), p. 75.
55 'More Information about: Christmas 1940'. See www.bbc.co.uk/history/topics, accessed 17 November 2012.
56 Cooper, 'Christmas Carols', p. 88.
57 Ben Bergman, 'On Commercial Radio, Christmas is Coming Early', www.npr.org, 24 November 2011.

58 Paul Farhi, 'All I Want for Christmas is Not to Hear that Song', *Washington Post* (14 December 2007).

59 Ibid.

60 Richard Stim, *Music Law: How to Run Your Band's Business* (Berkeley, CA, 2006), p. 178.

61 Jacqui Swift, '"Fairytale of New York" is a Great Record but I'm not the Only Person Responsible', *The Sun* (14 December 2012).

62 NPR Staff, 'Have Yourself a Sullen Little Christmas', www.npr.org, 20 December 2013.

63 Diane Werts, *Christmas on Television* (Westport, CT, 2006), pp. 14–15.

64 Ibid.

65 Ibid., p. 15.

66 Ibid., pp. 15–16.

67 Ibid., p. 167.

68 Ibid., p. 184.

69 Tara Brabazon, 'Christmas and the Media', in *Christmas, Ideology and Popular Culture*, ed. Sheila Whitely (Edinburgh, 2008), p. 153.

70 Adam Sherwin, 'Strictly, EastEnders, Doctor Who: Why the Christmas TV Schedules are Always a Repeat', *The Independent* (29 November 2013).

71 Stuart Heritage, 'It'll be Lonely this Christmas without Elf', *The Guardian* (19 November 2013).

72 Serri Graslie, 'The Good Old Yule Log Spreads to HDTV', ww.npr.org, 24 December 2011.

## FOUR: Christmas Outlawed

1 Chris Durston, 'Lords of Misrule: The Puritan War on Christmas, 1642–60', *History Today*, XXXV/12 (1985), p. 8.

2 Ibid.

3 Ibid.

4 Neil Armstrong, *Christmas in Nineteenth-century England* (New York, 2010), p. 5.

5 Durston, 'Lords of Misrule', p. 9.

6 John Storey, 'The Invention of the English Christmas', in *Christmas, Ideology and Popular Culture*, ed. Sheila Whitely (Edinburgh, 2008), p. 19.

7 Penne L. Restad, *Christmas in America: A History* (Oxford, 1995), p. 8.

8 Ibid., p. 7.

9 Durston, 'Lords of Misrule', p. 9.

10 Restad, *Christmas in America*, p. 8.

11 Ibid.
12 Martyn Bennet, *Oliver Cromwell* (New York and London, 2006), p. 137.
13 Elizabeth A. Dice, *Christmas and Hanukkah* (New York, 2009), p. 57.
14 Tara Moore, *Victorian Christmas in Print* (New York, 2009), p. 37.
15 Restad, *Christmas in America*, p. 9.
16 Ibid., p. 14.
17 Ibid., p. 11.
18 Robert Dirks, *The Black Saturnalia: Conflict and its Ritual Expressions on British West Indian Slave Plantations* (Gainsville, FL, 1987), pp. 168–70.
19 Edmund Gosse, *Father and Son* (London, 1989), p. 133.
20 Richard Pipes, *Russia under the Bolshevik Regime* (New York, 1993), pp. 357–8.
21 Ibid.
22 *Christmas in Russia* (Chicago, 2001), n.p.
23 Helene Henderson, *Holidays, Festivals, and Celebrations of the World Dictionary: Detailing nearly 2,500 Observances from all 50 States and More than 100 Nations: A Compendious Reference Guide to Popular, Ethnic, Religious, National, and Ancient Holidays* (Detroit, MI, 2005), p. 108.
24 Ibid., p. 108.
25 "Eight Lao Christians in Prison for Christmas', www.asianews.it, 22 December 2011.
26 'Chinese Police Shut Down Christmas Celebration', www.cbn.com, 16 December 2011.
27 Joe Perry, 'Nazifying Christmas: Political Culture and Popular Celebration in the Third Reich', *Central European History*, XXXVIII/4 (December 2005), p. 576.
28 Ibid., p. 578.
29 Ibid., p. 579.
30 Christine Agius, 'Christmas and War', in *Christmas, Ideology and Popular Culture*, ed. Sheila Whitely (Edinburgh, 2008), pp. 141, 143.
31 Ibid., p. 142.
32 Ibid., p. 142.
33 Perry, 'Nazifying Christmas', p. 574.
34 Stanley Weintraub, *Pearl Harbor Christmas: A World at War, December 1941* (Cambridge, MA, 2011), p. 25.
35 Gerry Bowler, *Santa Claus: A Biography* (Toronto, 2005), p. 166.
36 Ibid., pp. 593–4.
37 Ibid., p. 594.
38 Ibid., pp. 596–7.

39 Kathleen Stokker, *Folklore Fights the Nazis: Humor in Occupied Norway, 1940–1945* (Madison, WI, 1997), p. 95.

40 Kathleen Stokker, *Keeping Christmas: Yuletide Traditions in Norway and the New Land* (St Paul, MN, 2000), p. 48.

41 'Christmas Season Hits . . . Saudi Arabia?', www.msnbc.com, 23 December 2004.

42 Mauro Pianta Turin, 'Malaysia: No Christmas Carols without Police Authorization', *Vatican Insider* (2011).

43 'Christmas Bombers Target Christians in Iraq', www.aljazeera.com, 26 December 2013.

44 Jadaliyya Ezine, 'Muslim Brotherhood Call on Egypt's Military to Protect Egypt's Churches on Christmas', *Arab Stands* (2012). See www.arabstands.com.

45 Mohamad Atho Mudzhar, 'The Cof Indonesian "Ulama" on Muslims' Attendance at Christmas Celebrations', in *Islamic Legal Interpretation: Muftis and their Fatwas*, ed. Muhammad Khalid Masud, Brinkley Messick and David S. Powers (Cambridge, 1996), pp. 230–37.

46 Paula M. Cooey, 'What Child is This?': *Lynch v. Donnelly* and the Celebration of Christmas in the United States', in *Christmas Unwrapped: Consumerism, Christ, and Culture*, ed. Richard Horsley and James Tracy (Harrisburg, PA, 2001), p. 209.

47 Elizabeth Pleck, 'Christmas in the Sixties', in *Christmas Unwrapped*, ed. Horsley and Tracy, p. 27.

48 Cooey, 'What Child is This?', p. 201.

49 Ibid., p. 202.

50 Oliver Burkeman, 'The Phoney War on Christmas', *The Guardian* (8 December 2006).

51 John Coles, 'It's Silent Light after Gun Ban', *The Sun* (28 November 2008).

52 'PNP Chief Warns Men vs Firing Guns this Christmas Season', www.gmanetwork.com, 10 December 2010.

### FIVE: Christmas Away from Home

1 Mark Connelly, *Christmas: A Social History* (London, 1999), p. 108.

2 Rudyard Kipling, 'Christmas in India', in *The Collected Poems of Rudyard Kipling* (Ware, 2001), p. 57.

3 John Eldon Gorst, *New Zealand Revisited: Recollections of the Days of My Youth* (London, 1908), pp. 186–7.

4 Kathleen Stokker, *Keeping Christmas: Yuletide Traditions in Norway and the New Land* (St Paul, MN, 2000), p. 151.

5 Ibid., p. 117.

6 Ibid., pp. 120–24.

7 Ibid., p. 128.

8 Ibid., p. 134.

9 Brigitte Bönisch-Brednich, *Keeping a Low Profile: An Oral History of German Immigration to New Zealand* (Wellington, 2002), pp. 247–50.

10 Connelly, *Christmas*, pp. 108–9.

11 Ibid., p. 111.

12 *An Aussie Christmas: A Celebration of Down Under* (Greenwood, 2006), p. 59.

13 Simon Winchester, 'Have Pudding Will Travel', *The Times* (24 December 1985), p. 6.

14 'Christmas in the Heavens', www.nasa.gov, 18 December 2003.

15 Peter Warwick, *The South African War: The Anglo-Boer War, 1899–1902* (Harlow, 1980), p. 148.

16 Bruce Chadwick, *George Washington's War: The Forging of a Revolutionary Leader and the American Presidency* (Naperville, IL, 2004), pp. 10–17.

17 David Hackett Fischer, *Washington's Crossing* (New York, 2004), n.p.

18 Florence Nightingale, *Florence Nightingale: The Crimean War*, ed. Lynn McDonald (Waterloo, Ontario, 2010), p. 94.

19 Stanley Weintraub, *Silent Night: The Story of the World War I Christmas Truce* (New York, 2001), pp. 9–10.

20 Ibid., pp. 22–5, 102–3.

21 Ibid., pp. 121–55.

22 Mike Brown, *Christmas on the Home Front* (Stroud, 2004), pp. 29–30.

23 Ibid., p. 187.

24 Ibid., pp. 38, 117.

25 Ibid., p. 176.

26 Ibid., pp. 37, 72.

27 'St Paul's Survives London Fire Storm', *World War II Today*, www2today.com, accessed 12 November 2012.

28 Stanley Weintraub, *Pearl Harbor Christmas: A World at War, December 1941* (Cambridge, MA, 2011), p. 72.

29 Ibid., p. 81.

30 Ibid., p. 88.

31 Matthew Litt, *Christmas 1945: The Greatest Celebration in American History* (Palisades, NY, 2010), p. 32.

32 Ibid., p. 11.

33 Ibid., p. 9.
34 Ibid., p. 79.
35 Ibid., p. 86.
36 Ibid., pp. 44–5.
37 Ibid., p. 55.
38 Ibid., pp. 69–74.
39 Carol S. Slotterback, *The Psychology of Christmas* (New York, 2009), p. 6.
40 'Christmas Mail Pouring into the Hostages Overwhelms Iranians', *Lewiston Journal* (9 January 1980), p. 10.
41 Rocky Sickmann, *Iranian Hostage: A Personal Diary of 444 Days in Captivity* (Topeka, KS, 1982), pp. 298, 302.
42 Ingrid Betancourt, *Even Silence has an End: My Six Years of Captivity in the Columbian Jungle* (London, 2010), p. 243.
43 'More People Behind Bars in Britain this Christmas than Ever Before', *The Guardian* (23 December 2011).
44 'Around £25,000 Spent on Christmas Treats for Scots Prisoners', http://news.stv.tv, 16 January 2011.
45 'Montana Judge Orders Man to Report to Jail for Christmas for Next Five Years', *Star Tribune* (29 September 2010).
46 Diane Werts, *Christmas on Television* (Westport, CT, 2006), pp. 35–8.
47 Susan Gilmore, '90 Million Americans on the Road for Christmas', *Seattle Times* (14 December 2011).
48 Tamás Zonda, Károly Bozsonyi, Előd Veres, David Lester and Michael Frank, 'The Impact of Holidays on Suicide in Hungary', *OMEGA: Journal of Death and Dying*, LVIII/2 (2009), p. 154.
49 Gert Jessen and Borge F. Jensen, 'Postponed Suicide Death? Suicides around Birthdays and Major Public Holidays', *Suicide and Life: Threatening Behavior*, XXIX/3 (Autumn 1999), pp. 272–3.
50 Peter O. Peretti, 'Holiday Depression in Young Adults', *Psychologia*, XXIII/4 (1980), p. 254.
51 Daniel J. David, 'Christmas and Depression', *Journal of Family Practice*, XVII/6 (1983), p. 1084.
52 Dorothy S. Becvar, *In the Presence of Grief: Helping Family Members Resolve Death, Dying, and Bereavement Issues* (New York, 2001), pp. 225, 221.

## SIX: Commercial Christmas

1 Jennifer Rycenga, 'Dropping in for the Holidays: Christmas at the Precious Moments Chapel', in *God in the Details: American*

*Religion in Popular Culture*, ed. Eric Michael Mazur and Kate
McCarthy, 2nd edn (New York, 2011), p. 142.

2 Lee Anne Fenell, 'Unpacking the Gift: Illiquid Goods and
Empathetic Dialogue', in *The Question of the Gift: Essays across
Disciplines*, ed. Mark Osteen (New York, 2002), p. 99.

3 Tina M. Lowrey, Cele Otnes and Kevin Robbins, 'Values
Influencing Christmas Gift Giving: An Interpretive Study', in
*Gift Giving: A Research Anthology*, ed. Cele Otnes and Richard F.
Beltramini (Bowling Green, OH, 1996), p. 40.

4 Ibid., p. 46.

5 Ibid., p. 50.

6 Yvonne Jeffrey, *The Everything Family Christmas Book: Stories,
Songs, Recipes, Crafts* (Avon, MA, 2008), pp. 9–10.

7 Maymie R. Krythe, *All About Christmas* (New York, 1954), p. 37.

8 Roger Highfield, *The Physics of Christmas* (New York, 1999),
p. 51.

9 Carol S. Slotterback, *The Psychology of Christmas* (New York, 2009),
p. 35.

10 Natalie Zemon Davis, *The Gift in Sixteenth-century France*
(Madison, WI, 2000), pp. 23–4.

11 Bruce David Forbes, *Christmas: A Candid History* (Berkeley, 2007),
pp. 115–17.

12 John Storey, 'The Invention of the English Christmas', in
*Christmas Ideology and Popular Culture*, ed. Sheila Whiteley
(Edinburgh, 2008), p. 138.

13 Hugh Cunningham, *Leisure in the Industrial Revolution* (London,
1980), p. 62.

14 Storey, 'Invention', pp. 131, 141.

15 Forbes, *Christmas*, pp. 115–17.

16 Peter Kimpton, *Tom Smith's Christmas Crackers: An Illustrated
History* (Stroud, 2004), p. 85.

17 Christopher P. Hosgood, '"Doing the Shops" at Christmas:
Women, Men and the Department Store in England, *c.* 1880–
1914', in *Cathedrals of Consumption: The European Department
Store, 1850–1939*, ed. Geoffrey Cossick and Serge Jaumain
(Aldershot, 1999), p. 113.

18 Storey, 'Invention', p. 146.

19 Tara Moore, *Victorian Christmas in Print* (New York, 2009),
p. 109.

20 Ibid., p. 107.

21 Russell W. Belk, 'Materialism and the Modern U.S. Christmas',
*Advertising and Society Review*, I/1 (2000), p. 332.

22 Kathleen Stokker, *Keeping Christmas: Yuletide Traditions in Norway and the New Land* (St Paul, MN, 2000), p. 85.

23 Joe Perry, 'Nazifying Christmas: Political Culture and Popular Celebration in the Third Reich', *Central European History*, XXXVIII/4 (2005), pp. 140–41.

24 Rycenga, 'Dropping in for the Holidays', p. 147.

25 Max A. Myers, 'Santa Claus as an Icon of Grace', in *Christmas Unwrapped: Consumerism, Christ, and Culture*, ed. Richard Horsley and James Tracy (Harrisburg, PA, 2001), p. 190.

26 Stokker, *Keeping Christmas*, p. 50.

27 Ibid., p. 85.

28 Kathy Grannis, 'NRF: Black Friday Weekend Sees Bigger Crowds, $45 Billion in Spending', www.nrf.com, 2010.

29 Mitchell Hartman, 'Holiday Spending for People Who Don't Celebrate Christmas', www.marketplace.org, 24 December 2010.

30 Joel Waldfogel, *Scroogenomics: Why You Shouldn't Buy Presents for the Holidays* (Princeton, NJ, 2009), p. 11.

31 Ibid., p. 26.

32 Ibid., p. 27.

33 Ibid., pp. 62–3.

34 Ibid., p. 66.

35 Ibid., p. 61.

36 'Cheers or Jeers for Christmas 2010 and 2011 Sales', http://economists-pick-research.hktdc.com, 2010.

37 'Holiday Sales Shine', *Hong Kong Trader* (5 January 2011).

38 Peter Morris, 'Holiday Gift Card Sales', *ICSC Certified Professionals Newsletter* (2008). See www.icsc.org.

39 Donna Airoldi, 'Post 2010 Holiday Sales Show Returned Growth for Gift Cards', *Incentive* (2011). See www.incentivemag.com.

40 Ylan Q. Mui, 'Gift-card Sales Rise after Falling for Two Years', *Washington Post* (27 December 2010).

41 Tracy L. Tuten and Pamela Kierker, 'The Perfect Gift Card: An Exploration of Teenagers' Gift Card Associations', *Psychology and Marketing*, XXVI/1 (January 2009), p. 70.

42 Ibid., p. 88.

43 Loren Nikolai, John Bazley and Jefferson Jones, *Intermediate Accounting*, 11th edn (Mason, OH, 2010), p. 599.

44 Jennifer Pate Offenberg, 'Gift Cards', *Journal of Economic Perspectives*, XXI/2 (Spring 2007), p. 229.

45 Waldfogel, *Scroogenomics*, p. 11.

46 Ibid., pp. 11, 31.

47 Ibid., p. 37.

48 Haroon Siddique, 'Sales Begin Online as Retailers Look to Reclaim Snow-affected Revenue', www.guardian.co.uk/business, 25 December 2010.
49 Neil Armstrong, 'England and German Christmas Festlichkeit, *c.* 1800–1914', *German History*, XXVI/4 (2008), p. 491.
50 Samuel Taylor Coleridge, 'The Christmas Tree'. See http://classiclit.about.com.
51 Armstrong, 'England and German Christmas Festlichkeit', p. 493.
52 Ibid., p. 491.
53 Ibid., p. 498.
54 Ibid., p. 500.
55 Slotterback, *The Psychology of Christmas*, p. 25.
56 Karen J. Pine and Avril Nash, 'Dear Santa: The Effects of Television Advertising on Young Children', *International Journal of Behavioral Development*, XXVI/6 (2002), pp. 529–34.
57 Jo Robinson and Jean Coppock Staeheli, *Unplug the Christmas Machine* (New York, 1991), p. 22.
58 John F. Sherry Jr and Mary Ann McGrath, 'Unpacking the Holiday Presence: A Comparative Ethnography of Two Gift Stores', in *Consumption: Critical Concepts in the Social Sciences*, ed. Daniel Miller (New York, 2001), vol. III, pp. 165–6.
59 Laura Himmelreich, 'Noel and Glühwein: Germany's Christmas Markets Generate Billions in Revenues', *Spiegel Online International*, www.spiegel.de (2009).
60 Armstrong, 'England and German Christmas Festlichkeit', p. 486.
61 Ibid., p. 502.
62 'SPUGS Renew War on Christmas Graft', *New York Times* (3 November 1913).
63 Lowri Turner, 'Young, Indebted and Attached', *Western Mail* (16 December 2005).

SEVEN: Characters of Christmas

1 Martin Ebon, *Saint Nicholas: Life and Legend* (New York, 1975), p. 13.
2 Ibid., p. 35.
3 Gerry Bowler, *Santa Claus: A Biography* (Toronto, 2005), p. 17.
4 Ibid., p. 13.
5 Ibid., p. 21.
6 Ibid., p. 23.
7 Ebon, *Saint Nicholas*, p. 79.

8 Phyllis Siefker, *Santa Claus, Last of the Wild Men: The Origins and Evolution of Saint Nicholas, Spanning 50,000 Years* (Jefferson, NC, 1997), p. 12.

9 Ibid., pp. 39–61.

10 Ibid., p. 17.

11 Ibid., p. 19.

12 Ibid., p. 34; Nancy Smith Thomas, *Moravian Christmas in the South* (Winston-Salem, NC, 2007), p. 63.

13 Siefker, *Santa Claus*, p. 34.

14 Bowler, *Santa Claus*, p. 51.

15 Ibid., p. 62.

16 Tony van Renterghem, *When Santa was a Shaman* (St Paul, MN, 1995), pp. 52–3.

17 Bowler, *Santa Claus*, p. 121.

18 Ibid., p. 124.

19 Ibid., pp. 139–40.

20 David McLaughlan, *The Top 40 Traditions of Christmas* (Uhrichsville, OH, 2012), n.p. See http://tinyurl.com/afupsqh, accesed 27 July 2012.

21 Penn L. Restad, *Christmas in America: A History* (Oxford, 1995), p. 148.

22 Erica Marat, 'Nation Branding in Central Asia: A New Campaign to Present Ideas about the State and the Nation', *Europe-Asia Studies*, LXI/7 (2009), p. 1134.

23 Kathleen Stokker, *Keeping Christmas: Yuletide Traditions in Norway and the New Land* (St Paul, MN, 2000), p. 56.

24 Debra Jopson, 'Syd Cunningham OAM, Aboriginal Community Stalwart', *Sydney Morning Herald* (25 March 1999).

25 Theodora Papatheodorou and Janet Gill, 'Father Christmas: Just a Story?', *International Journal of Children's Spirituality*, VII/3 (2002), p. 330.

26 Carole S. Slotterback, *The Psychology of Christmas* (New York, 2009), p. 98.

27 Jacques T. Godbout and Alain C. Caille, *The World of the Gift* (Montreal, 2000), p. 44.

28 Ibid., *World of the Gift*, p. 44.

29 Stokker, *Keeping Christmas*, p. 99.

30 'Father Christmas', in *A Dictionary of English Folklore*, ed. Jacqueline Simpson and Steve Roud (Oxford, 2000), n.p.

31 Siefker, *Santa Claus*, p. 101.

32 'Father Christmas,' n.p.

33 Jóna Hammer, *Memoirs of an Icelandic Bookworm* (Bloomington, IN, 2006), p. 144.

34 Maurice Bruce, 'The Krampus in Styria', *Folklore*, LXIX/1 (1958), p. 45.
35 Ibid., p. 46.
36 Siefker, *Santa Claus*, pp. 9–10.
37 Bruce, 'Krampus in Styria', p. 45.
38 Mieke Bal, 'Zwarte Piet's Bal Masque', in *Zwarte Piet*, ed. Anna Fox (London, 1999), n.p.
39 MobileReference, *Encyclopedia of Observances, Holidays and Celebrations* (Boston, 2007), n.p.
40 Bowler, *Santa Claus*, p. 25.
41 Stokker, *Keeping Christmas*, p. 41.
42 Ibid., p. 45.
43 Helene Henderson, *Holidays, Festivals, and Celebrations of the World Dictionary: Detailing Nearly 2,500 Observances from all 50 States and More than 100 Nations: A Compendious Reference Guide to Popular, Ethnic, Religious, National, and Ancient Holidays* (Detroit, MI, 2005), p. 114.
44 Russell W. Belk, 'Materialism and the Making of the Modern American Christmas', in *Consumption: Critical Concepts in the Social Sciences*, ed. Daniel Miller (New York, 2001), vol. VI, p. 319.
45 Ibid., p. 215.
46 Fred Guida, *A Christmas Carol and its Adaptations: Dickens's Story on Screen and Television* (Jefferson, NC, 2000), p. 143.
47 Robert Louis Stevenson, *The Letters of Robert Louis Stevenson*, ed. Sidney Colvin (New York, 1911), vol. II, p. 178.
48 Belk, 'Materialism', p. 331.

### EIGHT: The Imported Global Christmas

1 Neil Armstrong, 'England and German Christmas Festlichkeit, *c.* 1800–1914', *German History*, XXVI/4 (2008), p. 503.
2 Michael Harrison, *The Story of Christmas* (London, n.d.), p. 264.
3 Trevor A. Harley, 'Nice Weather for the Time of Year: The British Obsession with the Weather,' *Weather, Climate, Culture*, ed. Sarah Strauss and Benjamin S. Orlove (Oxford, 2003), p. 109.
4 'Black Outlook for a White Christmas across Canada', Canadian Press, www.ctvnews.ca, 22 December 2011.
5 Malcolm McGregor and Rob Walls, *Christmas in Australia* (1990), pp. 140–41.
6 Andrew Hind, 'Native Canadian Voices: "The Huron Carol"', *History Magazine* (2011), pp. 29, 28.
7 Susan Topp Weber, *Christmas in Santa Fe* (Layton, UT, 2010), p. 22.

8 John Fischer, 'How Christmas Came to Hawaii',
http://gohawaii.about.com, 3 March 2013.

9 Maesyn, 'Have a Mele Kalikimaka' (2010), http://mauinow.com.

10 'The History of Parol Christmas Lanterns', www.myparol.com,
3 March 2013.

11 J. David Williams, 'Christmas in the Philippines: A Blend of
Malay, Spanish, and United States Customs', *Bulletin of the
American Historical Collection*, 11/4 (1972), p. 61.

12 Peter Millington, 'Mrs Ewing and the Textual Origin of the
St Kitts Mummies' Play', *Folklore*, cvii (1996), p. 78.

13 Ibid., p. 77.

14 Laurence Marshall Carucci, *Nuclear Nativity: Rituals of Renewal
and Empowerment in the Marshall Islands* (Dekalb, il, 1997), p. 171.

15 Ibid., p. 178.

16 Ibid., pp. 19–20.

17 Ibid., p. 29.

18 Ted C. Fishman, *China, Inc: How the Rise of the Next Superpower
Challenges America and the World* (New York, 2005), p. 162.

19 Ibid., p. 163.

20 John Vidal, 'How World's Biggest Ship is Delivering our
Christmas – All the Way from China', *The Guardian*
(30 October 2006).

21 John Storey, 'The Invention of the English Christmas', in
*Christmas Ideology and Popular Culture*, ed. Sheila Whiteley
(Edinburgh, 2008), p. 22.

22 'Christmas Sales Shine in Emerging Markets: Better Christmas
Sales Recorded in the u.s., uk and Germany', www.hktdc.com,
2010.

23 Huaiyuan Lu and James Melik, 'China Succumbs to the Glitz of
Christmas', www.bbc.co.uk/news, 2010.

24 'Christmas Drives Chinese People to Churches',
http://english.cri.cn, 26 December 2008.

25 Stephen T. Asma, *Why I am a Buddhist: No-nonsense Buddhism
with Red Meat and Whiskey* (Charlottesville, va, 2010).

26 'Chinese Celebrate Christmas with Oriental Twist', *China Daily*
(19 December 2011).

27 Kate Gillespie and H. David Hennessey, *Global Marketing*,
3rd edn (Mason, oh, 2011), p. 58.

28 Tiffany Tan, 'Christmas Village Opens at China's "North Pole"',
*China Daily* (25 December 2010).

29 Zach Epstein, 'PlayStation Vita Will Miss Christmas Shopping
Season in u.s., Europe', www.bgr.com, 4 August 2011.

30 Hideyo Konagaya, 'The Christmas Cake: A Japanese Tradition of American Prosperity', *Journal of Popular Culture*, XXXIV/4 (2001).
31 Ibid.
32 Lucy Craft, 'Christmas in Japan', www.npr.org, 25 December 2007.
33 Jonathan Head, 'No Room at Japan's Love Hotels at Christmas', http://news.bbc.co.uk, 24 December 2003.
34 'Hotel Chapel Christmas', http://unmissablejapan.com, 15 March 2013.
35 Katherine Rupp, *Gift-giving in Japan: Cash, Connections, Cosmologies* (Stanford, CA, 2003), p. 175.
36 Ibid., p. 145.
37 Helene Henderson, *Holidays, Festivals, and Celebrations of the World Dictionary: Detailing Nearly 2,500 Observances from all 50 States and More than 100 Nations: A Compendious Reference Guide to Popular, Ethnic, Religious, National, and Ancient Holidays* (Detroit, MI, 2005), p. 108.
38 Rupp, *Gift-giving in Japan*, p. 144.
39 Craft, 'Christmas in Japan'.
40 Henderson, *Holidays, Festivals, and Celebrations*, p. 108.
41 'Eel Lights Christmas Tree', www.npr.org, 4 December 2007.
42 Henderson, *Holidays, Festivals, and Celebrations*, p. 109.
43 'KFC Christmas Chicken Dinners a Big Hit In Japan', www.npr.org, 10 December 2008.
44 Konagaya, 'Christmas Cake'.
45 Ibid.
46 Vadim Yegorov, 'Christmas Japanese Style', *Asia and Africa Today*, VI (1991), p. 81.
47 Herbert M. Cole, 'Introduction: The Mask, Masking, and Masquerade Arts in Africa', in *I Am Not Myself: The Art of African Masquerade*, ed. Herbert M. Cole (Los Angeles, 1985), p. 19.
48 Ifeoma Onyefulu, *An African Christmas* (London, 2005), n.p.
49 Rainer Chr Hennig and Musa Saidykhan, 'Christmas "Unique in West Africa"', *Afrol News* (n.d.).
50 Ibid.

## NINE: Public Christmas

1 Richard Horsley, 'Christmas: The Religion of Consumer Capitalism', in *Christmas Unwrapped: Consumerism, Christ, and Culture*, ed. Richard Horsley and James Tracy (Harrisburg, PA, 2001), p. 168.
2 Ronald Hutton, *Stations of the Sun: A History of the Ritual Year in Britain* (New York, 1996), p. 70.

3 Iørn Piø, 'Christmas Traditions in Scandinavia', in *Custom, Culture and Community in the Later Middle Ages: A Symposium*, ed. Thomas Pettitt and Leif Søndergaard (Odense, Denmark, 1994), p. 59.

4 *Christmas in Russia* (Chicago, 2001), p. 1882.

5 Melvin M. Firestone, 'Mummers and Strangers in Northern Newfoundland', in *Christmas Mumming in Newfoundland: Essays in Anthropology, Folklore, and History*, ed. Herbert Halpert and G. M. Storey (Toronto, 1969), p. 75.

6 Phyllis Siefker, *Santa Claus, Last of the Wild Men: The Origins and Evolution of Saint Nicholas, Spanning 50,000 Years* (Jefferson, NC, 1997), pp. 22–3, 24–5.

7 Helene Henderson, *Holidays, Festivals, and Celebrations of the World Dictionary: Detailing Nearly 2,500 Observances from all 50 States and More than 100 Nations: A Compendious Reference Guide to Popular, Ethnic, Religious, National, and Ancient Holidays* (Detroit, MI, 2005), p. 111.

8 Ibid, p. 112.

9 *Christmas in Greece* (New York, 2000), vol. X, p. 17.

10 Henderson, *Holidays, Festivals, and Celebrations*, p. 113.

11 National Center for Statistics and Analysis, 'Fatalities Related to Alcohol-impaired Driving during the Christmas and New Year's Day Holiday Periods: A Brief Statistical Summary', www.nrd.nhtsa.dot.gov (Washington, DC, 2007).

12 Sarah Bell, 'The Death of the Christmas Party?', www.bbc.co.uk, 15 December 2009.

13 Patrick McGreevy, 'Place in the American Christmas', *Geographical Review*, LXXX/1 (1990), pp. 38, 35.

14 Bruce David Forbes, *Christmas: A Candid History* (Berkeley, 2007), p. 121.

15 Phillip V. Snyder, *The Christmas Tree Book: The History of the Christmas Tree and Antique Christmas Tree Ornaments* (New York, 1977), pp. 165–6.

16 Ibid., p. 169.

17 Stanley Weintraub, *Pearl Harbor Christmas: A World at War, December 1941* (Cambridge, MA, 2011), p. 77.

18 Roger Highfield, *The Physics of Christmas* (New York, 1999), p. 29.

19 Melanie Archer, 'Christmas', in *The Business of Holidays*, ed. Maud Lavin (New York, 2004), p. 237.

20 Tasneem Brogger and Frances Schwartzkopff, 'Christmas Tree Growers in Denmark See a Revival', *New York Times* (14 December 2007).

21 'Christmas Trees are Cloned', *Seattle Times* (4 October 2012).
22 Nancy Smith Thomas, *Moravian Christmas in the South* (Winston-Salem, NC, 2007), p. 36.
23 Forbes, *Christmas*, p. 122.
24 National Christmas Tree Association, 'Consumer Survey Results', www.realchristmastrees.org, 3 October 2012.
25 Archer, 'Christmas', p. 238.
26 Daniel J. Foley, *The Christmas Tree* (Detroit, 1999), p. 85.
27 See 'Chronology of Christmas Tree Lightings', www.nps.gov, 4 December 2012.
28 'White House Tree: 2011', www.christmastree.org.
29 Snyder, *Christmas Tree Book*, pp. 81–99.
30 Mike Brown, *Christmas on the Home Front* (Stroud, 2004), p. 59.
31 Kathleen Stokker, *Keeping Christmas: Yuletide Traditions in Norway and the New Land* (St Paul, MN, 2000), p. 65.
32 Ibid., p. 66.
33 Ibid., p. 68.
34 Jason Porterfield, *Scandinavian Mythology* (New York, 2008), p. 55.
35 'Swedish Christmas Goat Set on Fire – Again', *Huffington Post* (14 December 2012).
36 NPR staff, 'Christmas Trees around the World', www.npr.org, 24 December 2010.
37 Snyder, *The Christmas Tree Book*, pp. 101–28
38 Susan Topp Weber, *Christmas in Santa Fe* (Layton, UT, 2010), p. 22.
39 'Newcastle-under-Lyme Council Cuts Christmas Spending', www.bbc.co.uk/news, 24 February 2011.
40 The LawPhil Project, see www.lawphil.net.
41 Sheryll Bellman, *Through the Shopping Glass: A Century of New York Christmas Windows* (New York, 2000), p. 9.
42 Ibid., p. 13.
43 Ibid., p. 8.
44 Sandra Lawrence, 'Selfridges Christmas Windows', *British Heritage*, XXX/6 (2010).
45 'Myer Christmas Windows', www.onlymelbourne.com.au, accessed 16 December 2012.
46 Henderson, *Holidays, Festivals, and Celebrations*, p. 107.
47 Archer, 'Christmas', p. 239.
48 Oksana Yablokova and Kevin O'Flynn, 'Moscow to Pay a Price for Not Celebrating', *St Petersburg Times* (29 November 2002).
49 Horsley, 'Christmas', p. 169.
50 'Obama "Christmas" Party Season: 28 Events, 50,000 Guests', *Huffington Post* (1 December 2009).

51 Jill Dougherty, 'Baghdad Celebrates First Public Christmas Amid Hope, Memories', www.cnn.com, 21 December 2008.

52 Nancy Hellmich, 'Ringing in the Season with a Call for Giving', *USA Today* (24 December 2009).

53 Edna Barth, *Holly, Reindeer, and Colored Lights: The Story of the Christmas Symbols* (New York, 1971), p. 91.

54 Brian Shrader, 'Christmas Card Sales Decrease as Social Media Gains Popularity', www.wral.com, 20 December 2010.

55 Highfield, *Physics of Christmas*, p. 58.

## TEN: Christmas and the Church

1 Claude Lévi-Strauss, 'Father Christmas Executed', in *Unwrapping Christmas*, ed. D. Miller (Oxford, 1993), p. 51.

2 'Christmas', *Saturday Review* (26 December 1903), p. 788. See http://books.google.com, 14 January 2013.

3 Penne L. Restad, *Christmas in America: A History* (Oxford, 1995), p. 31.

4 Neil Armstrong, *Christmas in Nineteenth-century England* (New York, 2010), pp. 60–61.

5 Katherine Lambert Richards, *How Christmas Came to the Sunday-schools* (New York, 1934), p. 123.

6 Armstrong, *Christmas*, p. 59.

7 Joe Perry, 'Nazifying Christmas: Political Culture and Popular Celebration in the Third Reich', *Central European History*, XXXVIII (December 2005), p. 37.

8 Leigh Eric Schmidt, *Consumer Rites: The Buying and Selling of American Holidays* (Princeton, NJ, 1995), p. 179

9 Ibid., p. 179.

10 Ibid., p. 180.

11 Ibid., pp. 188–9.

12 Ibid., p. 189.

13 'Keep Christ in Christmas: Action Steps', www.kofc.org, 13 January 2013.

14 Amy Sullivan, 'Going to Church on Christmas: A Vanishing Tradition', *Time* (24 December 2008).

15 Alex Murashko, 'Churches Not Canceling Worship on Christmas Sunday; Will People Show Up?', *Christian Post* (30 November 2011).

16 Donald B. Kraybill and Carol F. Bowman, *On the Backroad to Heaven: Old Order Hutterites, Mennonites, Amish, and Brethren* (Baltimore, 2001), pp. 119, 120.

17 Ethan Cole, 'Bethlehem Sees Record-high Pilgrims for Christmas', *Christian Post* (26 December 2010).

18 Katie Kindelan, 'Rival Monks Brawl While Cleaning Bethlehem Church', http://abcnews.go.com, 29 December 2011.

19 William Ingraham Kip, *Christmas Holydays in Rome* (New York, 1846), p. 58.

20 Greg Tobin, *Holy Holidays!: The Catholic Origins of Celebration* (New York, 2011), pp. 3–4.

21 *Christmas in the Philippines* (Chicago, 1998), pp. 17–20.

22 Kathleen Stokker, *Keeping Christmas: Yuletide Traditions in Norway and the New Land* (St Paul, MN, 2000), p. 74.

23 *Christmas in Greece* (New York, 2000), vol. x, p. 60.

24 'Britons Spend "Million Pounds a Minute" in Christmas Sales', www.thaindian.com, 26 December 2008.

25 'Pagans Campaign for Census Voice', www.bbc.co.uk/news, 27 February 2011.

26 Jason Pitzl-Waters, 'Parsing the Pew Numbers', www.patheos.com, February 2008.

27 'Nativity Scenes in Spain: A Typical Christmas Tradition', www.spain.info, accessed 12 January 2013.

## Conclusion

1 'Why does Google's Christmas 2012 Doodle Say "Happy Holidays" instead of "Happy Christmas"?, http://productforums.google.com, accessed 10 February 2013.

# Further Reading

Hervey, Thomas, *The Book of Christmas* (London, 1836)
Kelly, Joseph F., *The Origins of Christmas* (Collegeville, MN, 2004)
Litt, Matthew, *Christmas 1945: The Greatest Celebration in American History* (Palisades, NY, 2010)
Moore, Tara, *Victorian Christmas in Print* (New York, 2009)
Parker, David, *Christmas and Charles Dickens* (New York, 2005)
Perry, Joe, *Christmas in Germany: A Cultural History* (Chapel Hill, NC, 2010)
Pimlott, J.A.R., *The Englishman's Christmas: A Social History* (Hassocks, 1978)
Seifker, Phyllis, *Santa Claus, Last of the Wild Men: The Origins and Evolution of Saint Nicholas, Spanning 50,000 Years* (Jefferson, NC, 1997)
Waldfogel, Joel, *Scroogenomics: Why You Shouldn't Buy Presents for the Holidays* (Princeton, NJ, 2009)
Weintraub, Stanley, *Silent Night: The Story of the World War I Christmas Truce* (New York, 2002)

# Photo Acknowledgements

The author and publishers wish to express their thanks to the below sources of illustrative material and/or permission to reproduce it. Some locations uncredited in the captions for reasons of brevity are also given below.

© The author: pp. 16, 19, 28, 34, 39, 43, 78, 82, 90, 91, 96, 134, 144, 147, 151, 157, 158, 162, 164, 175, 178, 193, 216, 227; Beinecke Rare Book and Manuscript Library, Yale University, New Haven, Connecticut: p. 54; Erics67, used with permission: p. 141; Mike Killar, used with permission: p. 181; Library of Congress, Washington, DC (Prints and Photographs Division): pp. 114, 121, 172, 187, 217; Anita Marintz, used with permission: p. 159; © NASA: pp. 31, 101; Leonard Shulman used with permission: p. 99; Stefan, used with permission: p. 201; © The Trustees of the British Museum, London: pp. 57, 123, 138; Thomas Stern, used with permission: p. 169; © Victoria and Albert Museum, London: pp. 21, 36, 55, 59, 61, 126, 129, 208.

# Index